arsenal

player by player

1 2 3 4 5 6 7 8 9 10 11

arsenal

player by player

IVAN PONTING

1 2 **3** 4 5 6 7 8 9 10 11

ACKNOWLEDGEMENTS

The author would like to thank the following: Pat, Rosie and Joe Ponting;
Bob Bickerton; George Armstrong; Matthew Impey;
Andy Cowie and the rest of the peerless Colorsport crew;
Steve Small; the late Jack Kelsey; David Herd; John Radford; Alan Skirton;
Geoff Strong; Julian Brown; Adam Ward; Rab MacWilliam;
Chris and Jo Forster; Les Gold; the late Bob Lewis; Simon Lewis; Fred Ollier,
whose book 'Arsenal: A Complete Record' is a towering work of reference for all
students of the Gunners (with apologies for not mentioning him in earlier
editions); George Herringshaw; Kenneth Prater; Bill Smith; Mark Leech; Action
Images; Barry Hugman; Jack Rollin; and as ever Robert Foulkes.

The author is also grateful for permission to reproduce photographs.
The vast majority are from Colorsport, with a sizeable contribution from
Associated Sports Photography. Also there are pictures from Kenneth Prater
Photography and Action Images.

First published in Great Britain by
Guinness Publishing in 1991

This revised and updated edition published in 1996 by Hamlyn an
imprint of Reed International Books Limited, Michelin House, 81
Fulham Road, London SW3 6RB and Auckland, Melbourne,
Singapore and Toronto.

ISBN 0 600 59258 8

Copyright © Ivan Ponting 1997

Printed and bound in Great Britain by
Butler & Tanner Ltd, Frome and London

INTRODUCTION

Exciting Arsenal, now there's a thought. As a catchphrase it won't have the same appeal to opposing fans as the old 'boring' tag, but with Arsene Wenger's revolution gathering pace, the Gunners' erstwhile critics just might have to get used to it.

Since the first edition of this book was published in 1991, and again in the mere 12 months since the second edition in 1996, the Highbury scene has been subject to almost continuous drama and kaleidoscopic change. Those six years have produced events triumphant and traumatic, tumultuous and tawdry, with two infamous individual cases verging on the tragic.

Just consider. Since 1991 the Gunners have become the first club to win the domestic double of FA Cup and League Cup; they have lifted a European trophy in stirring manner, then failed to retain it at the last moment only in highly bizarre circumstances; they have signed two of the world's most blindingly brilliant performers, Ian Wright and Dennis Bergkamp; they have acquired the services of an England captain, David Platt; they have witnessed improvements to their ground on the grand scale; and they have installed first Bruce Rioch, and then Arsene Wenger, as manager. Inevitably, but depressingly, mention must be made, too, of the unsavoury affair which culminated in the dismissal of George Graham for alleged financial irregularities in transfer dealings, and of the personal crises faced by Paul Merson and Tony Adams.

What Arsenal have *not* experienced in recent years is the excitement of a right-to-the-wire challenge for the League title, although Arsene Wenger's effort in 1996/97 was noble for a first attempt and bodes uncommonly well for the future. Indeed, at the time of writing, with more world-class recruits expected to join the likes of Vieira and Bergkamp, Wright and Seaman *et al*, the Gunners seem admirably equipped for a realistic tilt at that coveted crown, the premier benchmark of any leading club's success.

Mention of those players leads on to the prime concern of this book: to take a look, a positive one wherever possible, at the footballers who have worn the hallowed red-and-white strip. My interest in the game began as a wide-eyed youngster in the mid-fifties so I elected to start the main part of *Arsenal Player by Player* at the outset of Jack Crayston's managerial reign. Accordingly I have collected a picture of every individual who has pulled on an Arsenal shirt in the Football League, Premiership, FA Cup, League Cup (in all its manifestations) and European competition since October 1956. In almost every case, my personal assessment of the player appears alongside his photograph; where he has played so few matches as to render such coverage meaningless, only his career statistics are included. All records, including service with other clubs, are complete to May 17, 1997. I have attempted to depict in words the essence of each player and kept the general emphasis on footballing rather than personal matters. Because a number of first-class statistical works on Arsenal exist already, I have limited myself to basic numerical information - games played, with substitute appearances in brackets, goals scored, previous clubs, caps won etc - which are essential to place each man in context. Arsenal appearance and scoring figures refer to all matches (a breakdown for each competition begins on page 206) but under the heading of 'Other Clubs' the games and goals are in the League only. The dates in large type refer to the seasons in which each player appeared in the Gunners' first team, not when he joined or left the club. Under 'Honours' I have included only those won as an Arsenal player, except in the case of international caps, the figures for which cover complete careers to date.

Though the meat of *Arsenal Player by Player* concerns the past 40 years or so, I have set the scene with a look at famous names and teams from earlier eras. Then, in roughly chronological order, come my profiles of the characters who carried the Highbury flame through times both memorable and indifferent.

Many players who appeared in the first two editions are reassessed in the light of recent happenings, while others are included for the first time. These are the men in the vanguard of Wenger's Highbury revolution, the men who will seek European and domestic glory in 1997/98, the men of whom so much is expected by manager and fans alike. Boring Arsenal? Not any more.

Ivan Ponting
Chewton Mendip,
August 1997

CONTENTS

8	IN THE BEGINNING
10	THE ROARING TWENTIES
12	THE MEN WHO MADE ARSENAL GREAT
14	THE GUNNERS' SECOND COMING
16	JACK KELSEY
18	DAVE BOWEN
19	CLIFF HOLTON
20	PETER GORING
	DEREK TAPSCOTT
22	LEN WILLS
23	BILL DODGIN
24	GERRY WARD
25	DENNIS EVANS
26	STAN CHARLTON
27	JIM FOTHERINGHAM
	CON SULLIVAN
28	JIMMY BLOOMFIELD
30	GORDON NUTT
	JOHNNY PETTS
	MIKE TIDDY
	LEN JULIANS
32	DANNY CLAPTON
34	TOMMY DOCHERTY
35	JIM STANDEN
	LAURIE BROWN
36	JOE HAVERTY
37	JACKIE HENDERSON
38	DAVID HERD
40	MEL CHARLES
	JOHNNY BARNWELL
42	VIC GROVES
44	TONY BIGGS
	DENNIS CLAPTON
	MIKE EVERITT
	ROY GOULDEN
	PETER GOY
	PETER KANE
46	GORDON FERRY
	DANIEL LE ROUX
	FRANK O'NEILL
	RODNEY SMITHSON
	RAY SWALLOW
	BRIAN TAWSE
	ALAN YOUNG
48	DAVE BACUZZI
	EDDIE CLAMP
50	TERRY ANDERSON
	ARFON GRIFFITHS
51	BILLY McCULLOUGH
52	JIMMY MAGILL
53	GEOFF STRONG
54	JOHNNY MacLEOD
55	JOHN SNEDDEN
56	JACK McCLELLAND
	IAN McKECHNIE
54	GEORGE EASTHAM

56	ALAN SKIRTON
57	IAN URE
58	FRED CLARKE
	TONY BURNS
59	DAVID COURT
60	JOE BAKER
62	DON HOWE
63	JIM FURNELL
64	JON SAMMELS
66	TOMMY BALDWIN
	DAVID JENKINS
67	TERRY NEILL
68	JIMMY ROBERTSON
	BOBBY GOULD
69	COLIN ADDISON
	GEORGE JOHNSTON
70	BRENDON BATSON
	MICKY BOOT
	BRIAN CHAMBERS
	TOMMY COAKLEY
	ROGER DAVIDSON
	PAUL DAVIES
71	JIMMY McGILL
	GORDON NEILSON
	ROY PACK
	ALAN TYRER
	TOM WALLEY
	MALCOLM WEBSTER
	JOHN WOODWARD
72	FRANK McLINTOCK
74	JOHN ROBERTS
75	PETER MARINELLO
76	BOB McNAB
78	GEORGE GRAHAM
80	PETER SIMPSON
82	PETER STOREY
84	RAY KENNEDY
86	JOHN RADFORD
88	CHARLIE GEORGE
90	JEFF BLOCKLEY
91	EDDIE KELLY
92	BOB WILSON
94	GEORGE ARMSTRONG
96	PAT RICE
98	JIMMY RIMMER
99	BRIAN KIDD
100	DAVID PRICE
101	SAMMY NELSON
102	TERRY MANCINI
103	ALEX CROPLEY
	BRIAN HORNSBY
104	ALAN BALL
106	PAT HOWARD
	GEOFF BARNETT
107	JOHN MATTHEWS
	RICHIE POWLING
108	PAUL BARRON
	STEVE BRIGNALL

	JIMMY HARVEY
	MARK HEELEY
	JOHN KOSMINA
	KEVIN STEAD
109	TREVOR ROSS
	WILF ROSTRON
110	MALCOLM MacDONALD
112	ALAN HUDSON
113	WILLIE YOUNG
114	FRANK STAPLETON
116	STEVE GATTING
	STEVE WALFORD
117	PAUL VAESSEN
	BRIAN McDERMOTT
118	LIAM BRADY
120	PAT JENNINGS
122	JOHN DEVINE
	GEORGE WOOD
123	JOHN HOLLINS
124	PETER NICHOLAS
	VLADIMIR PETROVIC
125	COLIN HILL
	JOHN HAWLEY
	RAPHAEL MEADE
126	ALAN SUNDERLAND
127	TONY WOODCOCK
128	CHRIS WHYTE
	TOMMY CATON
129	IAN ALLINSON
	LEE CHAPMAN
130	BRIAN TALBOT
131	PAUL MARINER
132	STEVE WILLIAMS
133	STEWART ROBSON
134	GRAHAM RIX
136	NIALL QUINN
137	VIV ANDERSON
138	CHARLIE NICHOLAS
140	DAVID O'LEARY
142	KENNY SANSOM
144	GUS CAESAR
	COLIN PATES
145	MARTIN HAYES
146	PAUL DAVIS
148	JOHN LUKIC
149	KEVIN RICHARDSON
150	DAVID ROCASTLE
152	BRIAN MARWOOD
153	PERRY GROVES
154	LEE DIXON
156	ALAN SMITH
158	MICHAEL THOMAS
160	TONY ADAMS
162	NIGEL WINTERBURN
164	STEVE BOULD
166	PAUL MERSON
168	ANDERS LIMPAR
170	MARTIN KEOWN

171	ANDY LINIGHAN
172	PAL LYDERSEN
	ANDY COLE
173	KEVIN CAMPBELL
174	PAUL GORMAN
	RAY HANKIN
	JOHN KAY
	DANNY O'SHEA
	DAVID CORK
	DAVID MADDEN
	BRIAN SPARROW
175	RHYS WILMOT
	KWAME AMPADU
	SIGGI JONSSON
	LEE HARPER
	MATTHEW ROSE
	GAVIN McGOWAN
	NICOLAS ANELKA
176	JIMMY CARTER
	NEIL HEANEY
177	PAUL DICKOV
	MARK FLATTS
178	DAVID SEAMAN
180	IAN WRIGHT
182	DAVID HILLIER
183	RAY PARLOUR
184	STEVE MORROW
185	IAN SELLEY
186	JOHN JENSEN
187	STEFAN SCHWARZ
188	EDDIE McGOLDRICK
	GLENN HELDER
189	JOHN HARTSON
190	ALAN MILLER
	CHRIS KIWOMYA
	VINCE BARTRAM
191	STEVE HUGHES
192	ADRIAN CLARKE
	PAUL SHAW
193	SCOTT MARSHALL
	REMI GARDE
194	DAVID PLATT
196	DENNIS BERGKAMP
198	PATRICK VIEIRA
199	JACK CRAYSTON
	GEORGE SWINDIN
	BILLY WRIGHT
200	BERTIE MEE
201	TERRY NEILL
	DON HOWE
	STEVE BURTENSHAW
202	GEORGE GRAHAM
204	BRUCE RIOCH
	STEWART HOUSTON
205	ARSENE WENGER
	PAT RICE
206	STATISTICS

IN THE BEGINNING

The journey that was to end in the marbled splendour of Highbury began in a pub, the Prince of Wales at Plumstead, in 1886 when a group of workers at the Woolwich Arsenal, mainly Scots and northerners, banded together to form Dial Square FC. Later that year, boosted by the handsome gift of a set of red shirts from the already flourishing Nottingham Forest FC, the new club changed its name to Royal Arsenal. Operating from a succession of grounds in Plumstead, they made rapid progress, turning professional in 1891 and winning election to the Second Division of the Football League in 1893. Now calling themselves Woolwich Arsenal, they consolidated their new-found stature, steadily improving until 1903/04 when they earned promotion to the First Division as runners-up to Preston North End.

Despite increasing financial difficulties, they held their own in the top flight and reached FA Cup semi-finals in 1906 and 1907. However, the cash crisis had worsened dramatically by the end of the century's first decade and, understandably, that situation was reflected on the field.

Thus, season 1912/13 brought the club's first – and only – relegation. There had been moments when Woolwich Arsenal's very future had been in doubt, but the nadir of their fortunes had been reached and significant changes were afoot. They began 1913/14 at a new home, having headed north to Highbury, and with the 'Woolwich' accordingly removed from their title. Arsenal adapted admirably to life at the lower level, missing promotion only narrowly in each of the two following campaigns and raising hopes for the future. Then, of course, football was brushed to one side for the next four years as the world went to war.

ARSENAL IN 1914/15

Back row (left to right):

GEORGE GRANT (1911/12-1914/15, half-back, 57 games, 4 goals).

GEORGE HARDY (trainer).

JOE SHAW (1907/08-1921/22, full-back, 326 games, 0 goals).

JOE LIEVESLEY (1913/14-1914/15, goalkeeper, 75 games, 0 goals).

ROBERT BENSON (1913/14-1914/15, full-back, 54 games, 7 goals).

CHRIS BUCKLEY (1914/15-1919/20, centre-half, 59 games, 3 goals).

GEORGE MORRELL (secretary).

ALEX GRAHAM (1912/13-1923/24, half-back, 179 games, 20 goals).

Front row:

ALF FLETCHER (1914/15, wing-half, 3 games, 0 goals).

FRED GROVES (1912/13-1920/21, forward, 53 games, 7 goals).

JACK FLANAGAN (1911/12-1914/15, inside-forward, 121 games, 28 goals).

HENRY KING (1914/15, centre-forward, 39 games, 29 goals).

FRANK BRADSHAW (1914/15-1921/22, utility, 142 games, 14 goals).

JIM NORMAN (1914/15, outside-left, 4 games, 0 goals).

GEORGE FORD (1912/13-1914/15, full-back, 10 games, 0 goals).

Other leading lights:

JIMMY ASHCROFT (1900/01-1907/08, goalkeeper, 303 games, 0 goals).

JOHN DICK (1898/99-1909/10, half-back, 284 games, 13 goals).

ANDY DUCAT (1904/05-1911/12, half-back, 188 games, 21 goals).

RODDY McEACHRANE (1902/03-1913/14, half-back, 346 games, 0 goals).

PERCY SANDS (1903/04-1914/15, centre-half, 350 games, 12 goals).

THE ROARING TWENTIES

LESLIE KNIGHTON
(manager 1919/20-1925/26)

After the Great War, Arsenal found themselves back in the First Division without kicking a ball but amid blazin controversy. The Football League had decided to increase the size of the top flight by two clubs and the majority observers reckoned that Chelsea and Tottenham Hotspur, who had occupied the last two First Division slots at t end of 1914/15, were likely to benefit from the expansion.

However, after some discreet backstage lobbying, a place among the elite was allocated to the Gunners, who ha finished only fifth in the Second Division, to the exclusion of Spurs! Recriminations from the direction of Whi Hart Lane were predictably bitter, but Arsenal proceeded unabashed to set about cementing their new station.

To that end they appointed a new manager, Leslie Knighton, who presided over a nondescript period which threatened to get worse as the side slithered progressively closer to relegation. This culminated in a gruesome 1924/25 campaign in which the drop was avoided by only one place.

The following summer, Arsenal made the most important decision in their history to date - they appointed Herb Chapman as manager. Fresh from lifting two League Championships with Huddersfield Town, the inspirationa Yorkshireman transformed the North Londoners' fortunes, persuading the board to sign a clutch of new player including veteran inside-forward Charlie Buchan, winger Joe Hulme and full-back Tom Parker.

The result was the instant and hitherto unimaginable improvement to runners-up spot in the First Division an progress to that term's FA Cup quarter-final. The following year, 1927, the Gunners reached their first FA Cup Final, which they lost to Cardiff City, before continuing to consolidate less spectacularly over the next few seaso All the time, however, Chapman was building. As the twenties drew towards their close, such names as David Jac Alex James and Cliff Bastin appeared on the teamsheet. A truly memorable soccer force was about to be unleashe

THE GUNNERS IN 1919/20

Back row (left to right):

FRED GROVES (1912/13-1920/21, forward, 53 games, 7 goals).

ANGUS McKINNON (1908/09-1921/22, wing-half, 217 games, 4 goals).

JACK BUTLER (1919/20-1929/30, centre-half, 296 games, 8 goals).

J JEWETT (reserve who played no senior games).

JOE TONER (1919/20-1924/25, outside-left, 100 games, 6 goals).

JOE SHAW (1907/08-1921/22, full-back, 326 games, 0 goals).

Middle row:

ASSISTANT TRAINER (Name unknown).

FRED PAGNAM (1919/20-1920/21, centre-forward, 53 games, 27 goals).

FRANK BRADSHAW (1914/15-1921/22, utility, 142 games, 14 goals).

FRANCIS COWNLEY (1920/21-1921/22, full-back, 15 games, 0 goals).

STEVE DUNN (1919/20-1921/22, goalkeeper, 44 games, 0 goals).

ALF BAKER (1919/20-1930/31, utility, 351 games, 26 goals).

ALEX GRAHAM (1912/13-1923/24, half-back, 179 games, 19 goals).

LESLIE KNIGHTON (manager).

Front row:

CHRIS BUCKLEY (1914/15-1919/20, centre-half, 59 games, 3 goals).

JOCK RUTHERFORD (1913/14-1925/26, winger, 232 games, 27 goals).

HENRY WHITE (1919/20-1921/22, forward, 109 games, 46 goals).

JOE NORTH (1919/20-1921/22, forward, 23 games, 6 goals).

BILLY BLYTH (1914/15-1928/29, inside-left or left-half, 343 games, 51 goals).

WALTER COOPLAND (1919/20, outside-left, 1 game, 0 goals).

Pictured right (from left):

CHARLIE BUCHAN (1925/26-1927/28, inside-forward, 120 games, 56 goals).

JIMMY BRAIN (1924/25-1930/31, centre-forward, 231 games, 139 goals).

JOE SHAW

THE MEN WHO MADE ARSENAL GREAT

HERBERT CHAPMAN
(Manager, 1925-1934)

Arsenal won no major honours for the 44 years after their formation in 1886, but when the Gunners broke their duck, they shattered it with a vengeance.

The breakthrough came in 1930 when goals from free-scoring Jack Lambert and the schemer supreme, Alex James, secured a 2-0 victory over Huddersfield Town in the FA Cup Final at Wembley. Glorious, indeed, but merely a taster for the barely credible triumphs that lay ahead. The following season Arsenal became the first southern side to be crowned League Champions topping the table by the comfortable margin of seven points. There was a runners-up spot in 19 but then further titles were garnered in 1933, 1934, 1935 and 1938, with the little matter of another FA Cup win in 1936, when Ted Drake grabbed the only goal of the game against Sheffield United.

The one abiding sadness of this sensational period, when Arsenal became the most famous clu side in the world, was the death in January 1934 of Herbert Chapman. His successor was Georg Allison, already a club director, who would remain at the helm until after the war.

BOB JOHN

FA CUP WINNERS 1936

Back row (left to right):

WILF COPPING (1934/35-1938/39, left-half, 185 games, 0 goals).

GEORGE MALE (1930/31-1947/48, right-back, 314 games, 0 goals).

JACK CRAYSTON (1934/35-1938/39, right-half, 184 games, 17 goals).

ALEX WILSON (1933/34-1938/39, goalkeeper, 89 games, 0 goals).

HERBIE ROBERTS (1926/27-1937/38, centre-half, 333 games, 5 goals).

TED DRAKE (1933/34-1938/39, centre-forward, 182 games, 136 goals).

EDDIE HAPGOOD (1927/28-1938/39, left-back, 434 games, 2 goals).

Front row:

GEORGE ALLISON (manager 1934-1947).

JOE HULME (1925/26-1937/38, outside-right, 372 games, 124 goals).

RAY BOWDEN (1932/33-1937/38, inside-forward, 136 games, 47 goals).

ALEX JAMES (1929/30-1936/37, inside-forward, 259 games, 27 goals).

CLIFF BASTIN (1929/30-1946/47, outside-left or inside-forward, 392 games, 176 goals).

TOM WHITTAKER (trainer 1927-1946).

Above right (top left):

TOM PARKER (1925/26-1932/33, right-back, 292 games, 17 goals).

JACK LAMBERT (1926/27-1933/34, centre-forward, 159 games, 109 goals).

DAVID JACK (1928/29-1933/34, inside-forward, 206 games, 123 goals).

Right (in action, left to right):

ALEX JAMES

GEORGE MALE

Bottom row (left to right):

BERNARD JOY (1935/36-1946/47, centre-half, 92 games, 0 goals).

FRANK MOSS (1931/32-1935/36, goalkeeper, 159 games, 1 goal).

ALF KIRCHEN (1934/35-1938/39, winger, 99 games, 44 goals).

Left:

BOB JOHN (1922/23-1936/37, left-half, 467 games, 13 goals).

TOM PARKER

JACK LAMBERT

DAVID JACK

THE GUNNERS' SECOND COMING

TOM WHITTAKER
(Manager 1947-1956)

After the war, most of the players who had been riding high in 1939 were past their prime a Arsenal, in common with other clubs, faced a large-scale rebuilding programme. George Allis retained the managerial reins until 1947, when the responsibility passed to his assistant and th Gunners' one-time trainer, Tom Whittaker.

In harness with inspirational skipper Joe Mercer, the new boss led Arsenal to the League title 1948, the FA Cup in 1950 - when two Reg Lewis goals were enough to beat Liverpool - ar another Championship in 1953. After that the side began to break up and an era ended whe Tom died in 1956.

Here are the men who carried the Arsenal banner into a new age and played leading roles in club's second successful phase. The stories of those who followed them make up the main par this book.

REG LEWIS

LEAGUE CHAMPIONS 1952/53

Back row (left to right):

RAY DANIEL (1948/49-1952/53, centre-half, 99 games, 5 goals).

ALEX FORBES (1947/48-1955/56, wing-half, 239 games, 20 goals).

GEORGE SWINDIN (1936/37-1953/54, goalkeeper, 294 games, 0 goals).

LIONEL SMITH (1947/48-1953/54, left-back, 180 games, 0 goals).

ARTHUR SHAW (1949/50-1954/55, wing-half, 61 games, 0 goals).

Front row:

PETER GORING (1949/50-1958/59, centre-forward, 240 games, 53 goals).

DON OAKES (1952/53-1954/55, inside-forward, 11 games, 1 goal).

JOE MERCER (1946/47-1953/54, left-half, 273 games, 2 goals).

JOE WADE (1945/46-1954/55, full-back, 93 games, 0 goals).

DOUG LISHMAN (1948/49-1955/56, inside-forward, 243 games, 135 goals).

DON ROPER (1947/48-1956/57, utility forward, 319 games, 95 goals).

Also pictured, top row (left to right):

FREDDIE COX (1949/50-1952/53, winger, 94 games, 16 goals).

TOMMY LAWTON (1953/54-1955/56, centre-forward, 37 games, 14 goals).

LAURIE SCOTT (1945/46-1951/52, full-back, 126 games, 0 goals).

Middle row:

ARTHUR MILTON (1950/51-1954/55, winger, 84 games, 21 goals).

RONNIE ROOKE (1946/47-1948/49, centre-forward, 93 games, 69 goals).

WALLY BARNES (1946/47-1955/56, full-back, 292 games, 12 goals).

Bottom row:

BRYN JONES (1938/39-1948/49, inside-forward, 74 games, 7 goals).

DENIS COMPTON (1936/37-1949/50, outside-left, 59 games, 16 goals).

LES COMPTON (1931/32-1951/52, centre-half, 270 games, 6 goals).

Left:

REG LEWIS (1937/38-1951/52, inside-forward, 175 games, 116 goals).

Right: (left to right)

JIMMY LOGIE (1945/46-1954/55, inside-forward, 326 games, 76 goals).

ARCHIE MACAULAY (1947/48-1949/50, wing-half, 107 games, 1 goal).

JACK KELSEY

Great goalkeepers deserve to showcase their talents in successful sides; alas for Jack Kelsey, that was never to be. To be brutally frank, during the years when the Welshman was widely acclaimed as the most accomplished custodian in the land, Arsenal were nondescript in the extreme. Particularly in the late fifties and early sixties, Jack was the one world-class player at Highbury, and it was only he who stood between the Gunners and many a rout.

Throughout that trying time, the Kelsey presence was truly formidable. Tall and exuding an aura of imperturbable confidence, he was blessed with a pair of huge, apparently prehensile hands, and his speciality was plucking the most wicked of crosses out of the sky while besieged by marauding attackers. His natural strength, honed during teenage days as a steelworker, enabled him to withstand the attentions of dreadnoughts such as Nat Lofthouse and Trevor Ford in an era when knocking 'keepers flat was an essential part of the centre-forward's art.

Never unnecessarily showy, Jack made his job look deceptively easy through shrewd positioning, a fundamental but all-too-rare ability based on sound reading of the game. Not that he couldn't be acrobatic when the need arose. Indeed, he was dubbed 'the cat with magnetic paws' by the admiring Brazilians, ultimate connoisseurs of soccer excellence who would have purred with pleasure over one particularly agile display, against Manchester United in October 1960. That muddy afternoon at Highbury Jack won the match with a string of stupendous saves, including one gravity-defying mid-air flip to divert a Bobby Charlton thunderbolt.

Yet there had been a time when his future had seemed in doubt. After conceding five goals on his debut against Charlton Athletic in February 1951, the callow recruit from amateur club Winch Wen became the butt of a local music-hall comedian. Arsenal boss Tom Whittaker, to his eternal credit, would have none of it: outraged by the cheap jibes at the expense of a youngster, he declared that Jack had been blameless for the defeat and likened him to a pilot unluckily shot down on his first mission. Accordingly the rookie was soon back in the air, and was on hand to replace injured veteran George Swindin for most of the 1952/53 Championship campaign.

It wasn't long before he made the Gunners' green jersey his personal property, and although there were no more club honours, Jack made up for it on the international scene. As well as winning 41 caps - then a British record for a 'keeper - he played for Great Britain against the Rest of Europe in 1955 and was one of his country's stars in their progress to the last eight of the World Cup in 1958.

Only once was there a serious challenge to his Highbury position. On recovering from breaking his arm in 1959, Jack could not immediately oust his deputy, Jim Standen, and there were fears that his day was done. It wasn't long, however, before the Welshman was back in business, displaying majestic form for another two-and-a-half years, and it took a back injury, sustained diving at the feet of Brazilian centre-forward Vava in Rio in May 1962, to end his career.

Even then, his Arsenal days were far from over. Jack, a kind and loyal man, took over the club lottery and shop, and eventually retired as commercial manager in 1989 after 40 years at Highbury.

But it is for his deeds between the posts that he will be forever revered and, with due deference to the subsequent efforts of Messrs Jennings, Wilson and Seaman, there is only one place for Jack Kelsey on the Gunners' goalkeeping roll of honour - out on his own at the very top.

BORN: Swansea, 19.11.29. GAMES: 351. GOALS: 0.
HONOURS: League Championship 52/3.
41 Wales caps (54-62).
DIED: London, 18.3.92.

1950/51 — 1961/62

DAVE BOWEN

Arsenal needed a man of rare character to replace Joe Mercer when their inspirational wing-half and captain was forced out of the game by a broken leg in 1954. They found him in Welshman Dave Bowen, a motivator supreme whose storming, passionate performances in the Gunners' number-six shirt throughout the mid and late fifties did much to lift a rather ordinary side.

Fists clenched and vocal chords straining - it was said that Dave made more noise during a game than any dozen fans - he was a formidable adversary who packed a sturdy tackle, yet fire and brimstone were not his only assets. The man who became skipper during the frustratingly mundane campaign of 1957/58 was also a fluent passer, being particularly adept at the penetrating through-ball. This devastating ploy, however, was at its most effective when Dave was playing behind a direct, fleet-footed winger such as Cliff Jones, his Wales team-mate, and was less suited to the more intricate approach of Joe Haverty, his usual club partner.

Dave, who grew up in a rugby heartland and was a comparatively late starter at the round-ball code, arrived at Highbury from Northampton Town in July 1950 as a left-winger. He was converted quickly to wing-half and made his senior debut eight months later, but a sustained breakthrough was delayed by injuries and the stalwart Mercer.

On becoming an Arsenal regular, Dave soon made an international impact, and captained his country to the quarter-finals of the 1958 World Cup. The following year saw him return to Northampton, where he had always lived, and he became a successful team boss, leading the Cobblers from the Fourth Division to the top flight. He later served as general manager and director, and there are still those who maintain that Arsenal need have looked no further than Dave Bowen when, in the sixties, they sought a leader to restore their former eminence.

BORN: Maesteg, Glamorgan, 7.6.28.
GAMES: 162. GOALS: 2.
19 Wales caps (54-59).

OTHER CLUBS: Northampton Town 47/8-48/9 (12, 0) and 59/60 (22, 1).
MANAGER: Northampton Town 59-67 and 69-72 (general manager until 1985).
DIED: Northampton, 25.9.95.

1950/51 – 1958/59

CLIFF HOLTON

1950/51 – 1958/59

Cliff Holton was a rampaging, free-scoring centre-forward whom Arsenal saw fit to convert into a wing-half. Four seasons after the switch, he was allowed to leave Highbury, and called the Gunners' judgement into question by shattering records at a succession of clubs while adding a further 210 goals to his League tally.

When he was signed from non-League Oxford City in 1947, the big, raw-boned youngster was a full-back, but it wasn't long before manager Tom Whittaker realised that Cliff had all the attributes of an outstanding marksman. Accordingly, he led the line on his senior debut at Stoke on Boxing Day 1950, and was soon netting with gratifying regularity.

A magnificent all-round athlete, Cliff was blessed with one of the most explosive left-foot shots in living memory, and when the ball was played into his path anywhere within 35 yards of goal he offered a potent menace. Sadly, his form deserted him for the 1952 FA Cup Final, won by a Jackie Milburn-inspired Newcastle, but his 19 goals in 21 matches – including an emphatic Anfield hat-trick and a spectacular four-goal show at Hillsborough – were vital to the following year's title triumph.

Thereafter, Arsenal struggled and Cliff's progress was not helped by the purchase of fading England star Tommy Lawton, a Whittaker gamble that failed. Other strikers appeared and Cliff became a half-back, a role in which his passing skills improved and his tackling and aerial ability served him well.

He was appointed skipper for a brief stint but when new boss George Swindin revamped his staff in 1958, the 29-year-old was surplus to requirements and joined Watford. Although his subsequent feats were achieved in the lower divisions, there were many who believed that Cliff Holton would have been prolific at whatever level he played. How easy management seems, after the event.

BORN: Oxford, 29.4.29.
GAMES: 216. GOALS: 88.
HONOURS: League Championship 52/3.

OTHER CLUBS: Watford 58/9–61/2 (120, 84); Northampton Town 61/2–62/3 (62, 50); Crystal Palace 62/3–64/5 (101, 40); Watford 65/6 (24, 12); Charlton Athletic 65/6 (18, 7); Orient 66/7–67/8 (47, 17).
DIED: Spain, 30.5.96.

PETER GORING

Peter Goring's Highbury career was split into two distinct phases. Early in the first, as a brave and prodigiously industrious centre-forward, there were hopes that he might progress to international status; in the second, as a ball-winning wing-half, he became a bulwark of the side for several seasons and enjoyed a spell as captain.

The unassuming, blond West Countryman, known affectionately as 'The Butcher's Boy' in reference to his former occupation, joined Arsenal from Cheltenham Town in January 1948 on the recommendation of ex-Gunner Jimmy Brain, then boss of the Gloucestershire club.

After overcoming assorted fitness problems, Peter impressed on a 1949 summer tour of Brazil and forced his way into the first team for the following term. He scored the winner against Chelsea at Stamford Bridge on his senior debut, went on to net 21 times in 29 League outings, and gave a sterling display in the FA Cup Final victory over Liverpool.

It had been an enterprising, exhilarating first campaign: Peter had led his line intelligently, created frequent mayhem with bold solo runs into the penalty box, proved lethal with head and both feet, and showed himself willing to dive among the flailing boots. Understandably, the fans warmed to their burly young sharp-shooter; a glowing long-term future seemed assured.

Yet somehow, despite making a telling contribution to Arsenal's title triumph in 1953, Peter never quite recaptured that initial sparkle, and in 1953/54, troubled by injury and faced with stiff competition from Cliff Holton, he slipped out of the side. Manager Tom Whittaker was too shrewd to discard such a valuable asset, however, and converted him into a worthy successor to Alex Forbes at right-half. Peter revelled in his new role, toiling enthusiastically until his Highbury days ended with a free transfer back to non-League ranks in 1960.

BORN: Bishop's Cleeve, Gloucestershire, 2.1.27. GAMES: 240. GOALS: 53.
HONOURS: League Championship 52/3. FA Cup 49/50.
DIED: Bishop's Cleeve, Gloucestershire, December 1994.

1949/50 – 1958/59

DEREK TAPSCOTT

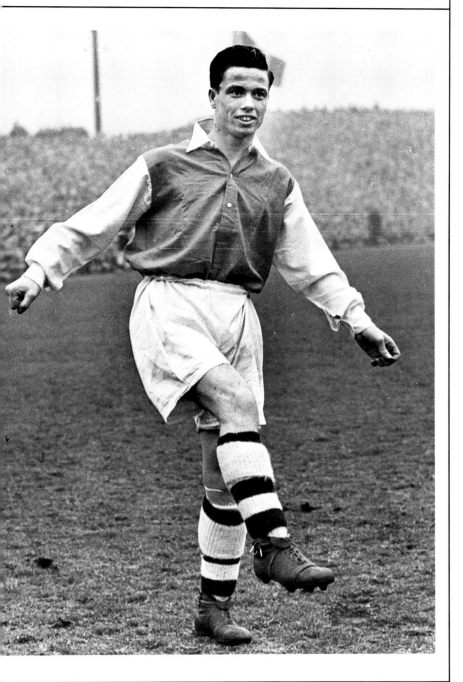

1953/54 – 1957/58

It was an unwise defender who took his eye off Derek Tapscott. The slight but wiry Welsh goal-poacher was a ball of energy whose speed and persistence was apt to hustle the calmest of opponents into unaccustomed errors.

A former builder's labourer who hailed from a family of 17, Derek was a £2,750 acquisition from amateurs Barry Town in October 1953. Within six months he had made an auspicious debut in a 3-0 victory against Liverpool, bringing a modicum of cheer to Arsenal fans who watched sadly as Joe Mercer's career was ended by a broken leg in the same Highbury encounter. Playing alongside Tommy Lawton, the newcomer scored twice, and then celebrated by winning his first Welsh cap three days later. He finished the season with five goals in as many matches, and Arsenal, it seemed, had unearthed a diamond.

During the next campaign, however, Derek's perpetual-motion style proved *too* frenetic for his own good, but as his experience grew so did his effectiveness, and he was the Gunners' leading scorer in both 1955/56 and 1956/57. Instead of rushing around with apparently aimless abandon, Derek was now reading the game, knowing when to hustle defenders and when to stand off, and picking up a high percentage of his goals through astute judgment of rebounds from the 'keeper. One of his most spectacular strikes – and certainly his most face-saving from the club's viewpoint – was a horizontal close-range header to win an FA Cup replay against non-League Bedford in 1956.

Cruelly, when playing at his peak in 1957, Derek underwent a cartilage operation and thereafter he never quite regained his old pizzazz. The following year, a £10,000 deal took him to Cardiff City, whom he supplied liberally with goals until the mid sixties.

BORN: Barry, Glamorgan, 30.6.32.
GAMES: 132. GOALS: 68.
HONOURS: 14 Wales caps (54-59).

OTHER CLUBS: Cardiff City 58/9-64/5 (194, 79);
Newport County 65/6 (13, 1).

LEN WILLS

Len Wills was a full-back of rare finesse in days when most supporters expected their defenders to offer passable impersonations of Desperate Dan. Neat and quick – he had been a champion hurdler as a boy – the amiable Londoner was a precise distributor who formed part of a particularly constructive right flank when he lined up with wing-half Gerry Ward and winger Danny Clapton, although vociferous elements among Gunners fans contended that the combination lacked bite.

An unflappable performer, Len refused to commit himself to rash tackles, preferring to jockey tricky opponents away from the danger area. This characteristic coolness was invaluable in his occasional role of penalty-taker, never more so than at Highbury in the dying seconds of a blood-and-thunder thriller against Wolves in January 1960. With the visitors 4–3 in front, Arsenal's Mel Charles was clattered and the referee pointed to the spot. The kick was delayed for the prostrate Welshman to be revived, and crowd pandemonium reached fever pitch as the seconds ticked by. But Len might have been carved from ice as he strode through the quagmire, deliberately cleaned the ball of mud and blasted the equaliser.

Yet for all his steady achievements, there had been a time when more had been expected of the versatile defender, who could readily fill in at left-back or wing-half. After a splendid start in 1953, he seemed set to become a fixture in the side, but mid decade saw him displaced by the more physical Stan Charlton. By the late fifties he was appearing regularly again, and in Febuary 1959 gave one of his finest displays, subduing the brilliant Cliff Jones in a 4–1 win at White Hart Lane.

As the sixties dawned, Len selflessly passed on his expertise to the young men who would replace him, a typically generous attitude from a true sportsman.

BORN: Hackney, London, 8.11.27.
GAMES: 208. GOALS: 4.

1953/54 – 1960/61

BILL DODGIN

1952/53 – 1959/60

There was an unmistakable aura of long suffering about centre-half Bill Dodgin. Although he stood tall at 6ft 4in and was rarely beaten in the air, he was spindly of build and lugubrious of countenance, thus conspicuously lacking the imposing physical presence the Highbury faithful demand of their stoppers.

It was all rather unfair, as it was not often Bill let the Gunners down. Like most defenders who are not of international class, he could be dominant on one occasion, seemingly hesitant the next, and if his footwork was occasionally clumsy then the same could be said of others who enjoyed the crowd's confidence and affection to a far higher degree.

He had encountered a similar reaction at Fulham, his first club, where frustrated fans had vented their spleen on him because his father, Bill Senior, was the manager. Such treatment must have been torture for the young Dodgin, a dedicated, intelligent professional who thought deeply about the game and was a thorough gentleman.

When drafted in as a replacement for departing Arsenal favourite Ray Daniel in 1953, he had shown encouraging form, and captained the England under-23 side during his first full campaign. But come the mid fifties he appeared to lose his way and was ousted by Jim Fotheringham, before fighting back strongly to reclaim his place in 1956/57. Despite facing frequent press speculation about an imminent successor, he struck up a solid understanding with goalkeeper Jack Kelsey, and towards the end of the decade had settled down as a capable, safety-first performer.

The end, however, was near. In 1960, with Mel Charles on the scene and young John Snedden developing promisingly, Bill fell out of favour for the last time at Highbury, and returned to Craven Cottage before embarking on a varied career in management.

BORN: Felling, Tyneside, 4.11.31.
GAMES: 207. GOALS: 1.

OTHER CLUBS: Fulham 51/2-52/3 (35, 0) and 60/1-63/4 (69, 0). MANAGER: Queen's Park Rangers 68; Fulham 69-72; Northampton Town 73-76; Brentford 76-80; Northampton Town 80-82.

GERRY WARD

When 16-year-old Gerry Ward ran out to face Huddersfield Town at Highbury in August 1953, his crisp red-and-white shirt bearing the number 11, he held centre stage as the Gunners' youngest-ever debutant. Less than two hours later, after charming the fans with a richly promising display, he was hailed, in some quarters, as 'the new Cliff Bastin'. It was a preposterous, cruelly unfair tag with which to saddle a young man, and, predictably, he did not live up to it.

Indeed, after two further matches, Gerry dropped out of the side, and, despite becoming an England amateur international, did not reappear until February 1958. Then, his National Service and a conversion to wing-half behind him, he faced Manchester United five days before the Munich air disaster in a classic confrontation which Arsenal lost by the odd goal in nine. Thereafter, without quite managing to cement a regular long-term place, he began to parade the skills which had prompted his early breakthrough.

A precise, intelligent passer, Gerry could tackle firmly and possessed a scorching shot, as all who saw his 25-yard strike at home to Spurs in September 1960 would testify. He was never the quickest of movers, however, and knee injuries around the turn of the decade were hardly conducive to advancement, especially with the likes of Tommy Docherty, Mel Charles, Vic Groves and others vying for midfield roles.

By 1963 it was clear that the likeable Londoner had little part to play in new manager Billy Wright's rebuilding plans, and he moved on to try his luck at Leyton Orient. Gerry, who later combined playing for non-League Cambridge City with a career in banking, could look back on a fitfully valuable but ultimately disappointing contribution to the Highbury cause.

BORN: Stepney, London, 5.10.36.
GAMES: 84. GOALS: 10.

OTHER CLUBS: Leyton Orient 63/4-64/5 (44, 2). DIED: Sheffield, January 1994.

1953/54 – 1962/63

DENNIS EVANS

1953/54 — 1959/60

Muscular Merseysider Dennis Evans deserves better than to be remembered for one freak own goal, yet his name remains linked inextricably to a bizarre incident in a First Division encounter with Blackpool at Highbury in December 1955. The Gunners were four up when the jubilant left-back, believing he had heard the referee blow for time, thrashed the ball past his own goalkeeper, Con Sullivan, from 25 yards. Alas for Dennis, he had been deceived by a phantom whistler in the crowd and, to his considerable chagrin, the goal stood.

In fact, such a piece of pantomime was the very antithesis of everything that the doughty defender stood for. Essentially, Dennis was a consistent performer who tackled ferociously, possessed commendable speed of recovery, was powerful in the air – where instinctive timing enabled him to reach crosses which seemed certain to pass over his head – and was a cool dispatcher of penalty kicks. Perhaps his most outstanding attribute, however, was a finely honed positional sense which made goal-line clearances a priceless speciality, and which enabled him to make a creditable fist of deputising between the posts for the injured Jack Kelsey in an FA Cup replay against Sheffield United in 1959.

Dennis, who had been on Wolves' books as a boy, made his first-team bow for Arsenal in a 1953 friendly against Grasshoppers in Zurich, before progressing steadily to become the long-term replacement for the distinguished Lionel Smith. A forceful yet thoughtful personality, he was one of several players tried as skipper by manager Jack Crayston in the mid fifties, and was ever ready to help youngsters. This latter trait helped to earn him a role as Highbury youth coach after two ankle fractures in 1959/60 precipitated the end of his playing days.

BORN: Ellesmere Port, Cheshire, 18.5.30.
GAMES: 207. GOALS: 12.

STAN CHARLTON

1955/56 – 1958/59

An afternoon in the company of Stan Charlton was not high on most wingers' lists of relaxing pastimes. It wasn't that the squarely-built Devonian was an unpleasant character; indeed, off the pitch Stan was affability itself. It was just that when plying his trade as the Gunners' right-back, he tackled with the subtlety of a runaway bulldozer, a method which made a lasting impression on all who experienced it.

Stan, who won four amateur international caps and played in the 1952 Helsinki Olympics before turning professional, moved to Arsenal from Leyton Orient in November 1955, accounting for a minor portion of the £30,000 package which also took Vic Groves to Highbury. It wasn't long before he had claimed a place at the expense of the more cultured but less robust Len Wills, and he maintained his first-choice status throughout most of his three years at the club.

True, his ball skills were rudimentary, and he could be outstripped by greyhound-like flankmen such as Nottingham Forest's Stuart Imlach. But Stan, as befitted a former regular soldier, was a never-say-die trooper who pulled his weight in the heat of battle, and was always ready to help out a beleaguered team-mate.

Like most full-backs in the fifties, he confined himself mainly to defensive duties but did venture forward occasionally, never to better effect than in an FA Cup quarter-final against Birmingham City in March 1956. That day at Highbury, in front of nearly 68,000 people, Stan lashed home a 30-yard thunderbolt that would have done credit to his sharp-shooting namesake, Bobby.

Arsenal presumably believing his best years were behind him, allowed Stan to return to the O's on Christmas Eve 1958, but he was far from finished. He put in a further six seasons' service, including a term in the top flight, before going on to manage non-League Weymouth.

BORN: Exeter, 28.6.29. GAMES: 110. GOALS: 3.

OTHER CLUBS: Leyton Orient 52/3-55/6 (151, 1) and 58/9-64/5 (216, 0).

IM FOTHERINGHAM

CON SULLIVAN

Jim Fotheringham had the height, but not the authority, to continue the Highbury tradition of distinguished centre-halves. When Tom Whittaker brought the spindly, 6ft 4in Scot into his side to replace out-of-form Bill Dodgin at Bolton in November 1954, the Arsenal boss believed he was launching the career of a stopper with the potential to match the deeds of Herbie Roberts in the thirties and Les Compton after the war.

But despite making a pluckily promising start against the formidable Nat Lofthouse, and retaining his place for 15 months, Jim rarely looked the part. Occasionally he would play a blinder and it would seem that Whittaker's faith was about to be repaid, but all too often he would follow it with an inept performance, revealing fragility in his aerial work and naivety in his positional play.

In January 1956 Jim was axed in favour of Dodgin, and was consigned to the reserves for the next season-and-a-half. A 19-match run as first choice in early 1958 produced little improvement, and after a disastrous showing in a 6-3 home defeat by Luton Town on Boxing Day, he was never picked again. Three months later, he joined Hearts for £10,000, but didn't settle and finished his career on an anti-climactic note with Northampton Town.

BORN: Hamilton, 19.12.33. GAMES: 76. GOALS: 0.

OTHER CLUBS: Heart of Midlothian 58/9; Northampton Town 59/60 (11, 0).
DIED: Kettering, Northamptonshire, September 1977.

Con Sullivan was a big, broad-shouldered goalkeeper who did a solid job as Jack Kelsey's deputy during the mid fifties. In fact, in the days following his arrival at Highbury from Bristol City in February 1954, there was speculation that he might even be a genuine contender for the senior slot, but such lofty aspirations proved beyond the Englishman with the Irish-sounding name.

Though he never let Arsenal down, and was an impressive performer on his line, Con was never the equal of Jack in claiming crosses and therefore never inspired the same confidence in his defenders.

Perhaps his finest hour between the Gunners' posts came in December 1956, when he made a series of brilliant saves against Cardiff City at Ninian Park to enable his team-mates to record a 3-2 victory. Undoubtedly his most irritating first-team moment was a year earlier when full-back Dennis Evans, wrongly believing a game against Blackpool to be over, blasted the ball past him for an own goal which ruined what would have been a second successive clean sheet. The unlucky custodian was not amused by the terrace whistler who caused the confusion.

Con's career ended in 1959, when he failed to recover from a back injury suffered in training, and he became a milkman.

BORN: Bristol, 22.8.28. GAMES: 32. GOALS: 0.

OTHER CLUBS: Bristol City 50/1-52/3 (73, 0).

1954/55 – 1958/59

1953/54 – 1957/58

JIMMY BLOOMFIELD

Jimmy Bloomfield was the midfield general who never won the battle honours his attacking prowess deserved. A shrewd tactician and a quite beautiful passer, he kept the Arsenal forward line ticking through the mid and late fifties, when one lean campaign followed another as the Gunners strove unavailingly to recapture past glories.

Total command of the ball was the essence of Jimmy's game, whether he was switching the angle of play through precise and imaginative distribution, leaving defenders helpless with the sweetest of body-swerves, or shooting for goal with a power that belied his spare, almost gangly frame. He also worked incessantly, possessed the resilience to soak up physical punishment, and had the gift, indispensable to schemers, for spotting the most fleeting of openings in an opposing rearguard. Unfortunately for Arsenal, sometimes he thought *too* quickly for less subtle team-mates to capitalise on his guile.

Jimmy sprang to the notice of Highbury boss Tom Whittaker through his enterprising efforts in a struggling Brentford side in 1953/54. When the Bees were relegated at the end of that campaign, a £10,000 fee was enough to ensure that their brightest prospect would not sink with them to the Third Division. With the Gunners undergoing a period of transition, Jimmy was tried in several forward positions, but spent most of his first term on the wing.

By mid 1955/56, however, he was a fixture at number ten, his left-sided inventiveness bringing much-needed poise and balance to a moderate team. In 1957 his progress was rewarded with two England under-23 caps, and the following year he represented the London side which lost to Barcelona in the first final of the Inter Cities Fairs Cup. Jimmy was a crucial factor in Arsenal's gratifying improvement in 1958/59, when they finished third in the Championship race, and but for his three-month absence to recover from a cartilage operation, they might have climbed even higher.

Sadly, the optimism of pundits who believed the Gunners were back as a major soccer power proved to be premature. The next season saw a slump to 13th place, despite some sparking Bloomfield contributions. Particularly memorable were an inspirational hat-trick in a 5-2 drubbing of Manchester United at Highbury - he invariably impressed against the Old Trafford club - and a magical dribble past four opponents to score in a home encounter with West Bromwich Albion. He was selected for the Football League and there were whispers about further international recognition, but then George Eastham was recruited and suddenly there was no place for Jimmy Bloomfield at Highbury. Accordingly, he moved to Birmingham City for £30,000 in November 1960, but never recaptured his earlier level of performance.

Eventually Jimmy, a deep thinker about the game, moved into management, taking a positive, attacking philosophy to Orient and Leicester. One of the game's most popular characters, he was much mourned when he died in 1983 after a lengthy illness.

BORN: Kensington, 15.2.34. GAMES: 227. GOALS: 56.

OTHER CLUBS: Brentford 52/3-53/4 (42, 5); Birmingham City 60/1-63/4 (122, 26); Brentford 64/5-65/6 (44, 4); West Ham United 65/6 (10, 0); Plymouth Argyle 66/7-67/8 (25, 1); Orient 67/8-68/9 (44, 3). MANAGER: Orient 68-71; Leicester City 71-77; Orient 77-81. DIED: Chingford, Essex, 3.4.83.

1954/55 – 1960/61

GORDON NUTT

Scampering flankman Gordon Nutt suffered an unlucky start to an Arsenal career which never quite took off. After arriving from Cardiff City in September 1955, the diminutive Brummie cracked his shin at Everton in his third match, and was sidelined for three months. When he recovered, his impact on the left side of the Gunners' attack was negligible, and apart from two spells in 1958, he was confined mainly to the reserves.

Gordon – valued at £10,000 in the package deal which also took Mike Tiddy to North London with a third winger, Brian Walsh, moving in the opposite direction – had speed and persistence, and was a fair crosser of the ball. Unfortunately his control was apt to let him down.

There were times, however, when his positive attitude paid dividends, never more memorably than in two high-scoring Highbury thrillers in February 1958. Against Manchester United, Gordon made two goals for Jimmy Bloomfield in an honourable 5-4 defeat, and against Spurs he looked even more dangerous, scoring in a 4-4 draw.

Sadly, such displays were too few, and five unsatisfactory years as a Gunner ended in 1960 with a transfer to Southend United. Subsequently, Gordon played in the Netherlands before emigrating to Australia.

BORN: Birmingham, 8.11.32. GAMES: 51. GOALS: 10.
OTHER CLUBS: Coventry City 51/2-54/5 (76, 13); Cardiff City 54/5-55/6 (17, 4); Southend United 60/1 (16, 2); PSV Eindhoven, Holland.

1955/56 – 1959/60

JOHNNY PETTS

There was a time when England youth international left-half Johnny Petts was seen at Highbury as the logical long-term successor to the faithful Dave Bowen. Unfortunately, the stocky sandy-haired Londoner, a tenacious marker whose gritty approach was spiced with more than a dash of creative knowhow, failed to build on his early promise and slipped away to the lower divisions.

There was no hint of such anti-climax when Johnny made his senior debut at home to Bolton Wanderers in February 1958. Though the Gunners lost 2-1, the young Petts took the eye with scurrying, combative performance, relishing an invigorating personal contest with the Trotters' highly-praised Dennis Stevens.

But after his progress was interrupted by National Service, Johnny was unable to claim a regular first-team spot. In 1958/59 a high-scoring run at inside-forward in the Football Combination hinted at a new direction, but it came to nothing, and he continued in his frustrating role as a stopgap wing-half for the senior side until new manager Billy Wright sold him to Reading for £5,000 in 1962.

Johnny, whose son Paul was to play on the wing for Bristol Rovers and Shrewsbury Town, later sampled management with Northampton Town.

BORN: Edmonton, London, 2.10.38. GAMES: 32. GOALS: 0.
OTHER CLUBS: Reading 62/3-64/5 (34, 0); Bristol Rovers 65/6-69/70 (92, 3).
MANAGER: Northampton Town 77-78.

1957/58 – 1961/62

MIKE TIDDY

LEN JULIANS

Mike Tiddy was a skilful winger whose rather dainty style was not always appreciated by vociferous sections of the Highbury crowd. Though he was hard-working, unselfish and an accurate crosser, he was inclined to wilt under the rumbustious attentions of the First Division's more physical full-backs, and his popularity suffered for it.

After arriving with Gordon Nutt as a £10,000 recruit from Cardiff City in September 1955, Mike was plunged straight into senior action, initially on his natural right side but later more often on the left. Despite enjoying a run of some 20 matches, the most settled sequence of his Highbury sojourn, he failed to establish himself, and was reduced to vying for a berth with Nutt and Joe Haverty.

His first full season, 1956/57, started encouragingly with five goals in ten games, including an adroit volley on the turn at Burnley and an acute-angle header at home to West Bromwich Albion. A subsequent knee injury did not help, and despite outstanding form on a European tour in the summer of 1957, Mike gradually drifted out of contention. The following year he joined Brighton, for whom he performed creditably, before becoming a village postmaster in his native Cornwall.

BORN: Helston, Cornwall, 4.4.29. GAMES: 52. GOALS: 8.

OTHER CLUBS: Torquay United 46/7-50/1 (5, 0); Cardiff City 50/1-54/5 (145, 19); Brighton and Hove Albion 58/9-61/2 (134, 11).

Len Julians was a goal-scorer of subtle skill who failed to find a niche at Highbury in a period when the Gunners were blessed with a plethora of strikers. With David Herd, Vic Groves, Jackie Henderson and Mel Charles all in contention for places, breaking through was never going to be easy for Len, who was recruited from Leyton Orient in December 1958 in exchange for Stan Charlton, Tony Biggs and a cash adjustment.

Yet the former star of Tottenham Schoolboys, who was effective both as leader of the line and inside-forward, had plenty to offer. Relying on precision of footwork and timing of runs more than on sheer power, left-sided Len was adept at peeling away from markers, dragging them out of position and creating space for colleagues.

After scoring on his debut at home to Luton Town, he found himself in and out of the side, despite underlining his value with a breathtaking strike at Blackpool in April 1959. Receiving the ball with his back to goal, he controlled it instantly and spun on the spot to hook a fierce, match-winning shot into the roof of the net.

The subsequent campaign brought only eight League appearances, however, and in the summer of 1960 Len joined Nottingham Forest for £10,000, later going on to excel for Millwall and coach in America.

BORN: Tottenham, 19.6.33. GAMES: 24. GOALS: 10.

OTHER CLUBS: Leyton Orient 55/6-58/9 (67, 35); Nottingham Forest 60/1-63/4 (59, 24); Millwall 63/4-66/7 (125, 58). DIED: London, 17.12.93.

1955/56 – 1957/58

1958/59 – 1959/60

DANNY CLAPTON

There was a touch of star quality about Danny Clapton; maybe even a faint hint of greatness. That he settled for something less reveals more about his complicated, contradictory character than any deficiency in a glorious natural talent. Not that Danny sold Arsenal short. For more than half a decade he entertained royally, if not always consistently, on the Gunners' right wing and, at his peak, was picked for England. Yet still there persisted the nagging feeling that he had more to give.

The young Clapton might never have become a professional footballer but for a sensible piece of self-help. He was working as a Billingsgate market porter, and playing for local amateurs Leytonstone, when he wrote to Tom Whittaker asking for a trial. The Highbury boss was instantly impressed and the enterprising Eastender was consigned to the junior ranks to develop his game. Fifteen months later, on Christmas Day 1954, he made his League debut at home to Chelsea, going on to claim a regular place as the manager sought to revamp a sadly lacklustre Arsenal team.

Danny's searing pace, devastating body-swerve and a penchant for cheeky back-heels soon made him a favourite with the fans, who revelled in his party piece of running along the byline towards the posts before dispatching the ball towards incoming colleagues. On his day he could torture any full-back, as the abrasive Tommy Banks of Bolton Wanderers discovered in September 1958 when he was on the receiving end of one of Danny's most dazzling displays, and the Gunners won 6-1. Like many wingers, however, he had an aversion to physical contact, and when Tommy took to the warpath in the return at Burnden Park the following week, Arsenal's number seven was hardly seen in a 2-1 defeat.

One oft-criticised aspect of the Clapton cocktail was his poor scoring record. His finishing tended to be wayward - despite an occasional knack of bending a shot with Garrincha-like prowess - though he might have improved his tally had he been more willing to cut inside. But such a flaw, hardly damning in a player who created so many chances for others, was not enough to explain why his international career was limited to one cap. No, Danny - whose selection in 1958 made him the first Gunner in five years to play for England, a telling comment on the sorry state of the club in the mid fifties - failed to reach the zenith of his profession for more fundamental reasons. He was a popular, outwardly casual personality who delighted in conferring nicknames on his team-mates - Jack Kelsey, of the receding hairline, was dubbed 'Yul Brynner' - but was nevertheless riven by self-doubt. He needed constant encouragement, responded negatively to a rollicking, and sometimes became sick with tension.

Danny left Highbury in 1962 and then, after a brief spell with Luton Town, emigrated to Australia where he played for Sydney Corinthians. He headed home in 1970 and, though troubled by ill health, took a pub in Hackney before dying, in tragic circumstances, in 1986.

BORN: Stepney, 22.7.34. GAMES: 225. GOALS: 27.
HONOURS: 1 England cap (58).

OTHER CLUBS: Luton Town 62/3 (10, 0); Sydney Corinthians.
DIED: Homerton, London, 22.5.86.

1954/55 – 1961/62

TOMMY DOCHERTY

1958/59 – 1960/61

It took Tommy Docherty only a few minutes of his Arsenal debut to incur the wrath of the Highbury fans; typically, he attracted the criticism by opening his mouth. On taking the field against Burnley in August 1958, the brush-topped extrovert lost no time in offering vociferous advice to his new colleagues. Accordingly, he was advised from the terraces to 'belt up and get on with the game'. Come the final whistle, however, the zestful wing-half had scored in a 3-0 win and was cheered off the pitch.

Having thus won recognition that although he made a lot of noise, he was certainly no empty vessel, Tommy went on to play a key role in transforming the Gunners from the mid-table non-entities of the previous term to a side that challenged for the title.

The astringent Glaswegian, who joined Arsenal for £27,000 after a dispute with former club Preston North End, commenced his Highbury career with conversion from attacking midfielder to one whose primary duties were defensive. But even though his lusty tackling and phenomenal work-rate were crucial in stiffening the team's spine, his passing skill ensured that he was also a creative influence.

Tommy's value was underlined by his absence for three months after breaking his ankle in October 1959. At the time of the accident, the side was fourth in the table; by his return they were in the lower reaches, and his springtime efforts as an emergency centre-half did much to right a boat that was rocking alarmingly.

Clearly, a young Tommy Docherty would have been a man around whom to build a new Arsenal, but he was 30 on his arrival at Highbury and already nursing management ambitions, so it was no surprise when he accepted the job of Chelsea coach in September 1961. His subsequent activities form one of soccer history's more lurid chapters.

BORN: Glasgow, 24.8.28.
GAMES: 90. GOALS: 1.
HONOURS: 25 Scotland caps (51-59).

OTHER CLUBS: Celtic 49/50;
Preston North End 49/50-57/8 (324, 5);
Chelsea 61/2 (4, 0). MANAGER: Chelsea 62-67;
Rotherham United 67-68; Queen's Park
Rangers 68; Aston Villa 68-70;
Oporto, Portugal, 70-71; Scotland 71-72;
Manchester United 72-77; Derby County 77-79;
Queen's Park Rangers 79-80; Sydney Olympic,
Australia, 80-81; Preston North End 81;
Wolverhampton Wanderers 84-85.

JIM STANDEN

LAURIE BROWN

[Ji]m Standen was a proficient goalkeeper who attracted widespread [s]ympathy for spending his Highbury years in the shadow of the magnificent Jack Kelsey. Yet as events turned out, the Londoner's [d]eparture was the most sensible of moves: Arsenal won nothing during the sixties, while Jim's distinguished service with West Ham United earned him FA Cup and European glory.

After recruitment from non-League Rickmansworth Town in 1952, he rose through the junior ranks before enjoying his first [s]ettled run in the senior side when Welsh star Jack broke his arm in 1959. Jim took his chance well, saving points with brilliant displays in several cliff-hanging encounters, notably at West [B]romwich and Blackburn. Jack returned in the autumn but was [b]elow par, and the younger man was selected on merit for eight [g]ames. Inevitably, however, the Kelsey touch came back and his frustrated deputy left for Luton Town in October 1960.

An accomplished shot-stopper whose occasional fallibility on [c]rosses hinted at an early lack of confidence, Jim improved with [m]aturity and his subsequent success with the Hammers was richly [d]eserved. He was also a gifted cricketer, and topped the national [b]owling averages while helping Worcestershire to win the County Championship in 1964.

[B]ORN: Edmonton, London, 30.5.35. GAMES: 38. GOALS: 0.

OTHER CLUBS: Luton Town 60/1-62/3 (36, 0); West Ham United 62/3-67/8 (179, 0); Detroit Cougars, USA; Millwall 68/9-69/70 (8, 0); Portsmouth 70/1-71/2 (13, 0).

Few people who knew Laurie Brown did not have a soft spot for the down-to-earth north-easterner, an endearing character who enjoyed both life and football to the very hilt. But while his reputation for filling the Highbury dressing-room with laughter was well founded, there was no more serious competitor than the versatile former amateur international.

Laurie, who played in the 1960 Rome Olympics during early days with Bishop Auckland, was not blessed with abundant natural ability, and everything he achieved was the product of fierce self-belief. This was reflected in the cumbersome six-footer's combative displays as a central defender after his £35,000 acquisition from Northampton Town – for whom he had played in six half-back and forward positions – in August 1961.

Relentlessly effective with his head, he was less impressive at ground level, and though his yeoman qualities offered much to admire, Arsenal were seeking to assemble a classier act. Thus in February 1964, with the expensive Ian Ure and several promising youngsters at manager Billy Wright's disposal, a £40,000 fee took Laurie to White Hart Lane, where he demonstrated his versatility with some storming performances at centre-forward. A much-loved personality had departed the Highbury scene.

BORN: Shildon, County Durham, 22.8.37. GAMES: 109. GOALS: 2.

OTHER CLUBS: Darlington (amateur) 58/9 (3, 0); Northampton Town 60/1 (33, 21); Tottenham Hotspur 63/4-65/6 (62, 3); Norwich City 66/7-68/9 (81, 2); Bradford Park Avenue 68/9-69/70 (36, 1). MANAGER: Bradford Park Avenue 69.

1957/58 – 1960/61

1961/62 – 1963/64

JOE HAVERTY

1954/55 – 1960/61

Joe Haverty was the laughing left-wing leprechaun who dribbled his way into all but the hardest hearts on the Highbury terraces. Inevitably, the affection sometimes wore a trifle thin when the 5ft 3½in Irishman overdid his impudent trickery and brought promising attacks to a standstill. But, on balance, the presence of 'Little Joe' – so dubbed after a character in the TV series, Bonanza – brought a welcome dash of high spirits to a rather cheerless period of Arsenal history.

The skilful Dubliner made his debut on the same day as Jimmy Bloomfield, at Goodison Park in August 1954, but it was to be another two years before he was to earn a settled run in the side. When he did, he impressed with his tight control and crossing ability, and it soon became evident that Joe had more to offer than his main mid-fifties competitors, Gordon Nutt and Mike Tiddy.

Results were poor, however, and a combination of managerial experiments and recurring back problems limited his appearances until 1959/60, when he produced his finest form and netted some opportunistic goals. Though never a prolific scorer, Joe lacked neither power nor accuracy in his shot, and he proved the quality of his finishing with two crisp strikes at Chelsea in November 1959, the second of which was squeezed audaciously into the net from the sharpest of angles.

Perhaps understandably in view of his size, the Eire international was not always keen on mixing it with hulking defenders, and he had a distinctive way of jumping from the path of lunging tackles, a habit marked one yuletide by the arrival at the ground of a Christmas card addressed to Joe and picturing a particularly athletic kangaroo. The tiny flankman, ever one to appreciate a joke, roared with laughter like everyone else. When he departed for Blackburn Rovers in a £17,500 deal in August 1961, Highbury became a duller place.

BORN: Dublin, 17.2.36. GAMES: 122. GOALS: 26. HONOURS: 32 Republic of Ireland caps (56–67).

OTHER CLUBS: Home Farm and St Patrick's Athletic, Republic of Ireland; Blackburn Rovers 61/2–62/3 (27, 1); Millwall 62/3–63/4 (68, 8); Bristol Rovers 64/5 (13, 1); Shelbourne, Republic of Ireland; Chicago Spurs, USA.

JACKIE HENDERSON

1958/59 – 1961/62

When Jackie Henderson announced his arrival at Highbury by scoring with two flashing headers in a 4–3 victory over West Bromwich Albion in October 1958, it seemed that manager George Swindin had pulled off an impressive coup. The chunky, muscular Scot, a dynamic raider who could play in any forward position but specialised on the left wing, had served Portsmouth with distinction throughout most of the fifties before enduring a short, unhappy stint with Wolves. Now a £20,000 fee had rescued him from Molineux and it was reckoned that if the Gunners could harness his undeniable verve, he would bring an exciting new dimension to their attack.

And, for a while, so it proved. Jackie netted 12 times in his 21 League games that term, his direct, hard-running style and blistering shot in either foot – his left was especially savage – being seen to maximum advantage. He could also cross the ball at high speed, was strong in the air, and was apt to pop up in the opposition goalmouth when least expected, assets which played a significant part in securing third place in the First Division for an improving side.

Jackie's enterprising displays even won him a fleeting return to international favour, but while he was usually in the Gunners' line-up during the next two campaigns, the team's form dipped distressingly and he failed to maintain consistency. In part, he was a victim of his own versatility, often being shifted in reshuffles dictated by injuries, and, in fairness, he was impressive at times in a deep-lying, creative role. But there is little doubt that Jackie, ever the dashing adventurer at heart, was at his all-action best when patrolling the flank.

In January 1962, with the Swindin era in its death-throes, one of the Highbury dressing room's liveliest characters bowed out with a £14,000 move to Craven Cottage, where he finished his League career.

BORN: Montrose, Scotland, 17.1.32.
GAMES: 111. GOALS: 29.
HONOURS: 7 Scotland caps (53–58).

OTHER CLUBS: Portsmouth 51/2-57/8 (217, 70); Wolverhampton Wanderers 57/8-58/9 (9, 3); Fulham 61/2-63/4 (45, 7).

DAVID HERD

The sale of David Herd did not represent Arsenal's finest hour on the transfer market. The sharp-shooting centre-forward was the Gunners' prime attacking asset, their leading scorer for four consecutive seasons, yet manager George Swindin made repeated attempts to offload him. In the 18 months before he joined Manchester United for £35,000 in the summer of 1961, David had been offered to Huddersfield Town in part-exchange for Denis Law, to Newcastle United as bait for George Eastham, and to Blackburn Rovers. It was hardly surprising, therefore, that the genial, unassuming Scot became unsettled and, ultimately, jumped at the chance to link up with Matt Busby, one of his boyhood heroes.

To the long-suffering Highbury fans, fed up with watching their once-great club floundering ineffectively in mid-table, the deal was as mysterious as it was galling. Why sell a man who, in what was to prove his farewell North London campaign, struck 30 League and FA Cup goals, including four hat-tricks, while none of his team-mates managed more than ten?

Whatever the answer, there was no doubt that the £10,000 which brought David south from Stockport County – for whom he had played alongside his father, Alex – had proved a shrewd investment. After completing the move in August 1954, the rookie striker spent two seasons on the fringe of the first team before claiming a regular place when Cliff Holton was switched to wing-half midway through 1956/57.

It wasn't long before he was paying his way with a steady supply of goals, many of them the product of one of British football's most powerful right feet. David's thunderous missiles rained in from all angles, and he had the priceless knack of keeping them low, an under-rated talent much feared by goalkeepers. He was also quick, strong and unfailingly enthusiastic, and if his aerial ability was less outstanding than his work on the ground, he could still take the breath away with an occasional gem, such as the diving header which clinched a 3–1 home victory over Spurs in October 1956.

David's progress was rewarded in 1958 with his first cap – against Wales in Cardiff – and as he continued his prolific leadership of the Arsenal front line, it seemed that the harassed George Swindin had solved at least one of his many problems. But whispers of imminent transactions involving the in-form marksman began to leak out and David, who would have been happy to stay at Highbury if only he had felt wanted, headed for Old Trafford.

With his new club, he maintained his strike rate, helping the Red Devils lift a succession of trophies until a broken leg signalled the end of his top-level exploits in the late sixties. After a short spell with Stoke City, David tried his hand at management with Lincoln before becoming a garage proprietor in Manchester. He remains a popular figure in the city of his greatest triumphs, and United fans still talk about his achievements; meanwhile long-time Arsenal supporters are left to rue the premature departure of a player who, it seems reasonable to suppose, would have left *them* with a treasure trove of golden memories.

BORN: Hamilton, Scotland, 15.4.34. GAMES: 180. GOALS: 107.
HONOURS: 5 Scotland caps (58-61).

OTHER CLUBS: Stockport County 50/1-53/4 (16, 6);
Manchester United 61/2-67/8 (202, 114); Stoke City 68/9-69/70 (44, 11).
MANAGER: Lincoln City 71-72.

1954/55 – 1960/61

MEL CHARLES

1959/60 – 1961/62

In a different era and with better luck, Mel Charles and Arsenal might have scaled the heights together. As events turned out, the multi-gifted Welshman's Highbury career was devastated by a succession of serious knee problems, and for much of the time when he *was* fully fit, he struggled to find the right niche in an unsettled side.

Expectations were sky high in April 1959 when Mel became a Gunner in a package deal which netted Swansea Town a cheque for £42,750 plus Arsenal youngsters Peter Davies and David Dodson. As a long-established international who could perform with equal dexterity at centre-half, wing-half and centre-forward, the strapping six-footer was seen as the man around whom George Swindin could build a title-winning combination.

But, it seemed, somebody up there had it in for Mel Charles. He was laid low by cartilage operations in 1959 and 1960, managing to start less than half the Gunners' games in his first two terms and often carrying injuries when he did turn out. There were several embarrassingly sluggish early outings in defence – notably at Newcastle, where Len White gave him a fearful chasing – though a match-winning double-strike when restored to the attack against Everton and a hat-trick against Blackburn did something to restore the balance.

The most frustrating aspect was that Mel, so majestic in the air and possessing amazingly intricate skills for such a big man, did just enough to hint at what might have been. Though not in the class of his famous brother John, he could be an exhilarating entertainer in his own right, as he proved in his farewell Highbury campaign, netting 17 times in 23 outings before moving to Cardiff City for £28,500.

A genial, happy-go-lucky soul who might have benefited from a touch more application, Mel later derived much satisfaction from the progress of his son Jeremy, the third member of the family to play for Wales.

BORN: Swansea, 14.5.35. GAMES: 64.
GOALS: 28. HONOURS: 31 Wales caps (55-62).
OTHER CLUBS: Swansea Town 52/3-58/9
(233, 69); Cardiff City 61/2-64/5 (81, 24);
Port Vale 66/7 (7, 0).

JOHNNY BARNWELL

1956/57 – 1963/64

The young Johnny Barnwell was a polished performer who carried the rare, unmistakable stamp of pure class: his ball control was magnetic, his passing and vision a delight to behold, and his shooting both powerful and accurate. Yet despite the stylish Geordie's enviable mastery of football's finer points, his game lacked the raw edge necessary to take him to the pinnacle of his profession.

Highbury had greeted few more exciting prospects than the flaxen-haired inside-forward when he left the amateur ranks of Bishop Auckland to sign for Arsenal in the mid fifties. After progressing apace in Army teams during his National Service, Johnny returned to find the play-maker's role in the possession of the experienced Jimmy Bloomfield. The ambitious rookie's chance came when the older man was injured early in 1959, and he took it with relish, earning a place alongside the Londoner for most of the following season.

When Jimmy was sold after the arrival of George Eastham in 1960, Johnny continued as a fairly regular member of the side and soon won England under-23 recognition. Somehow, though, he failed to exert an influence commensurate with his undoubted gifts. Although he was a fitness fanatic and didn't lack courage – he was undeterred by a fearsome early challenge on his debut, at Roker Park in 1957 – he was never the quickest of movers, and at times, perhaps, needed too long on the ball.

As George Swindin's managerial reign drew to a close, Johnny seemed to drift out of contention, but new boss Billy Wright was impressed by the Barnwell catalogue of skills and gave him new impetus with a switch to wing-half in October 1962. He did well enough, but couldn't establish a sufficiently dominant presence, and in March 1964 a £30,000 deal took him to Nottingham Forest, for whom he performed with credit for the remainder of the decade.

BORN: Newcastle, 24.12.38. GAMES: 151. GOALS: 24.

OTHER CLUBS: Nottingham Forest 63/4–69/70 (182, 22); Sheffield United 70/1 (9, 2). MANAGER: Peterborough United 77-78; Wolverhampton Wanderers 78-81; AEK Athens; Notts County 87-88; Walsall 89-90.

VIC GROVES

Ebullient Eastender Vic Groves exuded a passion for football in general and the Gunners in particular that communicated itself engagingly to the terraces and, allied to a generous helping of all-round ability, made the former eel-skinner a treat to watch. The fans warmed to his sheer love of life and jaunty, chase-everything attitude, both as a young centre-forward and, later, in his more influential role of wing-half.

Vic, who made a handful of unpaid appearances for Spurs in his fish-market days, began his Highbury career in November 1955 following a protracted fanfare of publicity over his on-off departure from Leyton Orient. Eventually, after Brisbane Road supporters had launched a fund to enable the hard-up O's to keep their most popular player, and Vic had spurned a tempting offer from Wolves, he crossed London with full-back Stan Charlton in a £30,000 package deal. The young striker – an amateur international who had played for Leytonstone and Walthamstow Avenue, and was newly capped as a right-winger at England 'B' level – was valued at £23,000.

He made a vibrant start in an Arsenal shirt, netting with a flourish on his debut at home to Sheffield United, but a sickening anti-climax was in store. A run of niggling injuries culminated in a cartilage operation during the 1956 close season and he was sidelined for most of the subsequent campaign. During this demoralising interlude, Vic was sorely tested as he fell victim to wild and iniquitous accusations of malingering, and it took all his natural buoyancy to carry him through.

Relief came in 1957/58 when, while not totally free of fitness problems, the stocky front-runner had the chance at last to demonstrate his long-term worth. There was much to admire in his ball skills, aerial power and ability to retain possession in the face of fierce pressure, but it was Vic's intelligent reading of the game which impressed most. His shrewd, off-the-ball runs created plentiful opportunities for David Herd, his usual partner, and such resourcefulness compensated amply for a lack of extreme pace.

Yet it was a master-stroke by manager George Swindin in the autumn of 1959 which realised the full Groves potential. Having acknowledged Vic's importance to the team by appointing him captain to succeed Dave Bowen during the previous term, George moved him back to midfield where his sharp tactical appreciation was seen to maximum advantage. A perceptive passer and sturdy tackler, he was always keen to experiment with new moves, and there were those who reckoned such enterprise might have earned him a chance in the England side.

It was not to be, however, although he continued to wear the red shirt with distinction until 1964, when – by then in his thirties and with new boss Billy Wright building for the future – he took a free transfer to non-League Canterbury City, later going on to become a publican and then work in insurance.

In his final years at Highbury, Vic – whose nephew Perry Groves is currently carrying on the family tradition – had been ever ready to lend his experience to the next generation, and the likes of George Armstrong remember him, both as a footballer and a character, with respect and affection. Few fans from his era would argue with that.

BORN: Stepney, London, 5.11.32. GAMES: 203. GOALS: 37.

OTHER CLUBS: Tottenham Hotspur (amateur) 52/3-53/4 (4, 3); Leyton Orient 54/5-55/6 (42, 24).

1955/56 – 1963/64

DENNIS CLAPTON

TONY BIGGS 1957/58 — 1958/59

Centre-forward. BORN: Greenford, London, 17.4.36.
GAMES: 4. GOALS: 1. OTHER CLUBS: Leyton Orient
58/9-59/60 (4, 1).

DENNIS CLAPTON 1959/60 — 1960/61

Centre-forward. BORN: Hackney, London, 12.10.39.
GAMES: 4. GOALS: 0. OTHER CLUBS: Northampton Town 61/2
(1, 0). Brother of Arsenal and England winger Danny Clapton.

MIKE EVERITT 1959/60 — 1960/61

Wing-half. BORN: Clacton, Essex, 16.1.41. GAMES: 9. GOALS: 1.
OTHER CLUBS: Northampton Town 60/1-66/7 (207, 15);
Plymouth Argyle 66/7-67/8 (29, 0); Brighton and
Hove Albion 68/9-69/70 (27, 1). MANAGER: Brentford 73-75.

ROY GOULDEN 1958/59

Inside-forward. BORN: Ilford, Essex, 22.9.37. GAMES: 1.
GOALS: 0. OTHER CLUBS: Southend United 61/2 (9, 2).
Son of West Ham United and England inside-forward Len Goulden.

PETER GOY 1958/59

Goalkeeper. BORN: Beverley, Yorkshire, 8.6.38. GAMES: 2.
GOALS: 0. OTHER CLUBS: Southend United 60/1-63/4 (118, 0);
Watford 64/5 (27, 0); Huddersfield Town 66/7 (4, 0).

PETER KANE 1960/61

Inside-forward. BORN: Petershill, Scotland, 4.4.39.
GAMES: 4. GOALS: 1. OTHER CLUBS: Queen's Park, Scotland;
Northampton Town 63/4 (18, 8);
Crewe Alexandra 63/4-66/7 (83, 31).

TONY BIGGS

PETER GOY

MIKE EVERITT

PETER KANE

ROY GOULDEN

GORDON FERRY

FRANK O'NEILL

DANIEL LE ROUX

GORDON FERRY 1964/65

Centre-half. BORN: Sunderland, 22.12.43. GAMES: 11.
GOALS: 0. OTHER CLUBS: Leyton Orient 65/6 (42, 0).

DANIEL LE ROUX 1957/58

Forward. BORN: South Africa, 25.11.33. GAMES: 5.
GOALS: 0. OTHER CLUBS: Queen's Park, Durban, South Africa.

FRANK O'NEILL 1960/61

Winger. BORN: Dublin, 13.4.40. GAMES: 2.
GOALS: 0. HONOURS: 20 Republic of Ireland caps (62-72).
OTHER CLUBS: Home Farm, Republic of Ireland.

RODNEY SMITHSON 1962/63

Wing-half. BORN: Leicester, 9.10.43. GAMES: 2. GOALS: 0.
OTHER CLUBS: Oxford United 65/6-74/5 (155, 6).

RAY SWALLOW 1954/55 — 1957/58

Forward. BORN: Southwark, London, 15.6.35. GAMES: 13.
GOALS: 4. OTHER CLUBS: Derby County 58/9-63/4 (118, 21).
Derbyshire cricketer.

BRIAN TAWSE 1964/65

Winger. BORN: Ellon, Scotland, 30.7.45.
GAMES: 5. GOALS: 0. OTHER CLUBS: Brighton and
Hove Albion 65/6-69/70 (102, 14); Brentford 69/70-70/1 (21, 1).

ALAN YOUNG 1960/61

Centre-half. BORN: Hornsey, London, 20.1.41. GAMES: 4.
GOALS: 0. OTHER CLUBS: Chelsea 61/2-66/7 (20, 0);
Torquay United 68/9-71/2 (59, 1).

RAY SWALLOW

BRIAN TAWSE

RODNEY SMITHSON   ALAN YOUNG

DAVE BACUZZI

Dave Bacuzzi was a tall, blond right-back whose early form in the senior side flattered to deceive. After making an accomplished debut at the Hawthorns in February 1961, when he refused to be ruffled by West Bromwich Albion's potent left-wing partnership of Clive Clark and Derek Kevan, he retained his place for the remainder of the campaign.

The critics – notably thirties Arsenal idol Joe Hulme – were beginning to predict a fruitful future for the former England youth international, and they remained full of praise when Dave reacted to a first-half run-around from Manchester United's Bobby Charlton by recovering his poise with a much improved showing after the interval.

But just as it seemed that he had inched ahead of Jimmy Magill in the struggle to become the long-term replacement for the veteran Len Wills, the cracks started to show. A dedicated athlete, his touch on the ball did not match his fitness, and when occasional mistakes crept in, his confidence appeared to deteriorate.

Eventually Dave – who was not helped by unfair comparisons with his father, Joe, a fine full-back with Fulham before and after the Second World War – slipped out of the first-team reckoning, and in April 1964 he joined Manchester City for £25,000.

BORN: Islington, London, 12.10.40. GAMES: 48. GOALS: 0.

OTHER CLUBS: Manchester City 64/5-65/6 (57, 0); Reading 66/7-69/70 (107, 1).

1960/61 – 1963/64

EDDIE CLAMP

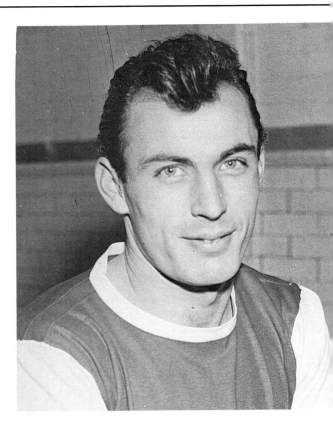

While reproving mothers once warned naughty children of the bogey-man, First Division managers of the mid fifties and early sixties might have threatened erring inside-forwards with the attentions of Eddie Clamp.

Arsenal boss George Swindin, believing that his hard-pressed midfield was in desperate need of extra steel, paid Wolves £34,500 for the combative wing-half in November 1961, but it was to prove a short-term arrangement. George was sacked and replaced by Billy Wright, who was not enamoured of his former Molineux team-mate's ferocious style. In his fourth match under the new regime, Eddie made a particularly crude challenge on Aston Villa's Charlie Aitken and was never picked again, moving to Stoke for a mere £14,000 in September 1962.

In fact, the former England international had far more to offer than the strength of his tackle. He possessed instinctive ball control and was a beautiful passer, but his occasional lack of self-discipline let him down.

Eddie is remembered by colleagues as a quiet man who would always look after them if they ran into trouble on the field. Opponents recall the Clamp glare and then, with an involuntary shudder, change the subject.

BORN: Coalville, Leicestershire, 14.9.34.
GAMES: 24. GOALS: 1.
HONOURS: 4 England caps (58).

OTHER CLUBS: Wolverhampton Wanderers 53/4-61/2 (214, 23); Stoke City 62/3-63/4 (50, 2); Peterborough United 64/5 (8, 0).
DIED: Wednesfield, Staffordshire, 14.12.95.

1961/62 – 1962/63

TERRY ANDERSON

Highbury has seen few more enigmatic figures than Terry Anderson, a leggy winger who failed to make the most of bounteous natural ability. An England youth international who progressed through Arsenal's junior sides, he was quick off the mark, boasted ball control which was the envy of many more successful players, and could operate on either flank.

But when he was given opportunities to fulfil his potential – usually as a deputy for either Alan Skirton or Johnny MacLeod – Terry offered only the briefest flashes of inspiration, often appearing to lose concentration and drift on the fringe of the action.

He was a quiet, self-effacing character, who was not over-keen on mixing it physically with some of the First Division's more zealous defenders, and might have benefited from a little of the zest and determination displayed by fellow rookie winger George Armstrong.

When it became clear that Terry was unlikely to prosper as a Gunner, manager Billy Wright sold him to Norwich City for £15,000 in February 1965. He served the Canaries admirably for nine years, eventually moving to midfield and helping them reach the top flight in 1972.

Terry, who later became a publican, was found drowned in 1980.

BORN: Woking, Surrey, 11.3.44. GAMES: 26. GOALS: 7.

OTHER CLUBS: Norwich City 64/5-73/4 (236, 16); Colchester United on loan 73/4 (4, 0); Scunthorpe United 74/5 (10, 0); Crewe Alexandra 74/5 (4, 0); Colchester United 75/6 (16, 0). DIED: Great Yarmouth, Norfolk, January 1980.

1962/63 – 1964/65

ARFON GRIFFITHS

The arrival of tiny Welsh inside-forward Arfon Griffiths was treated as a major event at Highbury. The Gunners had beaten off competition from Spurs, Everton, Newcastle and Preston to clinch the £14,000 signing of Wrexham's gingery-blond schemer in January 1961, and manager George Swindin announced proudly that he had acquired 'another George Eastham'. His judgement, alas, was to prove unsound.

Arfon was an industrious performer, neat, skilful and always on the move, and there were high hopes for him after he showed scintillating form on a pre-1961/62 European tour. Back in the more hectic environment of the First Division, however, he seemed out of his depth. One highlight was a headed goal against Manchester City at Highbury – team-mates marvelled at 5ft 5in Arfon's feat in outwitting giant German goalkeeper Bert Trautmann in the air – but it was an isolated triumph.

Accordingly, his North London sojourn ended in September 1962 with a £10,000 return to the Racecourse Ground. Back in his home town, he went on to complete a long and worthy career, as both player and manager, and was rewarded with an MBE.

BORN: Wrexham, 23.8.41. GAMES: 15. GOALS: 2. HONOURS: 17 Wales caps (71-76).

OTHER CLUBS: Wrexham 59/60-60/1 (42, 8) and 62/3-78/9 (550, 115). MANAGER: Wrexham 77-81; Crewe Alexandra 81-82.

1960/61 – 1961/62

BILLY McCULLOUGH

Billy McCullough was a footballing buccaneer who rejoiced in a cowboy's nickname. The slim Irishman was dubbed 'Flint' after a character in the TV series Wagon Train, the tag justified not only by a shared surname, but also by the sharp-edged tackles which he dispensed freely in his role of Arsenal's left-back throughout the first half of the sixties.

A £5,000 recruit from Portadown in September 1958, Billy was one of new manager George Swindin's first signings, and gave sterling value for such a modest investment. Just three months after checking in at Highbury, he made his senior debut in place of out-of-form Dennis Evans at home to Luton Town. On a chewing-gum pitch that put defenders at a distinct disadvantage, he eclipsed his countryman Billy Bingham, one of the most dangerous wingers in Britain, to play a stirring part in a narrow victory. He continued to make steady progress, and when injury ended Dennis' career in 1959/60, Billy became a first-team regular.

His trademark was aggression, both in his vigorous approach to opposing flankmen and his penchant for adventurous forays along his touchline. There were occasions, however, on which his heart ruled his head and he would find himself dispossessed deep in enemy territory. Then, his speed would be seen to full advantage as he sprinted back to make a recovering challenge. Perhaps a more serious weakness in the McCullough game was his distribution, which was inclined towards inaccuracy, though his bravery and endeavour were more than adequate compensations.

Billy, whose internationals were played mostly at left-half due to competition from the excellent Alex Elder, lost his Arsenal berth to Peter Storey in the autumn of 1965. He later served Millwall, and was a player-boss in Ireland before becoming an electrical engineer. At Highbury he is still recalled with warmth; mention 'Flint' McCullough there and conversation does *not* turn to wagon wheels and ornery injuns.

BORN: Woodburn, Northern Ireland, 27.7.35.
GAMES: 268. GOALS: 5. HONOURS: 10 Northern Ireland caps (61-66).

OTHER CLUBS: Portadown, Northern Ireland; Millwall 66/7 (19, 0). MANAGER: Cork Celtic, Republic of Ireland; Derry City, Northern Ireland.

1958/59 – 1965/66

JIMMY MAGILL

1959/60 – 1964/65

They were both Irish full-backs who cost Arsenal £5,000 from Portadown, they played together frequently, and there was a tendency among supporters of opposing teams to think of them as peas from the same pod; yet Jimmy Magill and Billy McCullough could hardly have offered a wider contrast.

While Billy's approach was based on fire and forcefulness, Jimmy was not noted for the ferocity of his tackles. He preferred, instead, to jockey his opponents away from the area of immediate peril, watching for an opportunity to nick the ball out of harm's way but relying on stealth rather than strength.

Perhaps he couldn't quite match his partner for speed, either – although he was no slouch in a race, being supremely fit – but Jimmy *could* offer better control and far more accomplished passing skills, being adept at sweeping the ball smoothly into the path of the Gunners' front-runners.

The younger man – he was nearly four years Billy's junior – made a traumatic start in First Division football, struggling to cope with Sheffield Wednesday's Alan Finney in a 5-1 trouncing at Hillsborough in December 1959. But he held on to his place for a 19-match run, and eventually fought off the challenge of Dave Bacuzzi to become first-choice right-back until Don Howe was signed in the spring of 1964.

With little option but to seek a future elsewhere, the Northern Ireland international made a £6,000 switch to Brighton, spending three seasons at the Goldstone Ground before taking up coaching and management in Denmark.

Jimmy will go down as a thoughtful, competent performer, his game complementary to Billy McCullough's but lacking the same keen edge.

BORN: Carrickfergus, Northern Ireland, 17.5.39. GAMES: 131. GOALS: 0. HONOURS: 26 Northern Ireland caps (61-66).

OTHER CLUBS: Portadown, Northern Ireland; Brighton and Hove Albion 65/6-67/8 (50, 1). MANAGER: Frederikshavn, Denmark.

GEOFF STRONG

Geoff Strong was a lean and lethal marksman who notched goals with the single-minded efficiency of some Wild West bounty hunter polishing off a desperado. In his last full season at Highbury, his scoring rate stood comparison with the best in the business, but what made him special was the proportion of chances that got away: it was awesomely low.

An exceptional athlete who had been a top schoolboy sprinter, Geoff joined Arsenal from northern amateurs Stanley United in September 1957, and it soon became apparent that the Gunners had recruited a gem. Quick, brave and carrying a savage shot in either foot, he was also a potent force in the air, controlled the ball smoothly, and showed a born striker's greed when in sight of the target.

On his senior debut at home to Newcastle in September 1960, Geoff grabbed an opportunist's goal from the edge of the box and showed the confidence to take on and beat opponents. But it was not until after completing his National Service in 1961, and pairing up with the newly-arrived Joe Baker the following year, that he blossomed fully. As a duo they terrorised First Division defences, and in 1963/64 became caught up in a thrilling race to top the Gunners' scoring list, eventually sharing the honour with 28 League and Cup strikes apiece.

One of Geoff's most eye-catching performances graced TV's first *Match Of The Day*, against Liverpool at Anfield in August 1964, when he helped set up a Baker goal and then netted smartly himself after a brisk exchange of passes with George Eastham. His creative talents were beginning to rival his scoring achievements, and Billy Wright gave him a run in midfield before yielding to the entreaties of Bill Shankly and dispatching him north for £40,000 in November 1964.

On Merseyside Geoff became one of Britain's finest utility players and won a stack of medals; at Highbury he and his goals were sorely missed as the Gunners continued the slide which was to cost the manager his job.

BORN: Newcastle, 19.9.37. GAMES: 137. GOALS: 77.

OTHER CLUBS: Liverpool 64/5-69/70 (155, 29); Coventry City 70/1-71/2 (33, 0).

1960/61 – 1964/65

JOHNNY MacLEOD

1961/62 – 1964/65

Great things were expected of Johnny MacLeod when he crossed the Scottish border to join the Gunners in the summer of 1961. Earlier that year, the 22-year-old winger had commenced what many pundits predicted would be an illustrious international career, and his £40,000 capture from Hibernian was seen as a major Highbury coup. Certainly, it was a vital transaction for manager George Swindin, whose team rebuilding plans were running out of time to bear fruit after two poor campaigns. As it turned out, Johnny failed to achieve the desired effect for his new employers, and his club form never earned him a further call to his country's colours.

It wasn't that he flopped, merely that his impact on the overall fortunes of a moderate side proved negligible. True, there were games, usually at home, when his speed and ability to beat defenders in confined spaces took the eye, and he was more adept at crossing the ball accurately than many First Division flankmen. His adaptability – usually he lined up on the right, but could switch wings when necessary – was another asset but, crucially, Johnny was rarely a match-winner. There was a feeling that he tended to play well only when in possession, perhaps lacking the tactical awareness to make the most of changing situations, and that he was not at his best against full-backs who countered his finesse with brute force.

While never a prolific marksman, Johnny managed a respectable strike rate, and can claim the honour of scoring Arsenal's first goal in European competition, in the ninth minute of the Inter-Cities Fairs Cup encounter with Staevnet of Denmark at Highbury in September 1963.

A year later he was transferred to Aston Villa for £35,000, later going on to sample Belgian football before finishing his playing days nearer home, with Raith Rovers.

BORN: Edinburgh, 23.11.38. GAMES: 112. GOALS: 28. HONOURS: 4 Scotland caps (61).

OTHER CLUBS: Hibernian 57/8–60/1 (85, 27); Aston Villa 64/5–67/8 (124, 16); K V Mechelen, Belgium; Raith Rovers 71/2 (15, 5).

JOHN SNEDDEN

A clod of upturned Hillsborough earth interrupted the burgeoning career of John Snedden at a crucial juncture. It happened in December 1960 during a 1-1 draw with Sheffield Wednesday: the 19-year-old Scot leapt to head the ball, landed awkwardly on the uneven ground and broke his ankle, sidelining him at a time when he had been showing the potential to become the outstanding centre-half Arsenal had lacked for so long.

Before the injury, John's progress had been quietly convincing. When only 17, he had performed nobly on his debut against Spurs, deputising for the injured Bill Dodgin and holding his own against England star Bobby Smith. Since then he had claimed a regular slot, displaying aerial power and a higher degree of ball skill than that traditionally associated with 6ft stoppers. Whenever possible he disdained the optimistic downfield punt, favouring instead a short-passing game and linking neatly with wing-halves Tommy Docherty and Vic Groves.

During 1961/62, having recovered from his accident, John returned to the side but seemed a little ponderous, and failed to recapture his confident form. In the following season, however, new Highbury boss Billy Wright played him as a defensive wing-half, sometimes with a one-on-one marking brief – he did a particularly fine job in one encounter with the tricky Bryan Douglas of Blackburn Rovers – and there was a marked improvement until he was scuppered again by injury. This time a knee operation cost him the last six weeks of the campaign and, with ever-increasing competition from emerging youngsters, John was squeezed out of the first-team frame.

Needing a fresh start, he accepted a £15,000 move to Charlton Athletic in 1965, but, still troubled by his fitness, he made little impact. After brief service with Orient, the young man who had once seemed to have the soccer world at his feet, left the game to work in Germany.

BORN: Bonnybridge, Scotland, 3.2.42.
GAMES: 94. GOALS: 0.

OTHER CLUBS: Charlton Athletic 64/5-65/6 (20, 0); Orient 66/7-67/8 (27, 3); Halifax Town *on loan* 67/8 (5, 0).

1959/60 – 1964/65

JACK McCLELLAND

IAN McKECHNIE

After a decade of savouring the talents of Jack Kelsey, most Arsenal fans were spoilt when it came to passing judgement on goalkeepers. It was hardly surprising, therefore, that Jack McClelland, once seen as the Welsh international's likeliest long-term replacement, should suffer in comparison with his illustrious predecessor.

Yet early omens had favoured the younger Jack, a £7,000 capture from Glenavon in October 1960. He won his first cap a week after becoming a Gunner and showed competent form in a handful of senior outings over the next two years. Then, when the Kelsey career was ended by injury, the slim, dedicated Irishman leapt ahead of fellow aspirant Ian McKechnie with an uninterrupted 34-game first-team sequence in 1962/63.

However, despite some dextrous displays in training, Jack appeared often to lose his confidence on match days. Though not lacking in courage, he could be hesitant at taking crosses, and had an occasional but disconcerting habit of diving feet-first at incoming forwards. Any impetus he might have built up was shattered by a broken collar-bone at Leicester in August 1963, and he gradually slipped out of the Highbury reckoning, moving to Fulham the following year.

Jack died in 1976, after a short illness.

BORN: Lurgan, Northern Ireland, 19.5.40. GAMES: 49. GOALS: 0. HONOURS: 6 Northern Ireland caps (60-66). OTHER CLUBS: Glenavon; Fulham 65/6-68/9 (51, 0); Lincoln City on loan 68/9 (12, 0). DIED: Northern Ireland, 15.3.76.

Ian McKechnie was a loveable character who was in the Bruce Grobbelaar class as a clown but not, unfortunately, as a goalkeeper. In fact, when Arsenal plucked the burly Scot from amateur football in September 1958, they had no reason to suspect that he might excel between the posts. Ian was signed as a promising left-winger, and was converted to a custodian only after a spectacular display of shot-stopping in a practice match.

Thereafter, he developed into a flashy 'keeper who delighted the fans with his antics but was never steady enough to make the grade in the top flight. The performance of Ian's life, which earned him one of soccer's more obscure nicknames, came in a friendly against a Swedish Select XI in 1961. That day in Gothenburg he made a succession of acrobatic saves that had his opponents gasping, and he was known henceforth as 'Yuri' - after the first man in space, Yuri Gagarin - because, his team-mates reckoned, he was up in the air with elation for days after the match.

However, brilliant though Ian could be at his best, he was prone to inconsistency and was given a free transfer to Southend United in 1964. A brief spell at Roots Hall was followed by eight seasons of reliable service with Hull City. In maturity, Ian had found his true level.

BORN: Lenzie, Scotland, 4.10.41. GAMES: 25. GOALS: 0. OTHER CLUBS: Southend United 64/5-65/6 (62, 0); Hull City 66/7-73/4 (255, 0). MANAGER: Sligo Rovers, Republic of Ireland.

1960/61 – 1963/64

1961/62 – 1963/64

GEORGE EASTHAM

When George Eastham stepped out at Highbury to make his League debut as a Gunner, he cut a delicate figure, appearing pale, even frail, as if the first full-blooded roar from the North Bank would blast him back down the dressing-room tunnel. He might have been more at home passing round the bone china at some elegant tea party than committing life and limb to confronting the notoriously rumbustious Bolton Wanderers defence. Soon, however, it transpired that the little man *did* have a talent for passing, though his particular expertise had nothing to do with dainty receptacles for Earl Grey.

George Eastham was blessed with a left foot like a magic wand. With it he could prise open cracks in the most clam–like of rearguards, and on that December afternoon in 1960 he contributed enough exquisite touches in Arsenal's 5-1 victory – as well as two goals – to convince all but his most persistent critics that here was a performer for whom it had been worth waiting while controversy raged over his £47,500 move from Newcastle United.

The delay had been due to a dispute between the Magpies and their player that was to prove a watershed in the battle to revolutionise footballers' pay and conditions. It led to the abolition of the outdated 'retain and transfer' system which gave the clubs total power over the so-called 'soccer slaves', although George had no such grand design at the outset, merely wanting to get away from Tyneside.

Yet the move was not an instant cure–all for his problems. When the euphoria of returning to the game after months on strike had subsided, George suffered an inevitable reaction to the tension, and struggled to find form. There were pessimistic predictions that he would prove a financial disaster, and hoots of derision at his 'butterfly tackling', but vindication of George Swindin's decision to pay dearly for quality was not long in coming. Ironically, the skilful schemer's path back to eminence began at St James' Park, Newcastle, where he was abused, roundly if predictably, by his former fans on his first return in an Arsenal shirt. He reacted by creating two goals for Geoff Strong and scoring a point-saving equaliser in his best Gunners display to date.

Thereafter, the famous Eastham artistry – his father, George senior, won an England cap in the thirties – began to emerge in its full glory. Though he was erratic at times, and he rarely recovered from a poor start to a match, he could charm dying games to life with moments of blinding insight. George was the master of the through-pass inside a full-back, luring hapless opponents into rash challenges and then stranding them in no-man's land as he slipped the ball deftly to his winger. He was the dream partner for hard-running flankmen such as Alan Skirton, and also brought the best out of strikers Joe Baker and Geoff Strong, setting up irresistible one-two combinations which produced a copious supply of scoring opportunities.

George, whose three years of England service ended immediately prior to the 1966 World Cup finals, parted company with Arsenal in August that year, new boss Bertie Mee selling him to Stoke City for £35,000. He served the Potters well, scoring their winning goal in the 1972 League Cup Final, and later becoming manager at the Victoria Ground before emigrating to South Africa.

There is no doubt, however, that his pomp was spent in North London, where a philistine minority may have viewed him as an expensive luxury, but most observers appreciated George Eastham as one of the finest play-makers in Highbury history.

BORN: Blackpool, 23.9.36. GAMES: 223. GOALS: 41.
HONOURS: 19 England caps (63-66).

OTHER CLUBS: Ards, Northern Ireland; Newcastle United 56/7-59/60 (124, 29); Stoke City 66/7-73/4 (194, 4). MANAGER: Stoke City 77-78.

1960/61 – 1965/66

ALAN SKIRTON

On the terraces they called him the 'Highbury Express', and Arsenal fans of the early sixties knew that when big, brawny winger Alan Skirton built up a full head of steam, there would be no stops en route to the byline; the only other possibility was a diversion towards goal.

In fact, with his powerful shot in either foot and formidable aerial strength, the affable West Countryman had most of the assets demanded of a traditional, bustling centre-forward. But his ball skills were unremarkable and he needed plenty of space to make the most of his startling speed, so it was on the flank that Alan was in his element.

His start with the Gunners was anything but auspicious. After a £5,000 move from Bath City made him the most expensive player ever recruited from non-League football, the raw 20-year-old managed two reserve games before falling prey to tuberculosis. He was out for 18 months and feared that he would never play again, but club physiotherapist Bertie Mee had him fit for 1960/61 and he made a favourable impression with a handful of dashing displays. During the following term he came of age, netting 21 times to head the Highbury scoring charts, though it wasn't until the December – when his glorious 25-yarder won the North London derby against Spurs – that he enjoyed the home crowd's whole-hearted support.

Alan in full flight was an exhilarating sight. The first sign of action was a dip of the shoulder, then the ball was pushed past his marker and he was off in full-blooded pursuit which was likely to end with a crisp cross or a pot at goal. He could play on either wing and had the talent – if not the total dedication – to have remained with Arsenal for the rest of the decade. But in 1966, while still only 27, Alan grew restless and joined Blackpool for £65,000, hardly the best of career moves. He continued to enjoy football, however, and after retirement he stayed in the game, going on to become commercial manager of Yeovil Town, a role in which he is both popular and successful.

BORN: Bath, 23.1.39. GAMES: 153 (1). GOALS: 54.

OTHER CLUBS: Blackpool 66/7–68/9 (77, 25); Bristol City 68/9–70/1 (78, 14); Torquay United 71/2 (38, 7).

1960/61 – 1966/67

IAN URE

1963/64 – 1969/70

The first time Arsenal fans saw Ian Ure in action, they could hardly believe their eyes. Billy Wright had just handed over £62,500, then a world record fee for a centre-half, to bring the big, bold stopper south from Dundee. The press had billed him as the great white hope who would shore up the Gunners' leaky defence, yet here he was, in his debut against Wolves on the opening day of 1963/64, playing like a no-hoper from the local park as the home side slid to humiliating defeat.

In fairness to the blond Scottish international, who had performed magnificently during Dundee's recent progress to the European Cup semi-finals, he was ring-rusty following a Dens Park dispute which had left him on strike. This did little to mollify his critics, however, as his torrid English baptism continued for several weeks. But gradually, as supporters realised that Ian was, at least, a born trier, the heat eased off and they came to accept him for what he was, a traditional central defender who was fine in the air, but limited on the ground. In fact, he had more skill than his public knew, often juggling the ball brilliantly in training, though that ability was not apparent in matches.

Ian's game was not helped by a natural impetuosity which allowed him, on occasion, to be lured out of position, and also resulted in repeated brushes with authority. He was sent off four times as a Gunner, the most infamous incident occurring at Old Trafford in 1967 when he was dismissed with Denis Law, both men being suspended for six weeks.

He left North London in August 1969, moving to Manchester United for £80,000, and later sampled management before becoming a social worker. A complex character, outspoken, intelligent and intense, he might have achieved more had he been able to relax more effectively. But whatever his shortcomings, Ian Ure was never dull, and he will go down as one of Highbury's most colourful figures since the war.

BORN: Ayr, Scotland, 7.12.39. GAMES: 202. GOALS: 2. HONOURS: 11 Scotland caps (61-67).

OTHER CLUBS: Dundee 58/9-62/3; Manchester United 69/70-70/1 (47, 1); St Mirren 72/3 (3, 0). MANAGER: East Stirling (75).

FRED CLARKE

Fred Clarke had more ability than his rather modest record might suggest. He was a small, fast left-back who was comfortable on the ball and worried away at opponents, attempting to harass them into errors.

What he lacked was the physical power and overall presence of, say, Billy McCullough, for whom he was an occasional deputy during the early sixties. Fred, who was at a distinct aerial disadvantage due to his diminutive stature, could never impose himself in the manner of his fellow Ulsterman, and was destined to bow out of Highbury as unobtrusively as he had conducted himself throughout his entire North London sojourn.

He had already won amateur international honours when George Swindin paid Glenavon £5,000 for his services in November 1960, just a month after Jack McClelland had joined Arsenal from the same club. Over the next few seasons, he won four under-23 caps but could not claim a regular place in the Gunners' side.

In 1964/65 Fred totalled 15 appearances, easily his highest in one campaign, but it was to be his final flourish, and in November 1965 he re-crossed the Irish Sea for a second stint with Glenavon.

BORN: Banbridge, Northern Ireland, 4.11.41. GAMES: 28. GOALS: 0.

OTHER CLUBS: Glenavon, Northern Ireland. (twice).

1961/62 – 1964/65

TONY BURNS

Lack of confidence was the only apparent reason for Tony Burn failure to establish himself as a top goalkeeper. He was brave, handled the ball safely and read the game astutely, yet he neve gave the impression that he was boss of his own penalty area.

Tony joined Arsenal from non-League Tonbridge United in March 1963 and took his place in the queue of hopefuls aiming t fill the void left by the injury-enforced retirement of Jack Kelse In his early days at Highbury, he showed immense potential an after benefiting from Jack's coaching, made encouraging strid towards realising his ambition.

His senior debut came in a friendly against Enschede in Hollar in August 1963, but it was not until 14 months later that Tony ma his League breakthrough, at home to Burnley. He kept his pla for 26 games before giving way to Jim Furnell, and despite hi fluctuating form, there were still those who thought he migh make the grade.

But the modest young man whose team-mates reckoned he w too good-looking to keep goal – they said he should have been film star – could not oust Jim, and in July 1966 he moved to Brighton. There followed a successful South African interlude some splendid service with Crystal Palace, and a spell in charge Southern League Gravesend.

BORN: Edenbridge, Kent, 27.3.44. GAMES: 33. GOALS: 0

OTHER CLUBS: Brighton and Hove Albion 66/7-68/9 (54, Charlton Athletic 68/9-69/70 (10, 0); Durban United, South Africa; Crystal Palace 74/5-77/8 (90, 0); Brentford on loan (6, 0 Plymouth Argyle 78/9 (8, 0).

1964/65 – 1965/66

DAVID COURT

1962/63 — 1969/70

David Court was an astute and gritty all-rounder who lengthened his Gunners career considerably by switching from the front line to midfield. He made his debut as an 18-year-old alongside Joe Baker at Villa Park in September 1962, but it was while deputising for the star centre-forward against Spurs a month later that he sprang to national attention. 'Boy Court in to stay' proclaimed one headline after he had scored twice, laid on another for winger Johnny MacLeod and repeatedly outwitted England stopper Maurice Norman in a pulsating 4-4 thriller.

However, it was not to be. David was a determined grafter who shielded the ball effectively and was adept at well-timed dummy runs which distracted attention from his fellow forwards, but his finishing was unreliable and he lacked pace. Thus, with John Radford emerging as a more likely partner for Baker, the future began to look distinctly bleak for the popular youngster.

Yet all was not lost. In 1964 manager Billy Wright – impressed by David's work-rate and shrewd reading of the game, and noting that he had more skill than he was given credit for – converted him into a half-back. The role suited him, and for the rest of the decade he was in the side more often than not, excelling particularly when asked to do a close-marking job on illustrious play-makers such as Manchester United's Bobby Charlton.

David, who picked up League Cup Final loser's medals against Leeds United in 1968 and Swindon Town the following year, joined Luton Town for £35,000 on the eve of the 1970/71 campaign which was to end in Arsenal lifting the League and FA Cup double. A congenital chatterbox off the field, he was much missed at Highbury, but doubtlessly brightened the dressing rooms of Brentford and non-League Barnet in later years. After retirement David went into the bakery business.

BORN: Mitcham, Surrey, 1.3.44.
GAMES: 194 (10). GOALS: 18.
OTHER CLUBS: Luton Town 70/1-71/2 (52, 0); Brentford 72/3 (12, 1).

JOE BAKER

More than a quarter of a century after exuberant centre-forward Joe Baker pulled on an Arsenal shirt for the last time, the mere mention of his name still has former team-mates and fans purring wistfully with pleasure. Joe was that sort of footballer, that sort of man. As a player, he could take the breath away with his audacious combination of speed and skill; as a character, he was mischievous and engaging, inspiring spontaneous affection in most people who knew him.

Joe joined the Gunners as a 22-year-old England international with a Scottish accent and an unusual pedigree. A Liverpudlian who grew up north of the border, he began his career with Hibernian – he was the first man to be capped by England while playing outside the Football League – and then he succumbed to the lure of the lire to pass an eventful, but often unhappy sojourn with Torino in Italy. When new Highbury boss Billy Wright hove into view with a £70,000 cheque in August 1962, Joe was delighted to make his escape, and rewarded his rescuer with a bountiful supply of goals which never dried up throughout his three-and-a-half years in North London.

Indeed, the effervescent marksman's prodigious natural talent was evident from the start. In his opening game, against Leyton Orient at Brisbane Road, he offered an enticing taste of riches to come by nutmegging a defender on the edge of the penalty box and driving a wicked, low shot into the bottom corner of the net for the winner.

Joe was a born crowd-pleaser, flamboyant, brave, and blessed with dynamic acceleration which was especially effective in short, sharp bursts. His close control was brilliant – he liked the ball played to his feet, no matter how tightly he was marked – and he revelled in quicksilver passing movements with Geoff Strong and George Eastham. There were even occasions, when Arsenal were already sure of victory, that the impudent trio would take a kick-off and set out to score without the opposition touching the ball.

But it wasn't just in slick approach play that Joe excelled; he was also a lethal finisher with both feet and his head. One gem which lingers in the memory came at Anfield in August 1964 when, after being caught on the wrong foot by a George Armstrong cross, he twisted in the air to head the ball emphatically past groping 'keeper Tommy Lawrence.

A fiery temperament led Joe into periodic scrapes, none better documented than his exchange of blows with Liverpool's Ron Yeats, which ended with both men being sent off in a tumultuous FA Cup tie in February 1964. Colleagues later recalled the confrontation's lighter side – Joe, at 5ft 8in, cut a comical figure squaring up to the colossal centre-half – but there was no doubting his seriousness at the time. Similar enthusiasm was evident in most areas of his life – the training ground might have been an occasional exception – and he positively relished the chance of a stint between the posts when Jack McClelland was injured at Leicester in August 1963. He conceded five that day, but no one questioned his commitment.

When Joe moved to Nottingham Forest for £65,000 in February 1966, he must have wondered why his prolific exploits had not coincided with success for the club, perhaps reflecting sadly on the shortcomings of a porous defence. He, at least, had not let Billy Wright down, his strike rate of a goal every one-and-a-half games speaking for itself. Sometimes Joe was accused of unpredictability, yet it was never hard to forecast whose name would be topping the Gunners' scoring charts at the end of the season. He was football's equivalent of the laughing cavalier and, for sheer excitement, Arsenal have not seen his like since.

BORN: Liverpool, 17.7.40. GAMES: 156. GOALS: 100.
HONOURS: 8 England caps (59-66).

OTHER CLUBS: Hibernian 57/8-60/1 (117, 102); Torino, Italy 61/2; Nottingham Forest 65/6-68/9 (117, 41); Sunderland 69/70-70/1 (40, 12); Hibernian 70/1-71/2 (25, 15); Raith Rovers 72/3-73/4 (49, 36).

1962/63 – 1965/66

DON HOWE

1964/65 – 1966/67

Don Howe was a thoroughbred footballer, a right-back whose smooth control and intelligent distribution made the game look deceptively easy. Whether defending or attacking, he relied on skill rather than strength and there is little doubt that, in his prime, the blond Black Countryman would have graced any team in the land.

However, it was argued by some observers that when Billy Wright paid West Bromwich Albion £35,000 for his former England team-mate in April 1964, Don was beginning to pass his peak, and evidence in support of this theory was quickly to hand. On his League debut for Arsenal, against Liverpool at Anfield on the opening day of 1964/65, he was on the receiving end of a severe chasing from tantalising winger Peter Thompson and there were fears that Billy had made an expensive blunder. But Don was too experienced to allow such a setback to wreck the final phase of his playing career, and he recovered his poise with a succession of classy performances, making up amply in craft what he lacked in speed.

Sadly, just when a lengthy and productive Indian summer was in prospect, the former Throstle broke his leg in an accidental collision with Blackpool goalkeeper Tony Waiters at Bloomfield Road in March 1966. When the bone had mended, new manager Bertie Mee gave Don a vote of confidence by making him club captain, but the injury had taken a grave toll of his mobility. An attempt at a comeback, against Manchester City at Maine Road in September 1966, proved abortive, and he never played League football again.

On retirement he remained at Highbury as chief coach, later managing West Bromwich Albion and coaching elsewhere in England and abroad, before returning to North London and inheriting the top job from his ex-colleague Terry Neill.

BORN: Wolverhampton, 12.10.35. GAMES: 74. GOALS: 1.
HONOURS: 23 England caps (57-59).
OTHER CLUBS: West Bromwich Albion 55/6-63/4 (342, 17).
MANAGER: West Bromwich Albion 71-75; Arsenal 83-86; Queen's Park Rangers 89-91; Coventry City 92.

JIM FURNELL

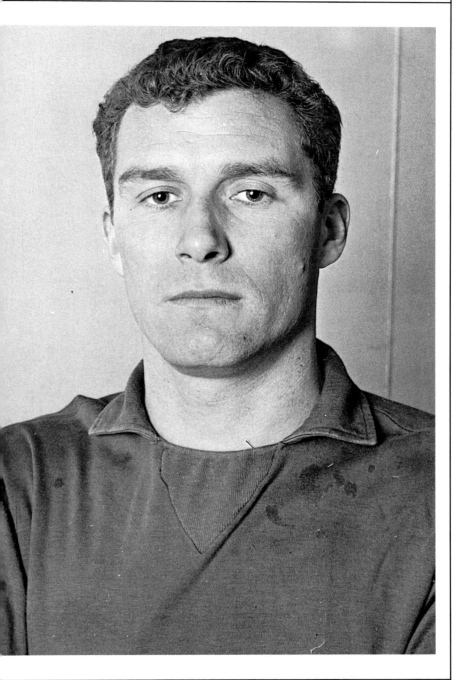

1963/64 – 1967/68

The mid sixties hardly represented a vintage period for Gunners goalkeepers. The likes of Jack McClelland, Ian McKechnie and Tony Burns were all found wanting, and although Jim Furnell retained the job for more than four years with only occasional interruptions, he never equalled the expertise of either Jack Kelsey or Bob Wilson, the men who held sway on either side of his reign.

Jim was a £15,000 recruit from Liverpool who had lost his Anfield place to the ever-improving Tommy Lawrence after breaking a finger. On arrival at Highbury in November 1963, he immediately established himself as manager Billy Wright's first choice, and had the dubious pleasure in the season's last game of conceding the five goals which wrapped up the Championship for his former club.

After settling in, the likeable left-footed Lancastrian revealed himself to be capable of spectacular action on his day, but with a disturbing tendency towards inconsistency. Though big and hefty, he didn't always command his penalty area, and gathering crosses was not his speciality.

Nevertheless Jim, a splendid improviser who was nothing loth to stop shots with his feet, was brave enough to dive head-first into the most fearsome of melees and his willingness to work ceaselessly at his game was an inspiration to youngsters.

He lost his place to Bob Wilson ten days after the 1968 League Cup Final defeat by Leeds United – in which many reckon Jim was impeded by two opponents seconds before Terry Cooper scored the only goal of the match – and never won it back. Six months later he accepted an £8,000 move to Rotherham United, before going on to guard Plymouth Argyle's net until he was 39. On retirement he became a coach, and subsequently managed Blackburn Rovers reserves.

BORN: Clitheroe, Lancashire, 23.11.37.
GAMES: 167. GOALS: 0.

OTHER CLUBS: Burnley 59/60-60/1 (2, 0);
Liverpool 61/2-63/4 (28, 0);
Rotherham United 68/9-69/70 (76, 0);
Plymouth Argyle 70/1-75/6 (183, 0).

JON SAMMELS

Jon Sammels' Arsenal career was sabotaged by a mindless section of the Highbury crowd, even as the Gunners approached their most glorious hour. For several years the terrace morons – and every club has their share – had singled out the skilful midfielder as a convenient scapegoat whenever events turned against their team. He would be baited mercilessly, often when he was playing well, until finally, unable to take any more, he was driven out of the club he had loved all his life. The decision to leave was taken in the weeks leading up to the famous League and FA Cup double and, poignantly, the £100,000 deal which took him to Leicester City was completed in the summer of 1971, when the subsequent euphoria was still at its height.

Perhaps others, blessed with more robust temperaments, would have shrugged off the unwarranted criticism, remained in North London, and continued to fight for his place. But Jon, a quiet, dedicated man who was popular with all who knew him, opted for peace of mind and a new start under one of his boyhood heroes, the former Highbury inside-forward Jimmy Bloomfield, who was then managing the Filberts.

Arsenal, who had sold the former England under-23 international only reluctantly and had publicly condemned the barrackers, were left to rue the premature departure of a richly gifted performer. Jon had been viewed as a potential star since his outstanding displays for the England youth team that won the 'Little World Cup' in 1963, and he duly impressed in early outings, scoring on his senior debut at Blackpool the following April.

By 1966 he had succeeded George Eastham as the Gunners' premier play-maker, and appeared to be maturing into a genuine top-liner with an enviable array of assets. Jon was a superbly accurate passer, he controlled the ball well with either foot, and packed a crisp shot, never seen to better advantage than in the home encounter with Manchester United in September 1969 when he curled a deliciously flighted 30-yarder past Alex Stepney. That same season he played a major part in the Gunners' European Fairs Cup victory, netting a late winner against Rouen, scoring in two other rounds, and then grabbing the goal that beat Anderlecht in the final.

All the while, however, he remained an aunt sally for the boo-boys, and his fortunes took a further dive when an ankle injury sidelined him for the first three months of 1970/71. George Graham took on the Sammels role with some aplomb, though Jon recovered his place for a midwinter spell that was just long enough to earn a title medal. In fact, although not as elegant as George, he was a busier player and at times just as subtle. But the Scot was clearly superior in the air and, in all fairness, the form of the future Arsenal manager could not be faulted in the hectic finale to the campaign, which also saw Charlie George return from injury to claim a place which might otherwise have been Jon's.

By then the Suffolk-born schemer – saddened, frustrated and still only 26 – knew that a break with his beloved Gunners was inevitable. Jon went on to serve Leicester with distinction, leaving those who had hounded him out to find new targets for their cowardly abuse.

BORN: Ipswich, 23.7.45. GAMES: 266 (4). GOALS: 52.
HONOURS: European Fairs Cup 69/70; League Championship 70/1.

OTHER CLUBS: Leicester City 71/2-77/8 (241, 21).

1962/63 – 1970/71

TOMMY BALDWIN

DAVID JENKINS

When Tommy Baldwin left Arsenal as a £25,000 makeweight in the deal which took George Graham from Stamford Bridge to Highbury, the young striker was written off by certain pundits who reckoned he was not good enough for the top flight. But the tenacious north-easterner confounded his critics by serving Chelsea with distinction for eight years, helping the Blues lift two major trophies and winning England under-23 honours.

Tommy, who rose through the Gunners' youth and reserve sides with John Radford but then failed to match his partner's progress, was endowed with moderate natural ability but was a tremendous trier. He was at his most dangerous when scurrying around the penalty area, harrying defenders into making mistakes, and he was nicknamed 'Sponge' for his ability to soak up punishment from rugged opponents.

West Ham were the victims of Tommy's finest performance in a red shirt, when he scored one and made another for John in a 2-1 home victory in August 1966. The following month, he made an indelible mark on Highbury history, netting the club's first three League Cup goals in a twice-replayed tie against Gillingham, but it was to be his Arsenal swansong. Two days later Tommy was bound for the Bridge.

BORN: Gateshead, 10.6.45. GAMES: 20. GOALS: 11.

OTHER CLUBS: Chelsea 66/7-74/5 (187, 74);
Millwall *on loan* 74/5 (6, 1); Manchester United *on loan* 74/5 (2, 0);
Brentford (non-contract) 77/8 (4, 1).

David Jenkins was a teenage prodigy who promised much but delivered little. The curly-haired Bristolian's form in the youth team suggested that Arsenal had a star striker in the making: he boasted a savage shot, excellent ball control and, though his pace was not outstanding, he seemed stronger than any of his contemporaries.

After breaking a leg in training during the summer of 1965, David recovered to make his senior debut in a League Cup encounter Gillingham 14 months later. He played in the 1968 League Cup Final defeat by Leeds United, but such was the competition for places that he wasn't offered an uninterrupted run until 1968/69 when he started the season in the number 11 shirt and retained for 16 matches.

The highlight of that sequence was a stunning hat-trick at Scunthorpe in the League Cup, featuring two 25-yarders and a glorious volley. But such stirring deeds were not to be repeated and that October he crossed North London to join Spurs in exchange for winger Jimmy Robertson. David made little impact either at White Hart Lane, or with his five subsequent clubs, and eventually took a job outside football. His was a sad story of a young man who had peaked too early.

BORN: Bristol, 2.9.46. GAMES: 24 (1). GOALS: 9.

OTHER CLUBS: Tottenham Hotspur 68/9-69/70 (14, 2);
Brentford 72/3 (18, 1); Hereford United 72/3-73/4 (22, 3);
Newport County *on loan* 73/4 (6, 1);
Shrewsbury Town 74/5 (2, 1); Workington Town 75/6 (6, 0).

1964/65 – 1966/67

1966/67 – 1968/69

TERRY NEILL

1960/61 – 1969/70

Terry Neill was not one of Arsenal's greatest players of the post-war era, but he was one of the more influential. The serious-minded, self-confident Ulsterman became, at 20, the youngest skipper in Gunners history, and he shouldered that responsibility for a major slice of the sixties. It was a period of disappointment in terms of results but one which laid the foundations for the club's finest hour, the League and FA Cup double of 1970/71, and he deserves a measure of credit for that.

From the moment he walked into Highbury as a 17-year-old recruit from Irish League Bangor City in 1959, there was no doubting Terry's dedication, and he moved quickly to the fringe of the first team. There followed two and a half years of steady but unspectacular progress, in and out of the League side, until his career gathered momentum with the appointment of Billy Wright. One of the new Highbury boss's first acts was to install the callow Irishman as captain, a bold move applauded by some, but by no means approved unanimously by the players.

Also there were slight reservations about his playing qualifications. He was versatile enough to fill any half-back position, but there was a feeling that he would always remain an adequate, rather than outstanding performer at the top level. Terry passed the ball well and tackled firmly enough, but he could be exposed for pace and was not always dominant in the air. Even allowing for injury and illness, he was not always an automatic choice, and as the decade drew to a close, he slipped out of the reckoning after an attack of jaundice.

A thoughtful and articulate captain of his country, Terry was clearly prime management material, and it was no surprise that when a £40,000 deal took him to Hull in 1970, he became player-boss, going on to assume the same dual role for Northern Ireland. Ahead of him was a stint in charge of Spurs, before his ultimate challenge, the Highbury hot seat.

BORN: Belfast, 8.5.42.

GAMES: 272 (3). GOALS: 10. HONOURS: 59 Northern Ireland caps (61-73).

OTHER CLUBS: Bangor, Northern Ireland; Hull City 70/1-72/3 (103, 4).

MANAGER: Hull City 70-74; Tottenham Hotspur 74-86; Arsenal 76-83; Northern Ireland 70-75.

JIMMY ROBERTSON

When Jimmy Robertson left White Hart Lane for Highbury in a straight swap for David Jenkins in October 1968, Arsenal got the better of the deal by a comfortable margin. While poor David was destined for almost instant obscurity, Jimmy was to make a positive, if rather fleeting contribution as the Gunners began to re-emerge as a major force.

The leggy Scottish winger, who could operate on either flank despite a heavy right-foot bias, was a busy raider of the speedy and direct variety. He relished knocking the ball past his marker and outstripping him in the race to the byline, but was also ready to forage in midfield. Jimmy was an expert crosser, specialising in deep balls to the far post, and also possessed a fierce shot, as he demonstrated with an unstoppable volley which put an FA Cup tie beyond the reach of Charlton Athletic at Highbury in January 1969.

The purchase of Peter Marinello signalled the end of his days as a Gunner, and Jimmy joined Ipswich for £60,000 in March 1970. In the two months remaining of the season, he became a local hero in East Anglia, helping Town retain top-flight status. But he didn't settle, serving a succession of clubs, notably Stoke City, before going into insurance.

BORN: Glasgow, 17.12.44. GAMES: 58 (1). GOALS: 8.
HONOURS: 1 Scotland cap (64).

OTHER CLUBS: Cowdenbeath 61/2 (25, 7); St Mirren 62/3-63/4 (52, 18); Tottenham Hotspur 63/4-68/9 (157, 25); Ipswich Town 69/70-71/2 (87, 10); Stoke City 72/3-76/7 (114, 12); Walsall 77/8 (16, 0); Crewe Alexandra 78/9 (33, 0).

1968/69 – 1969/70

BOBBY GOULD

Nature was less than bountiful in blessing Bobby Gould, that brave, irrepressible workhorse of a centre-forward, with football more subtle skills. But his desire to play the game, and to win, was second to none.

The swarthy, solidly-built Midlander made Arsenal the second stop on his eight-club playing tour of the Football League when Bertie Mee paid Coventry City £90,000 for his combative services in February 1968. Although he lacked genuine pace, Bobby chased so hard that often he would turn a team-mate's poor pass into a good one by hustling opponents out of their stride, and his finishing, while variable, could be deadly. Above all, his fiery enthusiasm was ideal for a team in the throes of clawing their way out of a decade-long trough of mediocrity, and his tears after the ignominious defeat by Swindon Town in the 1969 League Cup Final - he scored the Gunners' only goal - offered a graphic illustration of utter commitment.

Eventually, he was eased out by the emergence of gifted youngsters Ray Kennedy and Charlie George, and in June 1970 Bobby joined Wolves for £55,000, his Highbury holding-job complete successfully and with pride.

BORN: Coventry, 12.6.46. GAMES: 72 (11). GOALS: 23.

OTHER CLUBS: Coventry City 63/4-67/8 (81, 40); Wolverhampton Wanderers 70/1-71/2 (40, 18); West Bromwich Albion 71/2-72/3 (52, 18); Bristol City 72/3-73/4 (35, 15); West Ham United 73/4-75/6 (51, 15); Wolverhampton Wanderers 75/6-76/7 (34, 13); Bristol Rovers 77/8-78/9 (36, 12); Hereford United 78/9-79/80 (45, 13). MANAGER: Bristol Rovers 81-83; Coventry City 83-85; Bristol Rovers 85-87; Wimbledon 87-90; West Bromwich Albion 91-92; Coventry City 92-93; Wales 95-.

1967/68 – 1969/70

COLIN ADDISON

olin Addison was an accomplished goal-scoring inside-forward
ho never did himself justice at Highbury. When he was signed
rom Nottingham Forest for £45,000 in September 1966, there
seemed little doubt that he would play an integral part in new
anager Bertie Mee's vigorous campaign to lift the club out of its
stressing slump. The amiable West Countryman had established
glowing reputation at the City Ground and was seen as exactly
the type of skilful technician the Gunners needed.

ut somehow, as Bertie experimented with a variety of strikers,
Colin failed to come through. Troubled by niggling injuries, he
ever enjoyed a settled run in the side, and rarely performed to his
full potential when he did play. The thwarted marksman's
redicament was made all the more frustrating by scintillating
rm on the training ground, which was reproduced in just one
encouraging match-day sequence, when he scored in three
consecutive victories in September 1967.

After 15 months in which he had managed an average of
pproximately one goal every three games, a disappointing but by
no means disastrous record, Colin accepted a £40,000 move
to Sheffield United, later embarking on a varied career
in management.

ORN: Taunton, Somerset, 18.5.40. GAMES: 31 (1). GOALS: 10.

OTHER CLUBS: York City 57/8–60/1 (87, 27);
Nottingham Forest 60/1–66/7 (160, 61); Sheffield United 67/8–70/1
'94, 22); Hereford United 72/3 (23, 1). MANAGER: Hereford
United 71–74; Newport County 77–78; Derby County 79–82;
Newport County 82–85; Celta Virgo and Atletico Madrid, Spain;
Hereford United 90–91.

1966/67 – 1967/68

GEORGE JOHNSTON

There were shrewd judges at Highbury who thought little George
Johnston had the makings of a vintage, goal-poaching Gunner;
unfortunately he was destined to fizzle out like a prematurely
spent firecracker.

The slim Scot had come to Bertie Mee's attention through a
dazzling display for Cardiff City in a friendly against Arsenal to
raise money for the Aberfan disaster appeal in November 1966.
Four months later he had moved to North London in a £25,000
deal, and the initial impression was favourable.

George was a mobile operator with a fine touch in both feet, who
aimed to feed principally off knock-downs from the more robust
John Radford and to capitalise on rebounds from the goalkeeper.
He contributed several promising performances, and earned
kudos for snatching the winning goal in a 4–3 cliff-hanger at home
to Leeds United in May 1968.

But there was a feeling that he lacked maturity and didn't offer
enough to the overall team effort, so, with several other strikers in
contention for the role of John's partner, George was sold to
Birmingham City in 1969. However, he failed to make his mark
at St Andrews or with four further clubs, and drifted out of the
professional game.

BORN: Glasgow, 21.3.47. GAMES: 20 (5). GOALS: 3.

OTHER CLUBS: Cardiff City 64/5–66/7 (60, 21);
Birmingham City 69/70 (9, 1); Walsall *on loan* 70/1 (5, 1);
Fulham 70/1–71/2 (39, 12); Hereford United 72/3 (18, 5);
Newport County 73/4 (3, 0).

1967/68 – 1968/69

BRENDON BATSON

BRENDON BATSON 1971/72 — 1973/74

Full-back. BORN: Grenada, West Indies, 6.2.53.
GAMES: 6 (4). GOALS: 0. OTHER CLUBS: Cambridge United
73/4-77/8 (163, 6); West Bromwich Albion 77/8-82/3 (172, 1).

MICKY BOOT 1966/67

Forward. BORN: Leicester, 17.12.47. GAMES: 4 (1). GOALS: 2.

BRIAN CHAMBERS 1972/73 — 1973/74

Midfielder. BORN: Newcastle, 31.10.49. GAMES: 1 (1).
GOALS: 0. OTHER CLUBS: Sunderland 70/1-72/3 (63, 5);
Luton Town 74/5-76/7 (76, 9); Millwall 77/8-78/9 (59, 9);
Bournemouth 79/80-80/1 (42, 7); Halifax Town 80/1 (10, 0).

TOMMY COAKLEY 1966/67

Winger. BORN: Bellshill, Scotland, 2.5.47. GAMES: 13.
GOALS: 2. OTHER CLUBS: Motherwell.
MANAGER: Walsall 86-88.

ROGER DAVIDSON 1967/68

Midfielder. BORN: Islington, London, 27.10.48.
GAMES: 0 (1). GOALS: 0. OTHER CLUBS: Portsmouth 69/70
(3, 0); Fulham 70/1 (1, 0); Lincoln City 71/2 (6, 0);
Aldershot on loan 71/2 (12, 2).

PAUL DAVIES 1971/72

Striker. BORN: St Asaph, North Wales, 10.10.52.
GAMES: 0 (2). GOALS: 0. OTHER CLUBS: Charlton Athletic
72/3-74/5 (57, 9). Brother of Southampton and Wales
centre-forward Ron Davies.

MICKY BOOT

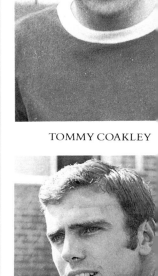

TOMMY COAKLEY

ROGER DAVIDSON

BRIAN CHAMBERS

PAUL DAVIES

70

GORDON NEILSON

ALAN TYRER

ROY PACK

JIM McGILL

TOM WALLEY

JOHN WOODWARD

JIM McGILL 1965/66 — 1966/67

Midfielder. BORN: Glasgow, 27.11.46. GAMES: 8 (4).
GOALS: 0. OTHER CLUBS: Huddersfield Town 67/8-71/2 (164, 8);
Hull City 71/2-75/6 (147, 2); Halifax Town 75/6-76/7 (32, 0).

GORDON NEILSON 1965/66 — 1966/67

Winger. BORN: Glasgow, 28.5.47. GAMES: 17. GOALS: 3.
OTHER CLUBS: Brentford 68/9-71/2 (91, 15).

ROY PACK 1965/66

Full-back. BORN: Islington, London, 20.9.46. GAMES: 1.
GOALS: 0. OTHER CLUBS: Portsmouth 66/7-68/9 (92, 0).

ALAN TYRER 1966/67

Midfielder. BORN: Liverpool, 8.12.42. GAMES: 1 (1). GOALS: 0.
OTHER CLUBS: Everton 59/60-61/2 (9, 2);
Mansfield Town 63/4-64/5 (41, 5); Bury 67/8 (2, 0);
Workington Town 68/9-75/6 (243, 18).

MALCOLM WEBSTER 1969/70

Goalkeeper. BORN: Rossington, Yorkshire, 12.11.50.
GAMES: 6. GOALS: 0. OTHER CLUBS: Fulham 69/70-73/4
(94, 0); Southend United 73/4-75/6 (96, 0);
Cambridge United 76/7-83/4 (256, 0).

TOM WALLEY 1965/66 — 1966/67

Wing-half. BORN: Caernarfon, North Wales, 27.2.45.
GAMES: 14 (4). GOALS: 1. HONOURS: 1 Wales cap 1971.
OTHER CLUBS: Watford 66/7-70/1 (203, 17);
Orient 71/2-75/6 (157, 5); Watford 76/7 (13, 0).

JOHN WOODWARD 1966/67

Midfielder. BORN: Glasgow, 10.1.49. GAMES: 3 (1).
GOALS: 0. OTHER CLUBS: York City 71/2-77/8 (166, 6).

MALCOLM WEBSTER

FRANK McLINTOCK

Frank McLintock was the Gunners' guiding light in their moments of greatest need on the road to League and FA Cup glory in 1970/71. He it was who sallied out of defence to score three crucial goals, including the winner at Southampton, on the Championship run-in; he it was again whose blazing defiance offered hope when his side fell behind in extra time at Wembley and their dream of the double seemed certain to be engulfed by Liverpool's red tide.

That sunny afternoon was to mark the climax of Arsenal's most triumphant campaign; it also underlined indelibly the North Londoners' debt to their inspirational captain. Refusing to contemplate the spectre of four previous defeats in the famous stadium, Frank rallied his sorely-pressed team-mates, even as time was running out. Fist aloft, he roared 'Come on, we *can* still win it', driving them forward to renewed efforts which produced two goals and a unique place in Highbury annals.

Such complete vindication of his belief, dedication and talent were all the more sweet for a spell of comparative travail after joining the Gunners from Leicester City. When Billy Wright paid £80,000 for the lean wing-half in October 1964, the Arsenal boss believed he was making the soundest of investments, and so he was, but it was to be five years before the Scottish international was seen to optimum effect. As an attacking midfielder, Frank offered passionate commitment and fine all-round skills; he was incisive in the tackle, passed the ball with precision, and possessed formidable stamina. But, too often, his anxiety to make a contribution in every corner of the pitch got the better of him, and his ill-advised wanderings left too many gaps.

He might have continued as a generally proficient, yet frustratingly unfulfilled performer but for a brainwave by coach Don Howe during an injury crisis in 1969/70. Frank was switched, somewhat reluctantly, to central defence and soon became the dominant influence that Billy Wright had always intended him to be. After a short period of adjustment, he began reading the game with a new-found maturity; where once he had been headstrong, he was now cool, but without losing the fire that made him special, and his forward forays were more telling for being rationed intelligently. Some feared that Frank, at 5ft 10in, would struggle in the air, but his instinctive timing, and the tactic of limiting the immediate goal threat by rarely retreating beyond the 18-yard line, quickly stilled such anxieties. As skipper, which he had been for two years, there was no doubting his qualities: he was a hard taskmaster who led by example and earned the respect of all who played under him.

Thus the stage was set for ultimate success, the despair of two FA Cup Final defeats with Leicester, and the Gunners' League Cup Final reverses of 1968 and 1969 placed firmly behind him. The former Gorbals boy had begun to suspect that he was a jinx on Arsenal and, at his lowest point, had even asked for a move. But leading the fight-back from a 3-1 first-leg deficit against Anderlecht to lift the European Fairs Cup in 1970 gave birth to renewed faith, and two personal honours – Footballer of the Year in 1971 and MBE in 1972 – were fitting rewards for a stirring renaissance.

In April 1973, a bargain £25,000 took Frank to Loftus Road, where he fuelled the arguments of fans who maintained he should never have been released, playing magnificently for three seasons and narrowly missing a Championship medal in 1976. But nothing could dim their memories of the man who had embodied the spirit of the Gunners. The North Bank swore Frank McLintock had the biggest heart in football; their case had much to commend it.

BORN: Glasgow, 28.12.39. GAMES: 401 (2). GOALS: 32.
HONOURS: European Fairs Cup 69/70; League Championship 70/1;
FA Cup 70/1. 9 Scotland caps (63-71).

OTHER CLUBS: Leicester City 59/60-64/5 (168, 25);
Queen's Park Rangers 73/4-76/7 (127, 5).
MANAGER: Leicester City 77-78; Brentford 84-87.

1964/65 – 1972/73

JOHN ROBERTS

The name of John Roberts won't appear on any list of the Gunners' most gifted players, the majority of fans remembering him as an archetypal stopper, a veritable Goliath in the air but awkward with the ball at his feet. In addition, the blond Welsh international tends to be classified along with numerous others who sojourned briefly at Highbury, making minimal impact before leaving for less illustrious fields.

Yet that does scant justice to John – or 'Garth', as he was widely known – who won a League Championship medal in 1970/71, playing in nearly half the season's matches, and who made Arsenal a tidy profit of £115,000 when he was sold to Birmingham City in October 1972.

A former railway fireman who started his League life as a centre-forward with Swansea Town, John had moved into defence when he caught the attention of Bertie Mee, who signed him from Northampton Town for £35,000 in May 1969. He was seen as a potential long-term successor to Ian Ure, but made a hesitant start with a handful of outings in which his rough edges and a certain lack of drive became apparent. Skilful coaching and brisk motivation by Don Howe and Steve Burtenshaw built up his confidence, however, and John started 1970/71 in the senior side.

For three months his towering presence helped to maintain the Gunners' interest in the title race, but then two erratic performances against Crystal Palace cost him his place. Henceforth, the new, more classy pairing of Peter Simpson and Frank McLintock was to leave the quiet six-footer on the sidelines, his earthy qualities offering little competition to their ability on the ball, and he missed out on the run-in to the League and FA Cup double.

But he remained in the squad, briefly regaining his place on merit in 1971/72, and when eventually he opted for a fresh start at St Andrew's, John could point to a significant contribution to the Highbury cause.

BORN: Abercynon, South Wales, 11.9.46.
GAMES: 77 (4). GOALS: 5.
HONOURS: League Championship 70/1.
22 Wales caps (71-76).

OTHER CLUBS: Swansea Town 65/6-67/8 (37, 16); Northampton Town 67/8-68/9 (62, 11); Birmingham City 72/3-75/6 (66, 1); Wrexham 76/7-79/80 (145, 5); Hull City 80/1 (26, 1).

1969/70 – 1972/73

PETER MARINELLO

1969/70 – 1972/73

Poor Peter Marinello, he never had a chance. Saddled with the ludicrous and impossible task of becoming London's answer to George Best, he faded inevitably into oblivion. Peter was yet another sad victim of media overkill, and the poignancy of his failure is hardly lessened by the feeling that, in less pressurised circumstances, the considerably gifted winger could have made the grade.

He had been coming along nicely with Hibernian, regularly captivating his home-town fans with a range of expressive skills, when the Gunners stepped forward, in January 1970, with a £100,000 offer which the Easter Road club could hardly refuse.

Perhaps it was fate that the long-haired 19-year-old should make his debut at Old Trafford, the home ground of the similarly hirsute Irish genius. Certainly it was the stuff of comic-strip fantasy when the fleet-footed Scot dribbled the ball for 50 yards, waltzed it around 'keeper Alex Stepney and placed it neatly in the net. Undoubtedly it signalled a bonanza for the image-makers, who latched hungrily on to Peter as an instant messiah for the success-starved south.

Soon Peter's cherubic features were staring down from the advertising hoardings, he cut a trial pop record, and was seen in all the most fashionable haunts. But one thing was missing: he wasn't fulfilling his potential on the field. By the start of the following season, he was out of the side – missing virtually all of the League and FA Cup double campaign – and then suffered a serious knee injury.

Come 1972/73, Peter was given another extended run in the team but, his initial impetus destroyed, he failed to make much impression, and joined Portsmouth for £80,000. It was an unsatisfactory exit, attracting little of the razzmatazz that had greeted his opening display. The publicity machine had moved on.

BORN: Edinburgh, 20.2.50.
GAMES: 43 (8). GOALS: 5.

OTHER CLUBS: Hibernian 67/8-69/70 (45, 5); Portsmouth 73/4-75/6 (95, 7); Motherwell 76/7-78/9 (89, 12); Fulham 78/9-79/80 (27, 1); Phoenix Infernoes, USA; Heart Of Midlothian 81/2-82/3 (22, 3).

BOB McNAB

When Bob McNab turned down the chance to join Liverpool, opting instead for a future at Highbury, Bill Shankly reacted to the disappointment with a typically mischievous barb. 'It's okay, I didn't really want him, he's not good enough for us anyway', rasped that most celebrated of soccer sages. But this was merely Shanks' inimitable way of admitting that, for once, he had been beaten, that his strenuous efforts in the autumn of 1966 to sign the 23-year-old full-back from Second Division Huddersfield Town had failed. The Anfield boss knew as well as everyone else in the game that the Gunners had captured one of England's brightest young defenders, a theory to which Bob's performances over the next nine seasons bore eloquent testimony.

The fee of £50,000 was then a record for a full-back, and the perky Yorkshireman set about justifying it with gusto, initially in the number-two shirt, but eventually in the left-flank slot where he was to win four England caps. Quick and brave, Bob tackled crisply and with admirable timing, and was also a potent attacking force, particularly when playing behind the prodigiously industrious George Armstrong, who dropped back to cover when the full-back took off on the penetrating overlaps he loved so dearly. In the early days, Bob's crossing and all-round distribution were a little wayward at times, but such was his dedication and aptitude that his technique improved rapidly. One of his most valuable sorties into opposition territory came against Anderlecht in the second leg of the European Fairs Cup Final at Highbury in April 1970, when he reached the byline to lay on John Radford's equaliser.

But for all his enterprise on the ball, Bob's most telling contribution to the Gunners' success was, arguably, his shrewd grasp of tactics and the ability to adapt sharply to the ebb and flow of the action. He was a constant caller, acting as an extra pair of eyes for each of his defensive colleagues, and his warning voice could often be heard above the buzz of the crowd. In his 'watchman' mode, he was the chief orchestrator of the team's offside trap, frequently urging Frank McLintock and company on a concerted charge forward, and when he was absent there was an unnerving lack of certainty about such delicate manoeuvres by the North Londoners' rearguard.

Bob's way with words earned him a place on ITV's panel of experts during the 1970 World Cup and his relative reticence in the role won him a spirited ribbing from club-mates accustomed to his prolific patter, both on and off the pitch. However, as he was sharing the screen with Messrs Jimmy Hill, Malcolm Allison, Paddy Crerand and Derek Dougan, he might have contended that he deserved congratulations, merely for getting a word in edgeways!

On the international scene, Bob's progress was blocked first by the excellence of Terry Cooper, and then by Don Revie's insistence on playing Emlyn Hughes out of position at left-back. At club level, there was no such impediment, and he played a full part in the European Fairs Cup victory in 1970, and the double triumph that followed. Bob missed much of 1971/72 with a deep-seated pelvic strain, but then recovered to remain first choice until mid decade. In July 1975, aged 32, he joined Wolves on a free transfer, subsequently playing in the United States and coaching in Canada. Arsenal missed him, both as a footballer and a character, and Highbury became a quieter place . . .

BORN: Huddersfield, 20.7.43. GAMES: 362 (3). GOALS: 6.
HONOURS: European Fairs Cup 69/70; League Championship 70/1;
FA Cup 70/1. 4 England caps (68-69).

OTHER CLUBS: Huddersfield Town 63/4-66/7 (68, 0);
Wolverhampton Wanderers 75/6 (13, 0); San Antonio, USA.

1966/67 – 1974/75

GEORGE GRAHAM

George Graham was a footballer of style and poise, whose finest displays brought a welcome reminder that the game, at its best, can be beautiful. He performed as though accompanied by the stirring theme music from *Chariots of Fire*, echoing the film's uplifting opening sequence not only in his grace and underlying power, but also in that, at times, he seemed to be playing in slow motion. Indeed, pace was the one attribute George lacked, and but for that he would surely have ranked with Arsenal's all-time greats. As it was, his rare combination of elegant ball skills and aerial strength made him one of the more eye-catching components in the Gunners' efficient machine of the late sixties and early seventies.

The gifted Scot became one of new manager Bertie Mee's earliest recruits when he was signed from Chelsea in September 1966, valued at £50,000 in a part-exchange deal that saw Tommy Baldwin move in the opposite direction. At that point, George was a prolific striker who had averaged a goal every two games for the Stamford Bridge club, and it was felt that he would be an ideal front-line partner for John Radford.

The strongly-built newcomer settled in well enough. He topped the North Londoners' scoring chart in each of his first two terms, attracted lavish praise for his majestic heading ability, and distinguished himself vividly from most contemporary marksmen by a seemingly adhesive first touch on the ball. But no amount of deft expertise when in possession could disguise a marked deficiency in acceleration which left him struggling if asked to sprint for a through-pass.

Accordingly, in early 1969, George was switched to a midfield role in which artistry would be prized above speed, and his career blossomed. At last he gave full rein to his subtle talents, spreading the play with smoothly-stroked passes and bringing much-needed creativity to an essentially workmanlike side. There were games which he ran with an apparent ease that bordered on arrogance, and he was dubbed 'Stroller' for his measured approach. Sometimes, not surprisingly, George's aura of casualness rebounded on him, and if he had a poor match his critics would call him lazy, which was far from the truth.

Overall though, the pundits, and more importantly the fans, were delighted with the Graham conversion. Not only was he scheming openings for others, he was also finding extra time and space for his own attempts on goal. George's shot was savage and his eye was sure - witness the unstoppable 25-yard volley that beat Ipswich Town at Highbury in October 1972 - but he could also caress the ball into the net, as he showed with a delicate floater at Goodison Park some two years earlier. However, some of his most spectacular goals continued to come from his head, many of them powered home from near the edge of the box, like the venomous strike from a George Armstrong corner against Stoke City in the 1971 FA Cup semi-final replay.

The Highbury play-maker was enormously influential in the League and FA Cup double campaign - responding with a vigour which belied his image to being dropped for six weeks in midwinter - and was the popular choice as man of the match in the Wembley defeat of Liverpool. It seemed inconceivable, then, that within a season and a half he would be leaving to join Manchester United's battle against relegation, but Tommy Docherty offered £120,000 for the 28-year-old he described as 'another Gunter Netzer', and Bertie Mee let him go. Whether George's aristocratic touches might have helped to avoid the anti-climax which gripped Highbury in the mid seventies, we shall never know. He was, of course, destined to return in the fullness of time, but that's another story.

BORN: Bargeddie, Scotland, 30.11.44. GAMES: 296 (12). GOALS: 77.
HONOURS: European Fairs Cup 69/70; League Championship 70/1; FA Cup 70/1. 12 Scotland caps (71-73).

OTHER CLUBS: Aston Villa 62/3-63/4 (8, 2); Chelsea 64/5-66/7 (72, 35); Manchester United 72/3-74/5 (43, 2); Portsmouth 74/5-76/7 (61, 5); Crystal Palace 76/7-77/8 (44, 2).
MANAGER: Millwall 82-86; Arsenal 86-95; Leeds United 96-.

1966/67 – 1972/73

PETER SIMPSON

There is a certain breed of footballer who turns in performances of exemplary quality for season after season, often making a more telling contribution than many so-called stars, yet who receives the merest smidgin of public acclaim. Such a player was Peter Simpson, one of the most accomplished central defenders of his generation.

The quiet man from Norfolk was the very antithesis of the hoof-it-and-hope school of stopper, so prevalent in the British game. Though he was strong in the air and an expert at the sliding tackle, Peter preferred to play his way out of difficult situations, relying on shrewd interceptions and calm, accurate distribution. Indeed, his left foot was a precision instrument which enabled him to initiate slick interchanges of short passes with the midfielders, or, with equal facility, set up attacks by sweeping crossfield balls to the wing.

Yet even in the League and FA Cup double-winning era, when the Gunners were constantly in the spotlight, Peter's excellence was overlooked with remarkable consistency. True, Alf Ramsey selected him in the preliminary squad for the 1970 World Cup, but the presence of Bobby Moore and Norman Hunter ensured that he didn't make the final 22. While no one could contend reasonably that the Arsenal number six was the equal of the England captain, there was a strong argument that he was more comfortable on the ball than the Leeds United dreadnought, and it was a travesty of justice that he was never given a chance at the top level.

Perhaps the key to his eternal exclusion is to be found in a comparison with Norman. Where the Hunter hallmarks were ruthlessness and certainty of purpose, there was a hint of diffidence to the Simpson psyche. Peter was a laid-back character who needed extra motivation at times, especially early in his career, and only after it was dispensed in liberal quantities by the likes of manager Bertie Mee and defensive partner Frank McLintock did he perform at his peak. The very fact that he was nicknamed 'Stan', after the passive half of Laurel and Hardy, spoke volumes.

Peter had risen to senior status via the Highbury youth system, making his debut at home to Chelsea in March 1964 and experiencing the trauma of watching his direct opponent, Bobby Tambling, score all four goals in the visitors' easy victory. There followed intermittent appearances over the next two campaigns before he became a regular first-teamer in the wake of Billy Wright's replacement by Mee in 1966. Peter, who was versatile enough to play at full-back or in midfield, made rapid strides under the new regime, and emerged as a more polished operator than either Ian Ure or Terry Neill. After sharing in the gloom of League Cup Final reverses in 1968 and 1969, he sampled glory for the first time in the 1969/70 European Fairs Cup, and having recovered from a cartilage operation which sidelined him for three months, he resumed duty as a back-four bulwark to help complete the famous double.

The stalwart 'Stan' maintained his lofty standards until the mid seventies, when injuries began to take their toll, and he was released by his only English club in the spring of 1978. His achievements had been immense, his permanent place in Highbury's hall of fame was assured; but had he been born with a more forceful outlook, the image of Peter Simpson in the white shirt of his country would not now require a flight of the imagination.

BORN: Gorleston, Norfolk, 13.1.45. GAMES: 458 (19). GOALS: 15.
HONOURS: European Fairs Cup 69/70; League Championship 70/1;
FA Cup 70/1.

OTHER CLUBS: New England Teamen, USA.

1963/64 – 1977/78

PETER STOREY

When it came to winning popularity contests outside North London, the Arsenal side that lifted the League and FA Cup double in 1970/71 were, to put it mildly, an unmitigated disaster. Around the country, Bertie Mee's men were the subject of scathing criticism – most of it the product of bitter jealousy – and no one came in for more comprehensive vilification than Peter Storey. Much of the flak directed at the Gunners was vague, hysterically condemning so-called boring tactics while conveniently ignoring the flair of Messrs Graham and George, but that which elevated the darkly menacing midfielder to the status of anti-hero was absolutely specific: he was denounced as a crude purveyor of violence to whom a football was scarcely relevant as he cut a swathe through hosts of squeaky-clean opponents.

In fact, while it would be absurd to discount the aggressive attributes of a performer from whom one stony stare was enough to make strong men wince, Peter was far from devoid of skill. In particular, his distribution was both smooth and accurate, especially with his right foot, and Highbury boasted few more accomplished exponents of the chipped pass. He had a knack of picking out his forwards with long, teasing crosses to the left edge of the penalty box, a ploy from which many goals resulted. Occasionally he would get in on the scoring act himself, never more famously than in the drawn FA Cup semi-final against Stoke City in March 1971. The Potters seemed Wembley-bound after taking a two-goal lead, but Peter pegged them back with a ferocious 20-yard drive, and then forced a replay in injury time by coolly sending Gordon Banks the wrong way from the penalty spot.

But whatever his all-round merits, it was as a formidable and utterly unflinching ball-winner that Peter earned his place in soccer folklore. He seemed to have no concept of danger to himself, the sort of man who would lose inches of skin in a tackle on icy ground without a flicker of expression, a genuinely tough nut. Many believed his methods to be over-zealous and saw his total of 19 England caps as a telling indication of declining international standards; others, almost exclusively Arsenal supporters, maintained that he was a 'hard but fair' practitioner of what was, after all, a man's game. Either way, his reputation fed on itself and he became the First Division's equivalent of the big, bad wolf.

There was little hint of such notoriety when Peter – ironically a shy, unassuming personality off the field – made his debut as a 20-year-old full-back at Leicester in October 1965. Quietly efficient and versatile enough to play on either flank, he became a first-team fixture, going on to pocket League Cup Final losers' medals in 1968 and 1969 before helping to win the European Fairs Cup the following season. His conversion to a midfield role came early in 1970/71, and by the end of that memorable campaign he had convinced both Highbury boss Bertie Mee and England manager Alf Ramsey that he had found his best position.

Seven months later, however, Peter's future seemed in jeopardy when he was replaced by new signing Alan Ball, and his name was linked with Manchester United. But it wasn't long before his steely presence was missed and he enjoyed another five years in the side before completing his career with a short stint at Fulham. Thereafter Peter, perhaps struggling to come to terms with life outside the game, encountered serious personal problems and got into difficulties with the law. Yet nothing could strip from him the achievements of his Gunners days, when his name was known, feared, and yes, respected, throughout most of the footballing world.

BORN: Farnham, Surrey, 7.9.45. GAMES: 494 (7). GOALS: 17.
HONOURS: European Fairs Cup 69/70; League Championship 70/1;
FA Cup 70/1. 19 England caps (71-73).

OTHER CLUBS: Fulham 76/7-77/8 (17, 0).

1965/66 – 1976/77

RAY KENNEDY

At the outset of 1970/71, rookie Ray Kennedy had started just two senior games and faced a daunting task if he was to gain a regular place in an Arsenal side made newly buoyant by lifting the European Fairs Cup. Less than nine months later he finished the League and FA Cup double campaign as the Gunners' top scorer and was being hailed as a future leviathan of English football.

It represented a remarkable transformation in the fortunes of the beefy north-easterner, who had been released by Port Vale several years earlier. The offer of an apprenticeship at Highbury in May 1968 rescued him from a job in a sweet factory and within 16 months he had made his first-team debut, as a Fairs Cup substitute at Glentoran. Again wearing the number 12 shirt, Ray confirmed his burgeoning promise with a headed goal in the away leg of the final against Anderlecht to keep Bertie Mee's team – 3-0 down and seemingly destined for defeat – in with a chance. He took no part in the subsequent second-leg victory, but eloquent notice of his capabilities had been served.

At this point, Ray might have expected a lengthy wait for an extended top-level opportunity, but an injury to Charlie George on the opening day of the season pitchforked him into the limelight. He responded with a succession of mighty performances, showing consistency that exceeded all expectations and maturity beyond his years, and didn't miss another match throughout that all-conquering term. Ray netted 26 times in the four major competitions – none more joyously remembered than the classic 87th minute header from a George Armstrong cross at White Hart Lane that set the seal on the Championship – and enjoyed a fruitful partnership with the ever-helpful John Radford.

Though neither the quickest nor the most graceful of movers, the 19-year-old newcomer had much to offer. Strong as an ox and a willing worker, he could control the ball instantly with his left foot, and was adept at retaining possession while colleagues poured forward to join the attack. He could deliver a fearsome shot with the minimum of backlift, his aerial power was formidable, and by offering such a potent central threat, he freed John to roam dangerously across the front line.

After such a scintillating start, Ray seemed set to tread a golden path to untold glory with the Gunners over the next decade, but alas, the soccer fates had other plans. Imperceptibly at first, his form began to wane, and despite winning England under-23 recognition in 1971/72, he was relegated to the substitutes' bench for the FA Cup Final against Leeds United. The eager young athlete had become a trifle sluggish, carrying a little extra weight and lacking his former punch, and soon there were whispers that he had enjoyed too much success too soon.

Salvation was at hand in the shrewd person of Bill Shankly, who bought Ray for £180,000 in July 1974 as his last act before resigning as Liverpool boss. However, it was the extrovert Scot's more downbeat successor, Bob Paisley, who did most to transform the Kennedy career by moving the out-of-sorts striker to midfield. In this new, creative role, and looking considerably more streamlined than in his final days at Highbury, he was a revelation, helping the Reds to garner ten major honours in six years and winning an England place.

His playing career drew to a close with brief contributions to Swansea City and Hartlepool United, before he sampled life as a publican, and then tried coaching with Sunderland. But heartbreak was lying in wait: Ray was found to have Parkinson's disease, a shattering blow which put all of sport's triumphs and so-called tragedies into stark perspective.

BORN: Seaton Delaval, Northumberland, 28.7.51. GAMES: 206 (6).
GOALS: 71. HONOURS: European Fairs Cup 69/70;
League Championship 70/1; FA Cup 70/1. 17 England caps (76-80).
OTHER CLUBS: Liverpool 74/5-81/2 (275, 51); Swansea City 81/2-83/4 (42, 2);
Hartlepool United 83/4 (23, 3).

1969/70 – 1973/74

JOHN RADFORD

'I used to keep going, didn't I?' Such was the matter-of-fact verdict by John Radford when asked to reflect on his contribution as centre-forward in the Arsenal team that won the League and FA Cup double in 1970/71. It was an unpretentious answer which somehow defined the man, and was an admirably blunt explanation of his habit of scoring late goals in important games. But it fell far, far short of his overall value to the North Londoners, both during the season of their ultimate triumph and for half a decade on either side.

Of course, John was fit and fast, big and strong, a born trier from first to last, but that was only the beginning of the story. Above all, he was intelligent, a tactician who brought often-unseen craft and subtlety to his work, a player who made it possible for others to shine. His career goal tally for the Gunners stands second only to that of the great Cliff Bastin, yet it was a succession of partners who profited most from his unselfish efforts. Joe Baker, George Graham, Ray Kennedy and Brian Kidd all fed voraciously from John's service, which not only afforded them a stream of opportunities, but also the time and space to make the most of them.

Perhaps the Yorkshireman's most priceless asset was his ability to time his off-the-ball runs to maximum advantage. When a colleague was poised to make a long pass out of defence, John would spin away from his marker, sprinting away from the spot he hoped to receive the ball, before changing direction abruptly at the last possible moment. Once in possession, his control rarely let him down, and his distribution was neat and unfussy, as he showed in the swift left-flank interchange with Charlie George which led to the young Londoner's double-clinching goal against Liverpool. John, who had earlier hooked the ball into the penalty box to lay on Eddie Kelly's equaliser, was the choice of many fellow professionals as man of the match, although the award went to George Graham.

It was a perfect example of the way in which the faithful front-runner missed out on public acclaim throughout his playing days, even when he scored spectacular goals such as the Gunners' second against Sporting Lisbon in the European Fairs Cup at Highbury in November 1969. With his back to goal, John deftly controlled a raking cross from Bob McNab with his left foot, before swivelling to crack a savage right-foot drive high into the net from 15 yards. His heading was equally accomplished, and it was his precise nod which put Arsenal on top against Anderlecht in the final of the same competition. Courage was another sterling Radford quality; he broke a bone in his wrist in the autumn of 1970, playing in subsequent matches despite severe pain, and also earned plaudits for his pluck as Bob Wilson's replacement between the posts during the last 15 minutes of the 1972 FA Cup semi-final against Stoke City.

By then, John had been based in North London for ten years, having started as an apprentice and been nurtured through Billy Wright's enterprising youth system. It wasn't long before he was showing such potential that Spurs made an inquiry about him, but the manager was hardly going to dispense with prime talent, however raw, and by the mid sixties the muscular marksman had come into his own at senior level. He went on to peak in the glory years, bowing out in December 1976 with an £80,000 transfer to West Ham United. There followed a stint with Blackburn Rovers and a spell as a publican before John took charge of Bishop's Stortford, later switching roles to become the non-Leaguers' commercial manager. It was a typically unobtrusive niche for one of the least showy, but most effective footballers in Arsenal history.

BORN: Pontefract, Yorkshire, 22.2.47. GAMES: 475 (6). GOALS: 149.
HONOURS: European Fairs Cup 69/70; League Championship 70/1;
FA Cup 70/1. 2 England caps (69-71).

OTHER CLUBS: West Ham United 76/7-77/8 (28, 0);
Blackburn Rovers 77/8-78/9 (36, 10).

1963/64 – 1976/77

CHARLIE GEORGE

Charlie George played his football with an insolent, rebellious swagger for a club that stood solidly for establishment values and the dignity of the game's hallowed traditions. Perhaps it was inevitable, therefore, that the North Bank's local hero, who hailed from deep in the Highbury heartland and had cheered the Gunners from the terraces as a boy, would never fit cosily into such a stately environment. The pity was that Arsenal, as one of the world's premier soccer institutions, offered the perfect setting for Charlie's prodigious flair, and it was a sorry day for the player, the club and most of all the supporters, when he left his greatest stage at the ludicrously premature age of 24.

From his earliest senior outings, it was blindingly clear that the tall, bony youngster with the lank, flapping locks was going to be special. In terms of natural ability, Charlie lacked nothing: his control was magnetic, his pace searing; he was a visionary passer and the most beguiling of dummy salesmen; his shot was startling in its sudden violence, and his headwork unusually subtle.

His temperament, however, was always going to be a problem. The habitually blank expression masked a volatile streak which made its initial major impact when he was sent off for swearing at a linesman during the European Fairs Cup clash with Glentoran in September 1969. At the time Charlie was less than two months into his debut campaign, and manager Bertie Mee reacted by dropping his *enfant terrible*, adding a severe injunction to seek maturity in the reserves.

But the George cocktail of skills was irresistible, and he was recalled in the spring, hitting ebullient form and helping the Gunners win the Fairs Cup. Hopes for his front-line link with John Radford were high as the 1970/71 season commenced at Goodison Park, but a painful setback was imminent. In the act of scoring, he broke an ankle in a collision with Everton 'keeper Gordon West and was sidelined until the New Year. By then, Ray Kennedy was established as John's partner, and when Charlie returned it was as an attacking midfielder, a role in which he gave a telling boost to Arsenal's double triumph. He was especially lethal in the FA Cup, scoring in the fourth, fifth and sixth rounds, and topped the lot with his history-making 20-yarder to sink Liverpool in extra time at Wembley, a stunning strike made in a state of near-exhaustion.

Such achievement should have provided the platform for greatness, but, sadly, Charlie never quite made it. During the early seventies, his highest total of League appearances in one term was a mere 28, his absences from a team he should have graced due either to inconsistent performances or the knee injuries which invariably laid him low whenever he seemed to be approaching his peak. His relationship with authority continued to be less than tranquil, and supporters grew critical of the management's failure to get the best from their fretful star.

Of course, there were some days, still, when Charlie delighted the senses with his freedom of expression, when an arrogant shrug of his sloping shoulders would remove defenders from his path as if by magic. But they became increasingly rare, and in the summer of 1975 it was decided that a parting of the ways would benefit all concerned. He came close to joining Spurs, which would have caused bitter furore on the North Bank, but Derby stepped in and Charlie accepted a £90,000 move to the Baseball Ground. With the Rams he came closer to realising his potential, and won a solitary England cap, before completing his career with a succession of short stints elsewhere. Back at Highbury, his devotees were left to lament a thrilling talent that was allowed to slip away. In retrospect, it would be kinder – and less frustrating – to dwell on his virtuoso contribution to the Gunners' finest hour.

BORN: Islington, London, 10.10.50. GAMES: 157 (22). GOALS: 49.
HONOURS: European Fairs Cup 69/70; League Championship 70/1;
FA Cup 70/1. 1 England cap (76).

OTHER CLUBS: Derby County 75/6–78/9 (106, 34);
Southampton 78/9–80/1 (44, 11); Nottingham Forest *on loan* 79/80 (2, 0);
Bulova, Hong Kong; Bournemouth 81/2 (2, 0); Derby County 81/2 (11, 2).

1969/70 – 1974/75

JEFF BLOCKLEY

Few players can have endured a more bewildering and ultimately depressing tenure at Highbury than the unfortunate Jeff Blockley. Yet when Bertie Mee paid Coventry City £200,000 for the spindly, curly-haired six-footer in October 1972, the Arsenal manager believed he had acquired a long-term successor to Frank McLintock as the linchpin of his defence. His judgment was confirmed, it seemed, when a few days after the deal was completed, the 23-year-old centre-half made his England debut, against Yugoslavia at Wembley.

It wasn't long, however, before there were audible rumblings of discontent. Many supporters were dismayed that the Gunners were preparing to dispense with their skilful, inspirational skipper, and planning to replace him with an old-style stopper of questionable all-round ability. To make matters worse, the terrace misgivings were mirrored in the dressing room, where several players greeted the move with ill-concealed consternation.

Jeff's form hardly helped. After an encouraging debut alongside Frank at Sheffield United, he appeared to lose confidence, even failing to achieve consistent dominance in the air, the one area in which he was supposed to excel. Lacking outstanding speed and any appreciable degree of dexterity on the ball, Jeff looked out of his depth at times, never more so than in the disastrous FA Cup semi-final defeat by Sunderland in the spring of 1973. Perhaps hampered by a niggling injury which had made him a doubtful starter before the match, he made a mistake which cost a goal and was never to be forgiven by the club's more critical fans.

He soldiered on, showing character and contributing some better performances, but Jeff was clearly not the answer to the Gunners' defensive problems, and in January 1975 he joined Leicester City, his home-town club, for £100,000.

BORN: Leicester, 12.9.49. GAMES: 62. GOALS: 1. HONOURS: 1 England cap (72).

OTHER CLUBS: Coventry City 68/9-72/3 (146, 6); Leicester City 74/5-77/8 (76, 2); Notts County 78/9-79/80 (59, 5).

1972/73 – 1974/75

EDDIE KELLY

1969/70 – 1975/76

If Eddie Kelly had been seen emerging from a gypsy's caravan in May 1971, his expression would probably have been glum. He had just helped the Gunners to complete the League and FA Cup double and, at 20, the Scottish midfielder who had already scored two of the most important goals in Arsenal history appeared to be on the threshold of a glittering future. But a crystal-ball session would have revealed that his career, while not unworthy, was destined to peter out in perplexing anti-climax.

Eddie's game was an unspectacular but effective fusion of strength and skill. Although a little short of pace, he was an accurate passer who controlled the ball neatly and rarely gave it away, while ensuring that he won his share of possession with Trojan-like tackling. Yet all this was overshadowed by a priceless knack of chipping in with crucial goals, such as the thunderous strike that transformed the 1970 European Fairs Cup Final. The Gunners were 3-1 down to Anderlecht at Highbury in the second leg when Eddie lashed home a 25-yarder, the prelude to a victory that signalled the rebirth of Arsenal as a major power.

But the Kelly *piece de resistance* was reserved for the 1971 FA Cup Final in which, with extra time ticking away and Liverpool a goal up, he prodded the ball through a ruck of bodies and into the net. Many maintained that George Graham got the last touch, but with neither the players nor the TV cameras able to offer conclusive proof, the goal was credited to Eddie, who had been called on to replace the injured Peter Storey. It was a rapturous finale to a term which he had begun as first choice on the right of midfield, before losing his place in December.

Newly capped at under-23 level, Eddie was expected to progress apace, but although he linked efficiently with Alan Ball in the early seventies, his form reached a plateau from which it did not advance. A stint as skipper did not provide further stimulus and in 1976 he joined Queen's Park Rangers for £60,000, before slipping out of the limelight.

BORN: Glasgow, 7.2.51. GAMES: 211 (11). GOALS: 19. HONOURS: European Fairs Cup 69/70; League Championship 70/1; FA Cup 70/1.

OTHER CLUBS: Queen's Park Rangers 76/7 (28, 1); Leicester City 77/8-79/80 (85, 4); Notts County 80/1 (27, 1); Bournemouth 81/2 (13, 0); Leicester City 81/2-82/3 (34, 0); Torquay United (non-contract) 84/5-85/6 (35, 1).

BOB WILSON

A combination of courage, intelligence and sheer hard graft transformed Bob Wilson from an enthusiastic, but undistinguished rookie goalkeeper into one of the First Division's master custodians. In fact, few who watched the blond, curly-haired six-footer's early, edgy performances between the Gunners' posts gave him much hope of making the grade; most believed that, as an eminently level-headed individual, he would recognise rapidly the futility of his football ambitions and turn instead to teaching, for which he was trained. But they had reckoned without the strength of character of a man who was to become a dauntless cornerstone of an Arsenal side destined for unprecedented glory.

Bob found his way to Highbury via Loughborough College and Wolverhampton Wanderers, whom he had served as an amateur, and made his League debut – his status unchanged – at home to Nottingham Forest in August 1963. His game at this time consisted of rough edges and fierce commitment in equal measure, but his unpaid efforts prompted the North Londoners to offer him a professional contract, which he signed in the spring of 1964 with Wolves receiving £5,500.

But the Wilson success story was not to be of the overnight variety. In fact, there was little immediate evidence that he would emerge from a rather motley collection of 'keepers aspiring to become the long-term replacement for Jack Kelsey. Though unfailingly valiant – his dives among the flailing feet became a trademark, and his shoulders were often a mass of bruises on the day after a match – he was prone to errors, particularly when dealing with crosses.

Accordingly, he remained as an understudy to Jim Furnell throughout the mid sixties, but anyone close to the former England schoolboy international knew he had not given up the classroom merely to mind a net in the Football Combination. His belief in himself unshaken, Bob worked ceaselessly, sought advice from the soundest sources and gradually improved until, in March 1968, he was given the chance to claim the senior slot. He responded by becoming the inspirational last line of defence the Gunners had lacked for half a decade, commanding his penalty area calmly and reading the game with an astuteness that was in stark contrast to more naive earlier displays.

Bob played a major part in the 1969/70 European Fairs Cup triumph, but it was during the following term that he reached his peak. Arsenal's form on the double trail was not *always* convincing, and their 'keeper's brilliance prevented a number of games from slipping away. Among his staunchest admirers was Bill Shankly – with whom he shared a deep passion for the game – and after the Reds had scuppered Arsenal 2-0 at Anfield, the Liverpool boss declared that Bob had saved the visitors from a six-goal thrashing. The two were in opposition again three months on at Wembley, where the Wilson clanger in allowing Steve Heighway to open the scoring at his near post was magnified unfairly, and two blinding stops which kept Arsenal hopes alive were invariably forgotten.

English-born Bob, whose parentage enabled him to win two caps for Scotland later that year, missed the 1972 final through injury, then returned for two more seasons of exemplary performances before retiring. He could reflect with pride on a career in which he had never revealed the style of a Gordon Banks, rarely indulging in picture-book exploits, but had been a truly formidable presence when it came to the crunch.

Unquestionably he could have played on longer, but with his future in mind he made the typically sensible decision to accept a job in television. His initial screen appearances struck many as rather shaky, but experience has brought increased appeal and authority. In the light of his previous achievements, the doubters should have known better.

BORN: Chesterfield, Derbyshire, 30.10.41. GAMES: 308. GOALS: 0.
HONOURS: European Fairs Cup 69/70; League Championship 70/1;
FA Cup 70/1. 2 Scotland caps (71).

1963/64 – 1973/74

GEORGE ARMSTRONG

There is no more important soldier in any battle than the man in charge of supplying ammunition to the front line; by that token, little George Armstrong was as crucial as any component in the Arsenal side that won the League and FA Cup double. It has been estimated that the workaholic winger had a hand in more than half the Gunners' goals during 1970/71, and there is a persuasive theory that opponents repeatedly presented Bertie Mee's team with the initiative by failing to stifle the threat posed by the unassuming north-easterner.

Not that bottling up 'Geordie', as he was affectionately known, was any simple matter. So perpetual was his motion, and so frequently did he turn up in every corner of the pitch, that harassed defenders could be excused for surmising that Mrs Armstrong had given birth to triplets and they all played for Arsenal. He was equally effective on either flank, though his habitual beat was on the left. There his capacity for tackling back frustrated countless opposition raids, while freeing his own full-back, Bob McNab, for a prominent attacking role and allowing midfielder George Graham extra scope to create.

It would be a gross misjustice, however, if tales of the phenomenal Armstrong industry and stamina should obscure his merits as a footballer of considerable all-round ability. He possessed a sure touch on the ball and had the skill and speed to run past defenders, but it was when he was anywhere in the proximity of the byline that he was at his most lethal. George was an inspired exponent of precision crossing, with either foot and whether under pressure or unattended. When he was in the side – and he didn't miss a match during the double campaign – there was no such thing as a wasted corner, his near-faultless delivery producing a rich return for Messrs Radford and Kennedy. Never a consistent scorer himself, he did contribute the occasional memorable strike, none more spectacular than the 30-yarder against Manchester United at Highbury in September 1965, and few more satisfying than the brace at home to Spurs in a 2-0 victory five years later.

George, who had been allowed to leave both Newcastle United and Grimsby Town after trials in his teens, joined Arsenal in 1961 as an inside-forward. He made an almost immediate transition to the wing and was introduced to League action at Blackpool the following February, going on to establish a regular senior slot over the next two terms. Maturing rapidly, the newcomer struck up a particularly fruitful understanding with prolific centre-forward Joe Baker, and by the turn of the decade he was reaching his peak.

Fittingly, his integral part in the Gunners' constant quest for trophies produced concerted calls for further international honours to add to his five under-23 outings in the mid sixties. But wingers were out of favour with England boss Alf Ramsey and George remains one of the most accomplished players never to have won a full cap. Characteristically undeterred by the lack of recognition, he continued to maintain lofty standards, and was one of the club's most reliable performers during their wretched mid-seventies slump, stretching his total of appearances beyond the 600 mark.

George's North London playing days ended on a slightly discordant note in 1977, when he was transferred to Leicester City for £15,000 following differences with manager Terry Neill. A stint with Stockport preceded coaching jobs in this country and Kuwait, before he returned to Highbury to run the reserve team. George Armstrong remains a sincere and generous man, universally liked and respected, and his young charges could hardly wish for a more impeccable role model. If just one of them manages to emulate his achievements, then Arsenal will be richly blessed.

BORN: Hebburn, County Durham, 9.8.44. GAMES: 607 (14). GOALS: 68.
HONOURS: European Fairs Cup 69/70; League Championship 70/1;
FA Cup 70/1.

OTHER CLUBS: Leicester City 77/8-78/9 (15, 0);
Stockport County 78/9 (34, 0).

1961/62 – 1977/78

PAT RICE

Nobody wanted to be a footballer more than Pat Rice. The problem was that even after being taken on as an Arsenal apprentice in December 1964, the squarely-built Irish teenager showed little of the natural talent normally deemed necessary to make the grade with a top club. But he refused to give up his dream, so he worked . . . and worked . . . and worked.

Endless hours of extra training were spent striving to increase his pace, hone the timing of his tackles, and improve his rudimentary ball control and wayward distribution. Away from the ground, he looked after himself in a manner befitting a professional athlete, and it slowly dawned on the Highbury coaching staff that they had a winner on their hands. As a result, Pat became the Gunners' regular right-back for a decade, which included three seasons as captain; he shared in the double triumph of 1970/71 and went on to appear in five FA Cup Finals; his total of European appearances (27) was a club record, and there was also the little matter of 49 matches for his country.

In fact, the effervescent Ulsterman, who had grown up in North London and been a boyhood supporter of Arsenal, was a full international before he made a major impact at club level. In the late sixties, Peter Storey was the undisputed occupant of the senior side's number two shirt, and it was only when the abrasive ball-winner was switched to midfield in August 1970 that the younger man became established.

Having broken through, Pat was not going to squander the achievement by adopting an over-ambitious mode of play. Sensibly he concentrated on doing the simple things well and minimising his weaknesses, attempting only the safest of passes and leaving most of the attacking overlaps to Bob McNab on the left flank. His rewards were immediate and vast: he finished his first full season with League and FA Cup winner's medals, and confounded critics who had forecast that he would suffer a Wembley runaround from Steve Heighway. Although the audacious new Merseyside hero escaped his minder's close attentions long enough to score the game's opening goal, the defender acquitted himself with honour on a stage which was to become increasingly familiar as his career wore on.

As he grew in experience, Pat became an accomplished all-round performer. He played a colossal part in steadying the Gunners rearguard during a shaky mid-seventies period and was the natural choice to succeed Alan Ball as skipper when the former England midfielder joined Southampton in 1977. A natural motivator who had been an apt pupil at the shoulder of Frank McLintock in earlier years, he enjoyed an exciting reign encompassing three consecutive FA Cup Finals, starting in 1978, and the European Cup Winners' Cup Final of 1980. One victory out of four, against Manchester United in 1979, was a disappointing return for such endeavour, but no one could cite leadership deficiencies as a reason for the reverses, and when Pat joined Watford for a bargain £8,000 in November 1980, he could leave Highbury secure in the knowledge of a task enterprisingly and faithfully fulfilled.

It was no surprise when, having assisted the Hornets' rise to Division One, he returned to his first love as youth coach in July 1984. No one was better qualified to instruct young men, whatever the level of their natural ability, on the qualities demanded of future Arsenal stars. Certainly, the Rice record offered vivid proof of the heights that can be scaled, if the desire burns strongly enough.

In 1996 a new instalment of Pat's service to the Highbury cause began with a brief stint as caretaker manager, followed by his appointment as Arsene Wenger's number two.

BORN: Belfast, 17.3.49. GAMES: 520 (7). GOALS: 13.
HONOURS: League Championship 70/1; FA Cup 70/1; FA Cup 78/9.
49 Northern Ireland caps (68-79).

OTHER CLUBS: Watford 80/1-83/4 (112, 1).

1967/68 – 1980/81

JIMMY RIMMER

1973/74 – 1976/77

Jimmy Rimmer was a splendid goalkeeper, but he was never a lucky one. At his first club, Manchester United, many sound observers reckoned he was unfortunate to lose out to Alex Stepney; years later with Aston Villa, he reached the European Cup Final, only to be injured and replaced after ten minutes; and in between, his stay at Highbury coincided with the Gunners' lowliest League positions since the twenties. In fact, Jimmy did more than most during the infuriatingly barren mid seventies to prevent the unthinkable - a slide into Division Two for the first time since the Great War.

Bertie Mee took the burly Lancastrian on loan from Old Trafford in February 1974, paying £40,000 to make the move permanent after two months, and plunging him into immediate action against Liverpool at Anfield. The new recruit impressed by keeping a clean sheet in an unexpected victory and, with Bob Wilson retiring at the end of the season, Jimmy grasped his opportunity.

Over the next three terms, he missed only two League games, displaying agility as a shot-stopper, dependability at taking crosses and bravery whenever it was necessary. He also offered an attacking bonus, sorely needed by Arsenal at that time, of instantly switching the scene of the action from one end of the pitch to the other with his mammoth drop-kicks. In training, he pushed himself to the limit, often doing extra work with coach Bobby Campbell before important matches, and richly deserved his election as Arsenal's player of the year in 1975.

Jimmy, whose enterprise had been rewarded by his sole England cap in 1976, left Highbury for Villa Park in a £70,000 deal on the same day in August 1977 that new manager Terry Neill signed Pat Jennings. His subsequent success, helping the Midlanders to the League title and triumph in Europe, was well overdue.

BORN: Southport, 10.2.48. GAMES: 146. GOALS: 0. HONOURS: 1 England cap (76).

OTHER CLUBS: Manchester United 67/8-72/3 (34, 0); Swansea City on loan 73/4 (17, 0); Aston Villa 77/8-82/3 (229, 0); Swansea City 83/4-85/6 (66, 0). MANAGER: Swansea City as caretaker 95 and 96.

BRIAN KIDD

1974/75 – 1975/76

Brian Kidd was a one-time Manchester United wonder-boy who moved to Highbury in search of new impetus after going off the boil during the death throes of a golden Old Trafford era. But no sooner had he left the newly-relegated Red Devils in August 1974 than he was caught up in Arsenal's own decline into the lower reaches of the First Division.

In the circumstances, the £110,000 striker acquitted himself well enough as a replacement for the recently departed Ray Kennedy, heading the Gunners' scoring list during both his campaigns in North London. Yet somehow Brian never seemed fully integrated into the team, always struggling without success to emulate his predecessor's fruitful rapport with front-running partner John Radford.

There was no doubt, certainly, that the slim, left-sided six-footer was well qualified in terms of natural ability. He was quick, skilful and had the confidence to run at defenders, often dropping his shoulder to confound the nimblest opponent with a sublime body swerve before finishing with a powerful shot. Against that, he appeared not always to show the physical resilience which had become an Arsenal trademark, and his single-minded approach in front of goal sometimes frustrated colleagues who felt they were better placed.

Brian's most impressive form was shown in his first term at Highbury, when he found the net 23 times in 50 outings despite Arsenal's chronic 16th position in the League table. There were grounds for hoping that the dashing Mancunian, once tipped to succeed Denis Law as 'King' of the Stretford End, might yet become the hero for which the North Bank yearned. But his tally was halved in 1975/76, and with the side slipping into the bottom six, swingeing changes were inevitable. That summer, when Manchester City bid £100,000 for his services, he decided not to await the appointment of new manager Terry Neill, and headed for home. After further travels, Brian returned to Old Trafford and excelled as assistant manager to Alex Ferguson.

BORN: Manchester, 29.5.49. GAMES: 90.
GOALS: 34. HONOURS:
2 England caps (70).

OTHER CLUBS: Manchester United 67/8–73/4 (203, 52); Manchester City 76/7-78/9 (98, 44); Everton 78/9-79/80 (40, 12); Bolton Wanderers 80/1-81/2 (43, 14); Atlanta Chiefs; Fort Lauderdale Strikers.
MANAGER: Preston North End 86.

DAVID PRICE

David Price was an ever-striving midfielder of limited natural talent but considerable thrust, whose achievements with the Gunners – holding a regular place for two-and-a-half seasons and playing in four cup finals – were a tribute to his tenacity. The blond former captain of England Schoolboys had spent five seasons on the outer fringe of the first team when, early in 1977/78, manager Terry Neill brought him in to operate wide on the right, in place of soon-to-be-sold Trevor Ross.

Despite being dispatched for a loan spell with Peterborough United in 1974/75 and suffering a broken leg during the following campaign, David had never lost sight of his ambition to make the grade at Highbury, and now he gave it his best shot. Making up in industry and courage what he lacked in the game's finer points, he proved an efficient link between defence and attack, invariably available to receive the ball and a reliable participant in neat passing triangles with the likes of Liam Brady and Alan Sunderland.

David also had a keen eye for an interception, as he showed when gaining possession to set up Frank Stapleton for the Gunners' first goal in the FA Cup semi-final against Wolves at Villa Park in March 1979. He impressed subsequently in the Wembley victory over Manchester United, again creating his side's opening goal, scored this time by Brian Talbot. It was the only time David pocketed a winners' medal in his four attempts: the previous year he had shared in the FA Cup defeat by Ipswich Town, and in 1980 was party to the debilitating double reverse against West Ham in the same competition and Valencia in the European Cup Winners' Cup.

As a new decade dawned, the battle for midfield places began to hot up, and David was squeezed out. In March 1981, he joined Crystal Palace for £80,000, going on to end his Football League days with Leyton Orient.

BORN: Caterham, Surrey, 23.6.55.
GAMES: 164 (11). GOALS: 19.
HONOURS: FA Cup 78/9.

OTHER CLUBS: Peterborough United *on loan* 74/5 (6, 1); Crystal Palace 80/1–81/2 (27, 2); Orient (non-contract) 82/3 (10, 0).

1972/73 – 1980/81

SAMMY NELSON

1969/70 – 1980/81

Highbury would have been an infinitely duller place in the seventies without the jaunty presence of full-back Sammy Nelson. The audacity of the Ulsterman's swashbuckling overlaps down Arsenal's left flank was equalled only by the corniness of his wisecracks, and he was held in genuine affection by team-mates and supporters alike.

Sammy had joined the Gunners as a left-winger, but was swiftly converted to the role in which he was to win more than half a century of international caps. He made his League debut at home to Ipswich Town in October 1969, but was to spend half a decade as a high-class deputy to Bob McNab before claiming a regular place.

Quick and agile, Sammy boasted a fine touch with his left foot, though his right was considerably less precise. He was capable of adding fire-power to the Gunners' attack – a scorcher in the 7-0 League Cup annihilation of Leeds United at Highbury in 1969 stays clear in the memory – and he could cross the ball reliably on his regular excursions into enemy territory. Unfortunately, however, Sammy did not read the game with the sureness of his predecessor and there were times when he was caught out of position. At the back, where his premier duty lay, he was effective in the air and a redoubtable tackler, unfailingly brave if a little inclined to make the occasional wild challenge.

This aggression in the heat of battle concealed a disarmingly gentle and humorous nature. Various antics – he once bared his behind to the crowd in a moment of levity – endeared him to the public, while his team-mates will never forget the night a fire alarm sounded at their hotel, and he emerged wearing only his underpants but clutching his wallet!

Sammy, an intelligent fellow behind all the clowning, eventually lost his place to Kenny Sansom, and joined Brighton for £35,000 in 1981. Have you heard the one about the Irish Seagull . . .

BORN: Belfast, 1.4.49. GAMES: 324 (14). GOALS: 12. HONOURS: FA Cup 78/9. 51 Northern Ireland caps (70-82).

OTHER CLUBS: Brighton and Hove Albion 81/2-82/3 (40, 0).

TERRY MANCINI

In ten years of management, Bertie Mee never made a shrewder investment than the £20,000 that persuaded Queen's Park Rangers to part with ebullient Cockney Terry Mancini. The deal was struck in October 1974, with Arsenal floundering near the foot of the First Division and a long, hard winter in prospect. Jeff Blockley had failed to fit the bill in the centre of the Gunners' defence, and now goals were being shipped steadily. At 32, Terry might have been past his prime, but he possessed two precious commodities that were desperately needed at Highbury during that dismal autumn – unshakeable self-confidence and a wicked sense of humour.

From the day he breezed into the famous old stadium, the atmosphere changed. Officials, team-mates and supporters alike were lifted by his infectious high spirits, and results began to improve. It wasn't as though Terry was an outstandingly gifted footballer, being dominant in most aerial duels but prone to erratic moments when the ball was on the ground. He knew his limitations, however, and played to his strengths, a positive attitude which rubbed off on everyone around him.

The Eire international – his broad East End accent must have raised a few laughs in Dublin, but he qualified for selection through Irish parentage – rarely threatened to breach opposing defences, though his only successful strike in an Arsenal shirt was a vital one, being the winner in a relegation-haunted encounter with Wolves in April 1976.

After twice helping to keep Arsenal in the top flight – yes, the mid-seventies situation was *that* dire – he was granted a free transfer and joined Aldershot in September 1976. Terry, or 'Henry' as he was inevitably dubbed, had proved an inspired short-term acquisition, and he left Highbury secure in the knowledge that he had achieved more than anyone had a right to expect.

BORN: Camden Town, London, 4.10.42.
GAMES: 62. GOALS: 1. HONOURS: 5
Republic of Ireland caps (74-75).

OTHER CLUBS: Watford 61/2-65/6 (67, 0);
Port Elizabeth, South Africa;
Leyton Orient 67/8-71/2 (167, 16);
Queen's Park Rangers 71/2-74/5 (94, 3);
Aldershot 76/7 (21, 0).

1974/75 – 1975/76

ALEX CROPLEY

BRIAN HORNSBY

Alex Cropley looked like a matchstick man but tackled like a tank, and therein, perhaps, lies the explanation of the crushing sequence of injuries that blighted his career. Bertie Mee paid Hibernian £50,000 for the 5ft 7in midfielder in December 1974, hoping that he would supply desperately-needed dynamism to his listless Gunners. Initial indications were encouraging as the blond Scottish international buzzed around incessantly, throwing himself enthusiastically into every challenge and also showing a high degree of skill, especially with his left foot.

However, it seemed remarkable that such a lightweight figure could muster so much force without ill effects, and sure enough, after a few matches, Alex was in trouble. The day after playing at Middlesbrough, he climbed from his car and felt something give in his leg. A break was diagnosed and he was sidelined for the rest of the season.

He recovered in time to start 1975/76 but it wasn't long before further knocks removed him from the side and impatient fans, believing Alex's absences made him a poor investment, began to complain. In September 1976, he accepted the chance to make a fresh start, joining Aston Villa for £135,000. He helped them to win the League Cup before more injuries led to early retirement.

BORN: Aldershot, 16.1.51. GAMES: 33 (1). GOALS: 6.
HONOURS: 2 Scotland caps (71).

OTHER CLUBS: Hibernian 69/70-74/5 (114, 24);
Aston Villa 76/7-79/80 (67, 7); Newcastle United *on loan* 79/80 (3, 0);
Toronto Blizzard, Canada; Portsmouth 81/2 (10, 2).

Brian Hornsby was a small, nippy striker with neat ball skills who lacked the physical thrust demanded of a top-line performer. At times he impressed with deft manoeuvres in crowded penalty areas, embarrassing big, sluggish defenders with his sharpness on the turn. However, he never looked likely to progress beyond the status of squad member, finding it difficult to achieve consistent form during a barren period for the Gunners in which opportunity was rife but morale was low.

The blond forward, a former England schoolboy and youth international, enjoyed two spells in the limelight. The first came in late 1973, when he deputised for the injured John Radford and contributed three goals in five games. For his next substantial chance, Brian had to wait until the end of the troubled 1974/75 campaign, when he partnered Brian Kidd for an uninterrupted run of 11 matches in which he netted three times but failed to convince the management of his long-term worth.

He was sold to Shrewsbury Town for £20,000 in June 1976, rapidly doubling his transfer value and going on to play the best football of his career with Sheffield Wednesday. Having found his true level, Brian became a key figure in the Owls' rise from the Third Division in 1980.

BORN: Cambridge, 10.9.54. GAMES: 23 (3). GOALS: 6.

OTHER CLUBS: Shrewsbury Town 76/7-77/8 (75, 16);
Sheffield Wednesday 77/8-81/2 (106, 25); Chester City *on loan* 81/2 (4, 0); Edmonton Drillers, Canada; Carlisle United 82/3-83/4 (10, 1); Chesterfield *on loan* 83/4 1, 0).

1974/75 – 1976/77

1972/73 – 1975/76

ALAN BALL

Arsenal and Alan Ball appeared to be made for each other. When Bertie Mee paid a British record £220,000 to Everton for the dynamic little Lancastrian in December 1971, the Gunners had gone stale in the afterglow of their League and FA Cup double, and were in urgent need of a tonic. Who better to provide it than the irrepressible redhead, a hero of England's 1966 World Cup triumph but, at 26, presumably on the threshold of his prime? Inevitably, it was predicted that Alan would spur the North Londoners to untold glories; yet in the course of five frustrating years, the union between a great club and one of the world's premier midfield talents was not to be blessed with a single trophy.

Indeed, a less positive character than the man who had formed such a potent creative trio with Howard Kendall and Colin Harvey at Goodison Park might have been dismayed by his initial experiences at Highbury. At that time, the long ball out of defence was beloved of the Gunners and Alan found himself being bypassed too frequently for his liking. Not exactly shy and retiring by nature, he was quick to state the case for fresh tactics, and it was not long before he was directing the short-passing game of which he was such an accomplished exponent.

The Ball technique was a delight to the eye. He specialised in startlingly slick one-touch interchanges which could demoralise opponents with their speed and efficiency. His control was instant, no matter at what angle he was required to receive the ball, and his fitness and industry were awesome. Alan was also a motivator supreme, alternately goading and cajoling his colleagues, his relentlessly forthright approach bringing out the best in many players while possibly alienating others.

After sharing in the disappointments of FA Cup Final defeat in 1972 and a League runners-up spot in the following campaign, Alan took on the captaincy as Arsenal regrouped in 1973/74. But key men had been allowed to depart - too soon, according to some judges - and when the Gunners' slide began, little went right for their most influential performer. After breaking a leg in April 1974, he made a lightning recovery, only to fracture his ankle three months later on a pre-season tour of Holland. Results were poor in the skipper's absence, and tensions began to mount, culminating in a row between Alan and the management when the club refused to back his appeal against a sending-off early in 1975. Relegation was averted, but the bitterness lingered on and the volatile star was axed for the opening games of 1975/76. Soon he returned, but the team continued to flounder and Alan, by now dropped from the England side he had once led, found himself caught up in a second successive battle to survive in the First Division.

The mission was accomplished, and the appointment of Terry Neill signalled a new era at Highbury, but not for Alan Ball. In December 1976, after several differences of opinion with his new boss, he joined Southampton for £60,000, going on to give some of the most inspiring displays of his career as the Saints rose to the top flight.

In retrospect, his move from Everton - according to the grapevine, he came close to joining Manchester United instead of heading south - proved more beneficial to Arsenal than to the player himself. His spirit and ability were of paramount importance during a period of rebuilding, and youngsters such as Liam Brady derived enormous benefit from his presence. It is even plausible to speculate that without Alan, Arsenal might have tasted Second Division football for the first time since 1919. Yet it remains inescapable that his Highbury sojourn did unexpectedly little to enhance the stature of a talent which, as his subsequent achievements proved, was far from spent.

BORN: Farnworth, Lancashire, 12.5.45. GAMES: 217. GOALS: 52.
HONOURS: 72 England caps (65-75)

OTHER CLUBS: Blackpool 62/3-65/6 (116, 41); Everton 66/7-71/2 (208, 66); Southampton 76/7-79/80 (132, 9); Philadelphia Fury; Vancouver Whitecaps; Blackpool 80/1 (30, 5); Southampton 80/1-82/3 (63, 2); Hong Kong; Bristol Rovers 82/3 (17, 2). MANAGER: Blackpool 80-81; Portsmouth 84-89; Stoke City 89-91; Exeter City 91-94; Southampton 94-95; Manchester City 95-96.

1971/72 – 1976/77

PAT HOWARD

GEOFF BARNETT

Pat Howard had precious little chance to make a significant impact at Highbury. New Arsenal manager Terry Neill paid Newcastle United £50,000 for the forceful, blond central defender in September 1976, intending him as a replacement for the departing Terry Mancini. But when Willie Young became available during the following spring, Pat was hastily jettisoned, and 11 months after arriving in North London he was on his way to Birmingham City for £40,000.

In truth, the Yorkshireman who had formed such an effective Magpies partnership with Bobby Moncur had never looked to have the class for a long-term Gunners future. It was the old story of a stopper being amply competitive in the air, but rather too basic for comfort with the ball at his feet.

His failure to find a niche in the south was ironic in view of the public outcry that had surrounded his departure from St James' Park, following, as it did, so closely on Arsenal's capture of Tyneside idol Malcolm Macdonald.

After a short stay at St Andrews, Pat gave doughty service to Bury, staying in the town on retirement to run a sports equipment business.

BORN: Dodworth, Yorkshire, 7.10.47. GAMES: 19 (1).
GOALS: 0.

OTHER CLUBS: Barnsley, 65/6-71/2 (177, 6);
Newcastle United 71/2-76/7 (184, 7); Birmingham City 77/8-78/9 (40, 0); Bury 79/80-81/2 (118, 5).

Geoff Barnett was the eternal understudy: his early years we spent in the shadows of Gordon West and Andy Rankin at Everton, then he became Arsenal's deputy net-minder, first Bob Wilson and later to Jimmy Rimmer. After the Gunners p £35,000 for the former England schoolboy and youth internatio in October 1969, he made the most of an early first-team chan saving a penalty in the goalless first leg against Sporting Lisbon the European Fairs Cup. At that time, Bob was only newly established as a first-team regular, and there were those who that the recruit from Goodison might offer serious competitio

But although he never let the team down, Geoff was really m more than a steady performer. He handled the ball deftly an distributed it with precision – his drilled clearances to the left wi were especially relished by George Armstrong – but he lacked t senior man's dominant physical presence. In the circumstance Geoff might have been expected to seek a move, but he elected stay and reaped the reward of an FA Cup Final appearance agai Leeds United in 1972, being blameless for the game's only go Geoff – dubbed 'Marty' for a supposed resemblance to comedi Marty Feldman – left Arsenal in 1976 to play and coach in Amer

BORN: Northwich, Cheshire, 16.10.46. GAMES: 49. GOALS
OTHER CLUBS: Everton 65/6-67/8 (10, 0);
Minnesota Kicks, USA.

1976/77

1969/70 – 1975/76

JOHN MATTHEWS

RICHIE POWLING

John Matthews was a dark, spidery six-footer endowed with superior passing skills, but cursed by a lack of pace which destroyed his chance of winning a regular place in the Arsenal midfield.

The quiet Londoner, who joined the Gunners as an apprentice in 1971, made his First Division debut at Leicester in August 1974, deputising in the back four due to a crop of injuries. In the course of that troubled season, when team changes were frequent and results depressing, the versatile teenager made 26 senior starts – comfortably the highest total during his four years in the senior squad – and must have felt optimistic about his Highbury future.

But a broken ankle in December 1975 set him back, and on his return he seemed ponderous and awkward, needing too much time on the ball to succeed in the top flight. Nevertheless, John continued to hover on the fringe of the team for the next two and a half years, his most notable mark on the record books being his two-goal contribution to the Gunners' 5-1 League Cup drubbing of Hull City in November 1977.

He joined Sheffield United for £90,000 in the following August and continued to play in the lower divisions until 1990.

BORN: Camden, London, 1.11.55. GAMES: 48 (9). GOALS: 5.

OTHER CLUBS: Sheffield United 78/9-81/2 (103, 14); Mansfield Town 82/3-83/4 (72, 6); Chesterfield 84/5 (38, 1); Plymouth Argyle 85/6-88/9 (135, 4); Torquay United 89/90 (25, 0).

A knee injury ended the career of Richie Powling shortly after his transformation from a distinctly limited central defender to a midfielder of considerable promise. The chunky all-rounder played most of his senior football at the back, where his lack of stature – at 5ft 7½in he was accustomed to enter aerial duels with a six-inch disadvantage – made it unlikely that he would progress beyond stopgap status, despite possessing a commendable turn of pace and a shrewd sense of anticipation.

A former England youth international, he tasted League action for the first time at Loftus Road in October 1973, but it wasn't until 1975/76 that he was given a settled run, partnering first David O'Leary and then Terry Mancini. However, at a time when Arsenal were faced with the unwelcome novelty of a relegation battle, Richie never really convinced, and as new faces arrived, he dropped down the pecking order. His midfield breakthrough came at the outset of 1977/78, when he netted twice in four League games and impressed with his energetic contribution before being laid low. Richie finally gave up his fight for fitness in 1981, though later he managed a comeback for non-League Barnet.

BORN: Barking, Essex, 21.5.56. GAMES: 54 (5). GOALS: 3.

1974/75 – 1977/78

1973/74 – 1977/78

PAUL BARRON

MARK HEELEY

PAUL BARRON 1978/79 — 1979/80

Goalkeeper. BORN: Woolwich, London, 16.9.53. GAMES: 8.
GOALS: 0. OTHER CLUBS: Plymouth Argyle 76/7-77/8 (44, 0);
Crystal Palace 80/1-82/3 (90, 0); West Bromwich Albion 82/3-84/5
(63, 0); Stoke City *on loan* 84/5 (1, 0); Queen's Park Rangers
85/6-86/7 (32, 0); Reading *on loan* 86/7 (4, 0).

STEVE BRIGNALL 1978/79

Defender. BORN: Ashford, Kent, 12.6.60.
GAMES: 0 (1). GOALS: 0.

JIMMY HARVEY 1977/78 — 1978/79

Midfielder. BORN: Lurgan, Northern Ireland, 2.5.58.
GAMES: 3 (1). GOALS: 0. OTHER CLUBS: Glenavon, Northern
Ireland; Hereford United 79/80-86/7 (278, 39); Bristol City
86/7-87/8 (3, 0); Wrexham on loan 87/8 (6, 0); Tranmere Rovers
87/8-92/3 (184, 18); Crewe Alexandra 92/3 (17, 0).

MARK HEELEY 1977/78 — 1978/79

Winger. BORN: Peterborough, Cambridgeshire, 18.9.59.
GAMES: 13 (7). GOALS: 1. OTHER CLUBS: Peterborough United
75/6-76/7 (17, 3); Northampton Town 79/80-82/3 (92, 3).

JOHN KOSMINA 1978/79

Forward. BORN: Australia, 17.8.56. GAMES: 1 (3).
GOALS: 0. OTHER CLUBS: Polonia, Australia.

KEVIN STEAD 1978/79

Defender. BORN: West Ham, 2.10.58.
GAMES: 1 (1). GOALS: 0.

JIMMY HARVEY

JOHN KOSMINA

STEVE BRIGNALL

KEVIN STEAD

TREVOR ROSS

Not many England schoolboy internationals go on to play for *Scotland* under-21s, but such was the unusual experience of Trevor Ross. The Lancashire-born midfielder was allowed the distinction because his parents hailed from north of the border - his father, William Ross, played for Third Lanark - but, alas, he did not progress to the top level for either country.

Trevor, a product of the Arsenal youth system and a fine athlete, made his first League appearance as a substitute for Alan Ball at home to Liverpool in February 1975. His big chance came a year later when Bertie Mee gave him an extended run in place of Eddie Kelly on the right of the Gunners' middle line.

He proved to be a solid, direct performer who tackled firmly, passed competently and packed a tremendous shot - the crowd often bayed for a thunderbolt when he gained possession - and new boss Terry Neill persisted with him in 1976/77. But Trevor never exuded class, and he was ousted by David Price before joining Everton for the substantial fee of £170,000 in November 1977. A creditable spell at Goodison Park ensued, and he later saw out his League days in his home county, with Bury.

BORN: Ashton-under-Lyne, Lancashire, 16.1.57.
GAMES: 66 (1). GOALS: 9.

OTHER CLUBS: Everton 77/8-82/3 (126, 16); Portsmouth on loan 82/3 (5, 0); Sheffield United on loan 82/3 (4, 0); AEK Athens 82/3; Sheffield United 83/4 (4, 0); Bury 84/5-86/7 (98, 11).

1974/75 − 1977/78

WILF ROSTRON

There was a time when the Gunners harboured high hopes for diminutive Wearsider Wilf Rostron. A former England schoolboy international, he was an outside-left who could dribble past defenders and then use the ball intelligently, yet also boasted the tenacity to make tackles when possession was lost. A similar cocktail of skill and bravery had proved fruitful at Highbury for George Armstrong, but Wilf couldn't equal the consistency of his fellow north-easterner and failed to maintain his exciting early progress.

The curly-haired flankman scored on his League debut at home to Newcastle United in March 1975, and followed that with another goal at Burnley four days later. But competition for places was extremely brisk, and Wilf was unable to claim a regular berth as Bertie Mee tried a variety of combinations in successive battles to avoid relegation.

In the summer of 1977, he accepted a £40,000 move to Sunderland, his hometown club, but it was back in the south that he was to enjoy most success. Having been converted to left-back, Wilf helped Watford reach the First Division, and then became captain as the Hornets remained among the elite for six seasons.

BORN: Sunderland, 29.9.56. GAMES: 14 (5). GOALS: 2.

OTHER CLUBS: Sunderland 77/8-79/80 (76, 17); Watford 79/80-88/9 (317, 22); Sheffield Wednesday 88/9 (7, 0); Sheffield United 89/90-90/1 (36, 3); Brentford 90/1-92/3 (42, 2).

1974/75 − 1976/77

MALCOLM MacDONALD

Few new arrivals at Highbury have produced a greater thrill of expectation than Malcolm Macdonald, and seldom has a prospective hero lived up to his reputation in more spectacular fashion. It follows, with depressing logic, that rarely have Arsenal supporters been plunged into deeper desolation than when an arthritic knee robbed them of their rampaging centre-forward after only two full seasons.

Malcolm became new manager Terry Neill's flagship signing when he was snatched from under the noses of neighbouring rivals Tottenham Hotspur in a swiftly concluded £333,333 deal with Newcastle United in August 1976. He was the emblem of a fresh order, dedicated to sweeping away the cobwebs that had gathered at the club during two consecutive relegation battles, and his swaggering statements of intent hogged the back-page headlines. In fact, one of Malcolm's early boasts rebounded on him when, on his Gunners debut, he was shackled by Bristol City's Gary Collier and outshone by the Robins' richly promising striker Paul Cheesley. There was heart-rending irony in the circumstance: young Paul's career was to be ended by a knee injury received in his next game.

For Arsenal's muscular marksman, however, such agony was well in the future and he responded to his temporary setback in typical style, amassing 29 goals during his opening North London campaign. The Macdonald method was based on pace and power, and he was at his most effective when running on to through-balls. Once he got ahead of a defender he was never caught, and his sledge-hammer left foot was a weapon of awesome ferocity. Though only 5ft 8in, Malcolm was also majestic in the air, often out-climbing far bigger men, as he demonstrated with an adroit looping header from an Alan Ball chip against his former Newcastle colleagues in December 1976.

His second term at Highbury was almost equally prolific, but the New Year brought danger signs when his knee began to seize up during games. The resultant reduction in Malcolm's mobility was a drastic blow to a side which perhaps relied on him too heavily for comfort, and was the cause of his ineffective showing in the Gunners' 1978 FA Cup Final defeat. This reverse, at the hands of Ipswich Town, was especially galling to the one-time Tyneside idol, who had twice finished on the losing side at Wembley in his days as a Magpie. Possessed by insatiable ambition, Malcolm was also frustrated by his failure to add to his total of England caps after joining the Gunners, but could at least look back on one feat denied to most international stars, a five-goal haul against Cyprus in 1975.

However, the man who had been converted from full-back to front-runner at Fulham, his first League club, had to prepare himself for even more distressing news. After managing just a handful of appearances and undergoing a series of operations in 1978/79, he was forced to quit.

Never slow to let team-mates know when they had failed to fulfil his requirements, Malcolm was portrayed by some as a selfish player. Indeed, his attitude to scoring goals *was* single-minded, but that didn't mean he had nothing to offer young colleagues in terms of knowhow and experience, and Frank Stapleton, in particular, learnt much from their association. On occasion, the outspoken Londoner lacked discipline and one clash with Terry Neill resulted in a spell on the transfer list. But neither fans nor manager had any doubt about the value of a fit Supermac. He was a match-winner supreme and his loss, at a time of re-awakening Championship aspirations at Highbury, was a blow of savage proportions.

BORN: Fulham, 7.1.50. GAMES: 107 (1). GOALS: 57.
HONOURS: 14 England caps (72-75).

OTHER CLUBS: Fulham 68/9 (13, 5); Luton Town 69/70-70/1 (88, 49);
Newcastle United 71/2-75/6 (187, 95). MANAGER: Fulham 80-84.
Huddersfield Town 87-88.

1976/77 – 1978/79

ALAN HUDSON

When future generations scan the football history books, the name of Alan Hudson will *not* crop up as one of the great players – and the infuriating Londoner should kick himself for the omission. Nature endowed him bounteously with talent and Arsenal offered him the perfect stage on which to parade it, yet he allowed the chance of soccer immortality to pass him by.

It was not as though the former Chelsea prodigy even came close to fulfilling his potential after the Gunners paid Stoke City £200,000 for his silky midfield services in December 1976. At the time, he was only 25, and despite a record in which immaturity was prominent, his pedigree was mouth-watering. At Stamford Bridge, shrewd observers had described Alan as one of the most brilliant teenagers the game had seen, and he emerged as the premier play-maker in an exciting side before a rebellious attitude curbed his progress; at the Victoria Ground, he appeared to grow up, played an inspirational part in the Potters' title challenge, and was picked for England.

But after a bright enough start at Highbury, during which he was paired with Liam Brady in the club's most skilful creative combination since the war, a familiar story began to unfold. The exquisite right-foot distribution, which could so deftly change the point of attack, was in evidence at times; so were his close control in confined spaces and his clever support play.

But these attributes tended to become prominent at non-vital moments, and when Arsenal were in a tight spot Alan's influence was apt to decline significantly.

There were also disciplinary difficulties – manager Terry Neill sent him home from the 1977 summer tour – and it was hardly a shock when, five months after a wan performance in the 1978 FA Cup Final, he joined Seattle Sounders for £95,000. A golden gift had gone to waste.

BORN: Chelsea, 21.6.51. GAMES: 46 (1). GOALS: 0. HONOURS: 2 England caps (75).

OTHER CLUBS: Chelsea 68/9-73/4 (145, 10); Stoke City 73/4-76/7 (105, 9); Seattle Sounders, USA; Stoke City 83/4-85/6 (39, 0).

1976/77 – 1977/78

WILLIE YOUNG

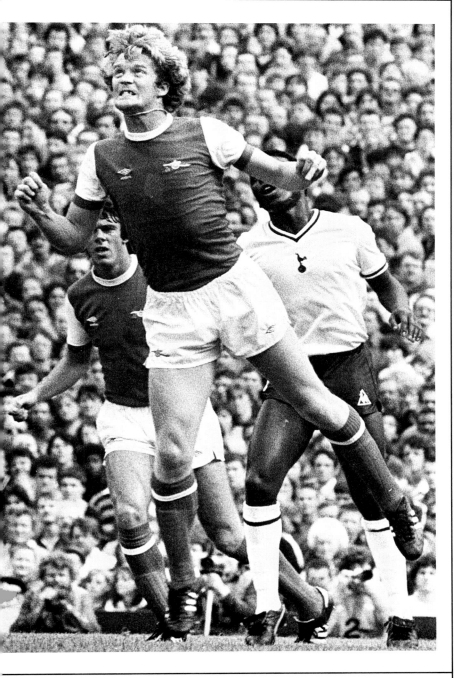

1976/77 – 1981/82

Red of hair, hearty of commitment and outspoken of character, Scottish stopper Willie Young was much loved on the Highbury terraces. His vociferous supporters gloried in his aerial might, made allowances for his indelicacy on the ball, and hailed him gleefully for his brusque dealings with authority.

In fact, they might have had the chance to adopt Willie as a folk hero some 18 months *before* his £80,000 move from Tottenham Hotspur in March 1977. The Gunners had monitored his progress with Aberdeen, but decided against making a bid after John Radford gave him a chasing in a friendly at Pittodrie. As it was, Arsenal boss Terry Neill, who as Spurs' manager had introduced the promising under-23 international to English football in 1975, was happy to sign him for a second time.

The newcomer slotted into central defence alongside David O'Leary, a player whose cultured talents were in sharp contrast to his own yeoman qualities, yet with whom he achieved an effective blend. Though slow on the turn, Willie could attack the ball with gusto, safe in the knowledge that the Irishman was admirably equipped to retrieve most situations. The Young passing repertoire was not extensive, the long punt forward being his preferred tactic, but he came into his own in physical duels with the likes of Manchester United's fearsome Joe Jordan, whom he did much to subdue in the 1979 FA Cup Final. Yet there were instances when the 6ft 3in centre-half, always a danger-man in opposing penalty areas at set pieces, astonished even his most rabid fans with an uncharacteristically subtle touch, such as the precise chip which won the UEFA Cup home encounter with Hadjuk Split in November 1978.

After a disagreement with Terry Neill, Willie joined Nottingham Forest in December 1981 for £170,000. An inimitable personality had departed, and the Highbury scene was less colourful for his absence.

BORN: Edinburgh, 25.11.51. GAMES: 236. GOALS: 19. HONOURS: FA Cup 78/9.

OTHER CLUBS: Aberdeen 70/1-75/6 (132, 10); Tottenham Hotspur 75/6-76/7 (54, 3); Nottingham Forest 81/2-82/3 (59, 5); Norwich City 83/4 (6, 0); Brighton and Hove Albion *on loan* 83/4 (4, 0); Darlington (non-contract) 84/5 (4, 0).

FRANK STAPLETON

The full measure of Frank Stapleton's contribution to the Arsenal cause cannot be gauged merely by his achievements in a Gunners shirt, magnificent though they were. More telling, still, was the frantic quest for an acceptable replacement when the dark-haired Dubliner joined Manchester United, a mission that was not accomplished with complete satisfaction until the signing of Alan Smith . . . six years later.

Many maintained that when Frank left Highbury for Old Trafford in August 1981, he was the equal, at least, of any centre-forward in Europe. Others, while accepting that he was on the verge of the top international bracket, felt that such a rating was a little extravagant. Either way, there was no denying that the Republic of Ireland star had undergone a remarkable transformation from the raw, rather ponderous teenager who had crossed the Irish Sea in the early seventies.

As his rapid progress was to prove, Frank had abundant natural talent, but it was sheer hard graft which brought it to the fore. A serious young man of level temperament, he laboured ceaselessly to improve his ball control and all-round technique, and when he was drafted in for a lengthy spell in place of the injured John Radford in 1975/76, his form offered grounds for increasing optimism.

But it was when Frank linked up with Malcolm Macdonald over the next two campaigns that he flowered as a performer of genuine stature. His touch, once average, had been honed to an impressive degree, enabling him to find colleagues with a subtle array of first-time flicks, or retain possession until reinforcements arrived. Though not blessed with outstanding pace, he was a selfless runner, often drifting to the wings and then crossing the ball accurately. He carried a splendid shot in either foot and, while not the most deadly of finishers – his scoring record was steady rather than prolific – Frank compensated royally by laying on untold chances for Malcolm and company. However, the most arresting asset in the Stapleton armoury was his aerial ability, which was matched by few, if any, of his contemporary peers. Plenty of them could offer equal power, but the Irishman's secret lay in immaculate timing, an instinctive gift which turned many a match the Gunners' way.

Frank, who was partnered by Alan Sunderland in his later days at Highbury, appeared in all four of the North Londoners' major finals between 1978 and 1980, playing a crucial role in their solitary triumph in the 1979 FA Cup. He netted five times on the way to Wembley, including a low drive from outside the penalty box to open the semi-final scoring against Wolves, and then helped to frustrate his future employers, Manchester United, with a precise header on the big day.

Come the summer of 1981, Frank's contract had expired, and when the Londoners could not meet his wage demands, he headed north amid widespread vilification from Arsenal fans. The bitterness was fanned by the clubs' failure to agree a fee for the 25-year-old striker, and reached a peak when a transfer tribunal ruled that the Red Devils could have their man for just £900,000, less than half the asking price.

It was an unsatisfactory exit for a dedicated athlete – Frank never smoked and rarely touched alcohol – who had given half a decade of admirable service, and was now seeking, like any family man, the maximum financial return for his skills. Without quite attaining the giddy heights predicted for him, he went on to win more honours with United, captain his country through the 1988 European Championships, and sample the European scene, before returning to bolster a succession of English clubs in the evening of his career. A promising first attempt at management ended somewhat harshly when he was sacked by Bradford City, then one of the game's most consummate professionals accepted a coaching post in the United States.

BORN: Dublin, 10.7.56. GAMES: 296 (3). GOALS: 108.
HONOURS: FA Cup 78/9.
70 Republic of Ireland caps (76-90).

OTHER CLUBS: Manchester United 81/2-86/7 (223, 60); Ajax, Holland, 87/8 (4,0); Derby County 87/8 (10, 1); Le Havre, France 88/9; Blackburn Rovers 89/90-90/1 (81, 13); Aldershot 91/2 (1, 0); Huddersfield Town 91/2 (5, 0); Bradford City 91/2-93/4 (68, 2); Brighton 94/5 (2, 0). MANAGER: Bradford City 91-94.

1974/75 – 1980/81

STEVE GATTING

Enthusiasm and competitive spirit are the attributes which spring most readily to mind at the mention of Steve Gatting. That is not to belittle the skill of the determined Londoner, who featured periodically in Arsenal's midfield as the seventies drew to a close; in fact, his left-sided distribution was more than adequate. But few would dispute that it was the first-mentioned traits - so well known in his older brother Mike, the former England cricket captain - which did most to establish him as a professional footballer.

Steve's initial senior run came in 1978/79 at a time when manager Terry Neill was experimenting with a variety of young hopefuls. While lacking polish, he gave a good account of himself and surrendered his place only with the arrival of the England player, Brian Talbot.

Undismayed by the setback, Steve soldiered on, drifting to the edge of the squad during the following campaign but bouncing back with 23 League starts in 1980/81. He was destined to lose out to another expensive international, however - this time it was Welshman Peter Nicholas - and that March joined Brighton for £200,000. At the Goldstone Ground, he became a reliable central defender, giving the Seagulls his best days before ending his League career with Charlton Athletic.

BORN: Willesden, London, 29.5.59. GAMES: 65 (11). GOALS: 6.

OTHER CLUBS: Brighton and Hove Albion 81/2-90/1 (316, 19); Charlton Athletic 91/2-92/3 (64, 3).

1978/79 − 1980/81

STEVE WALFORD

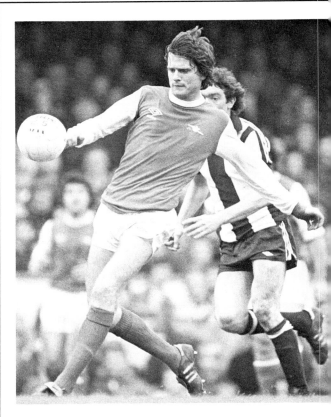

When willowy Steve Walford crossed North London from Whit Hart Lane to Highbury in August 1977, there were hopes that the £25,000 local boy could be groomed as a long-term succes sor to central defender Peter Simpson. A former England youth international, Steve was reminiscent of the Arsenal stalwart in hi skill on the ball, which allowed him to extract himself smoothl from tight corners, and his perceptive reading of the game. He was also quick for a six-footer and versatile enough to turn ou at full-back or in midfield. Unfortunately, he lacked the physica presence to dominate bustling opponents, creating a rather lightweight impression that was not reassuring.

Steve made his League debut in the number-12 shirt, replacing John Matthews at Norwich in September 1977, and then enjoyed a relatively encouraging 1978/79. That term he made 3 First Division appearances and pocketed an FA Cup winners' medal for coming on as a Wembley substitute when David Pric was withdrawn from the fray against Manchester United.

Thereafter, Steve was used principally as cover for centre-backs David O'Leary and Willie Young, and in March 1981 he joined Norwich City for £175,000, later serving West Ham with some success.

BORN: Highgate, London, 5.1.58. GAMES: 77 (20). GOALS: 4 HONOURS: FA Cup 78/9.

OTHER CLUBS: Tottenham Hotspur 75/6 (2, 0); Norwich City 80/1-82/3 (93, 2); West Ham United 83/4-86/7 (115, 2); Huddersfield Town on loan 87/8 (12, 0); Gillingham on loan 87/8 (4, 0); West Bromwich Albion on loan 87/8 (4, 0).

1977/78 − 1980/81

PAUL VAESSEN

Paul Vaessen experienced both extremes of the emotional pectrum during his cruelly brief football career. The promising striker revelled in the ecstasy of scoring the goal that took the Gunners to a European final, then suffered the devastation of being forced to quit the game at the age of 21.

His golden moment came two minutes from the end of Arsenal's 1980 European Cup Winners' Cup semi-final against uventus in Turin. The scores were level but the hosts seemed set to go through on the away goals rule when Paul, who was on the field as a substitute for midfielder David Price, netted with a simple header from a Graham Rix cross. Thus the Italian side asted defeat in a European tie on their own soil for the first time n a decade, and the 18-year-old who sent them reeling must have dreamed of many more glorious days to come.

Alas, it was all an illusion. Not long after, Paul received a severe nee injury, precipitating a heart-rending two-year battle for fitness which ended in failure during 1982/83. The son of Leon Vaessen, a former Millwall and Gillingham wing-half, was left to ponder on what he might have achieved if the fates had been kinder.

BORN: Gillingham, Kent, 16.10.61. GAMES: 27 (14). GOALS: 9.

1978/79 – 1981/82

BRIAN McDERMOTT

Forward Brian McDermott failed to capitalise on repeated opportunities to claim a regular place in the Gunners' attack. Tricky but lacking composure, he gave the same impression of youthful inexperience in his sixth season on the fringe of the League side as he did during his first, and rarely seemed likely to progress beyond the status of a 'bits and pieces' player at Highbury.

A former England youth international who could fulfil both front-line and midfield duties, he made his senior debut as a substitute for Mark Heeley, another youngster destined not to make the grade, at home to Bristol City in March 1979. But Brian was not given a protracted chance at the top level until 1980/81, when he made 16 starts and showed enough promise to earn first shot at partnering Alan Sunderland – in the slot made vacant by the departure of Frank Stapleton – at the start of the following campaign.

The chance passed him by, however, and after two more terms of occasional call-ups, Brian joined Oxford for £40,000 on the last day of 1984. After helping United reach the top flight, he switched to the lower divisions before serving non-League Yeovil Town with distinction.

BORN: Slough, Berkshire, 8.4.61. GAMES: 44 (28). GOALS: 13.

OTHER CLUBS: Fulham *on loan* 82/3 (3, 0); Oxford United 84/5-86/7 (24, 2); Huddersfield Town *on loan* 86/7 (4, 1); Cardiff City 87/8-88/9 (51, 8); Exeter City 88/9-90/1 (68, 4).

1978/79 – 1983/84

LIAM BRADY

Men who have made their livings from football are not easy to impress, and their praise for most players from any era is invariably studded with reservations. But talk to anyone in the game about Liam Brady and, at least in this writer's experience, the superlatives start to flow. Without attempting to disguise their sense of wonder, hard–bitten professionals speak of the cleverest play–maker of a generation, indeed the most gifted Gunner since the war. Draw the threads of their admiration together and they constitute a warm and fitting tribute to an uplifting talent whose sublime skill and vision crossed that subtle boundary between sport and art.

Liam's rare abilities were evident from his earliest days at Highbury. Former youth team opponents, who in the early seventies were dumbfounded by the unerring accuracy of his left foot and his capacity to glide past defenders, declare that such was his impact as a 16-year-old that nothing he achieved thereafter could surprise them. Clearly, such prodigious potential was not going to linger in Arsenal's junior sides, and the slightly-built Dubliner was given his League baptism, at the age of 17, in October 1973. By the following season he was a first-team regular, learning voraciously from his midfield partnership with Alan Ball and bringing incongruously joyful touches to a side struggling perilously close to the foot of the First Division.

Maturing rapidly as a player and assuming extra responsibility after Alan departed in 1976, 'Chippy' began to contribute performances that many described as world class. Moving smoothly and easily, always well balanced and in total command of the ball, he was an inscrutable adversary. When he seemed certain to hit a cross, he would probably shoot; if a square pass appeared inevitable, he would like as not shrug his shoulders and slip past several defenders into a goal-scoring position; he might be hemmed in on all sides, on the verge of losing possession, then suddenly strike a 40-yard pass through the narrowest of openings. Part of the Brady secret was minimal backlift, which disguised his intention until the last moment, but more relevant was a less tangible factor, something akin to genius.

Liam was the inspiration of many a triumph, but none illustrated his value more vividly than the 1979 FA Cup Final defeat of Manchester United, in which he was the architect of all three Gunners goals. Sadly for Arsenal, however, with the fans still marvelling at the unfettered brilliance of his Wembley display, the newly-crowned players' player of the year stilled the celebrations by announcing that after one more season at Highbury he would join Juventus. The vast financial rewards to be found on the continent were obviously important but Liam, a modest and likeable fellow, seemed genuinely keen for the stimulus of testing his talents against the world's best. Some questioned whether he could withstand the physical rigours of the Italian League, but he was to cope superbly, serving four major clubs before returning to England to finish his career with West Ham United.

The Republic of Ireland star's splendid form in his farewell North London campaign rubbed salt in the wounds of his loyal supporters, who retained two heartfelt gripes about his departure. The first was the fee of £600,000, the maximum allowed under EEC regulations but derisory for the likes of Liam. The second was manager Terry Neill's failure to find an adequate successor to the man who had given them six seasons of breathtaking entertainment. But, in all fairness to the harassed Highbury boss, how do you replace the best there is?

BORN: Dublin, 13.2.56. GAMES: 294 (12). GOALS: 59.
HONOURS: FA Cup 78/9. 72 Republic of Ireland caps (74–90).

OTHER CLUBS: Juventus, Sampdoria, Inter Milan and Ascoli, all of Italy;
West Ham United 86/7-89/90 (89, 9).

MANAGER: Celtic 91-93; Brighton and Hove Albion 93-95.

1973/74 — 1979/80

PAT JENNINGS

Every manager makes mistakes, but once in a while comes a blunder of such magnitude that it is emblazoned forever on the collective consciousness of his club and returns to haunt him with merciless cruelty. Such was Tottenham boss Keith Burkinshaw's decision to sell Pat Jennings in August 1977 when, as it transpired, the 32-year-old Ulsterman had more than a third of his playing days in front of him. Had the goalkeeper whom many reputable pundits rated above Peter Shilton and Ray Clemence been allowed to join any other club but local rivals Arsenal, and had the fee been commensurate with his ability, then Spurs fans – already outraged by relegation to the Second Division – might have been more inclined to bite the bullet. But Pat had been dispatched for a mere £45,000 and the White Hart Lane terraces seethed with unrest.

Later, Keith was to own up to his error and go on to become one of Tottenham's most successful managers; meanwhile the doubts of those Arsenal supporters who worried that Terry Neill might have acquired a talent in decline were laid to rest, both swiftly and emphatically. Pat, who had recovered from a serious ankle injury earlier that year, was as awesomely effective at Highbury as he had been on the other side of North London. Calm, almost stately, in bearing, he rarely shouted for the ball, yet infused his fellow defenders with the supreme confidence that came from playing in front of a proven master. Crowds were enraptured as hands like prehensile shovels plucked swirling crosses from the sky, or seemingly-impossible saves offered comprehensive proof that the passing years had served only to hone those renowned reflexes.

Yet Pat was essentially an economical performer who never made his job look more difficult than necessary, thanks mainly to an incomparable positional sense. His art was seen at its most subtle in one-on-one situations, in which he endeavoured to stand up as long as possible, knowing that to commit himself early against a high-class adversary was to be lost. Countless opponents found themselves beguiled into shooting from unpromising angles or delaying their strikes until it was too late, enabling the courageous Irishman – for whom risking his neck had been a pastime ever since his teenage exploits in the rough-and-tumble of Gaelic football – to dive and smother the threat.

As the seasons went by, and despite being ousted by George Wood for much of 1982, he made his meagre fee look an ever-more-sickening joke at the expense of his former club. While Spurs tried a succession of replacements – in fact, the Jennings jersey was not to be filled satisfactorily until the arrival at White Hart Lane of Ray Clemence, four years later – Pat helped Arsenal reach four finals, and made a further 42 appearances for Northern Ireland. That he picked up only one winner's medal, against Manchester United in the 1979 FA Cup, was through no fault of his own, and it is a tribute both to his fitness and undying hunger for success that even after giving up top-line club soccer in June 1985, he was not finished on the international scene. Having returned to Tottenham at the age of 40 as first-team cover, he went on to serve Northern Ireland nobly during the 1986 World Cup Finals, and set a record of 119 caps, later to be overhauled by Peter Shilton. It was a stirring finale to the career of a quiet man whose demeanour offered no hint of swagger despite a fabulous record encompassing four major medals, player of the year awards and an MBE as a Spur; further glories as a Gunner; and an OBE in 1987, after his retirement. Pat Jennings ranks among the greatest footballers of any era, and was one of sport's finest ambassadors.

BORN: Newry, Northern Ireland, 12.6.45. GAMES: 326. GOALS: 0.
HONOURS: FA Cup 78/9. 119 Northern Ireland caps (64–86).

OTHER CLUBS: Watford 62/3-63/4 (48, 0);
Tottenham Hotspur 64/5-76/7 (472, 0).

1977/78 – 1984/85

JOHN DEVINE

GEORGE WOOD

When the increasingly proficient displays of John Devine persuaded Arsenal manager Terry Neill that it was safe to part with the faithful Pat Rice in November 1980, there seemed little doubt that the 22-year-old Dubliner would occupy the Gunners' right-back slot for the foreseeable future. A slender lad who had arrived at Highbury with David O'Leary but turned professional a year later than the central defender, he had built up his strength through weight training and worked assiduously to improve his control and distribution. The most eye-catching part of his game, however, was his high-speed overlapping, which grew ever more potent as the quality of his crosses improved.

Somehow, though, having established himself in the senior side, John failed to progress. He was not the most lethal of tacklers, perhaps lacking ruthlessness, and the same happy-go-lucky character that was so charming off the pitch might not have been ideal for the rigorous business of top-level football. John was never happier than when playing his guitar, which travelled everywhere with him, and some thought he should have been a pop star. The Eire international's footballing fortunes declined steadily until he joined Norwich on a free transfer in 1983, later moving to Stoke, where a broken leg ended his League career.

BORN: Dublin, 11.11.58. GAMES: 108 (3). GOALS: 0.
HONOURS: 12 Republic of Ireland caps (79-84).
OTHER CLUBS: Norwich City 83/4-84/5 (53, 3); Stoke City 85/6 (15, 1).

There could be no more eloquent testimony to the goalkeeping prowess of George Wood than his achievement in depriving Pat Jennings of his Arsenal place for the better part of a year. Yet the big, blond Scot, a £150,000 capture from Everton in August 1980, rarely enjoyed the unanimous support of his home crowd. At the first suggestion of a fumble - and George, like all 'keepers, dropped the occasional clanger - he would be subjected to scathing criticism from a faction of Gunners' fans who persisted in comparing him unfavourably to the brilliant Irishman, an attitude scarcely calculated to bolster his confidence. In fact, while the former stone-mason was more impressive as a shot-stopper than a claimer of crosses, it was not often that the ball eluded his grasp and in 1982, his year of eminence, he gave enough outstanding performances to join his country's party for the World Cup Finals.

George began his fine run in the January, after Pat was injured and he remained first choice until December, when he was suspended after being sent off for a so-called professional foul on Aston Villa's Peter Withe. In the following May, he accepted a free transfer to Crystal Palace, and he was still gracing the lower divisions in the early nineties.

BORN: Douglas, Lanarkshire, 26.9.52. GAMES: 70. GOALS: 0.
HONOURS: 4 Scotland caps (79-82).
OTHER CLUBS: East Stirlingshire 70/1-71/2 (44, 1); Blackpool 71/2-76/7 (117, 0); Everton 77/8-79/80 (103, 0); Crystal Palace 83/4-87/8 (192, 0); Cardiff City 87/8-89/90 (67, 0); Blackpool on loan 89/90 (15, 0); Hereford United 90/1 (41, 0).

1977/78 – 1982/83

1980/81 – 1982/83

JOHN HOLLINS

1979/80 – 1982/83

Football would be a healthier, happier game for the presence of more men like John Hollins. When the stocky, bright-eyed midfielder joined Arsenal on the day before his 33rd birthday in July 1979, there were those who questioned the Gunners' wisdom in parting with £75,000 for a man presumably at the tail-end of his career. But they had reckoned without the astonishing vitality of a model professional who, after a dozen distinguished campaigns with Chelsea and four more at Loftus Road, still had five seasons of high-class competition ahead of him.

In his first year at Highbury, John scrapped for a place with David Price, who kept him out of the FA Cup Final against West Ham United. However, the older man earned a regular berth in 1980/81, thanks to a persuasive combination of incisive passing, waspish tackling and a work-rate that would have done credit to a teenager.

Come the following term and John was better than ever. After switching to right-back during an injury crisis in the January, he remained in defence to such effect that he was voted player of the year by Arsenal supporters. In 1982/83, now aged 36 but with eagerness undiminished, he took on the captaincy and helped the North Londoners reach the semi-final stage of both major domestic cups. As well as setting an impeccable example on the field, John produced an uplifting effect on the club as a whole. He never had a bad word for anyone, was ready with a quip for most occasions, and was invariably prepared to pass on his experience to any young players with sense enough to listen.

In the summer of 1983, he returned to Stamford Bridge as player-coach, and wore his Blues' shirt with distinction as John Neal's men took the Second Division title. Subsequent trauma as Chelsea manager was scant reward for the honesty, enthusiasm and intelligence that John Hollins had lavished on the game for so long.

BORN: Guildford, Surrey, 16.7.46.
GAMES: 164 (8). GOALS: 13.
HONOURS: 1 England cap (67).

OTHER CLUBS: Chelsea 63/4–74/5 (436, 47); Queen's Park Rangers 75/6–78/9 (151, 5); Chelsea 83/4 (29, 1). MANAGER: Chelsea 85–88.

PETER NICHOLAS

Few newcomers to Highbury have equalled the instant impact of Peter Nicholas. When Terry Neill paid Crystal Palace £400,000 for the midfield ball-winner in March 1981, the Gunners were wallowing ineffectively in mid-table and had won just three of their previous 14 League outings. Enter the blond, curly-haired Welshman and the side dropped only two points in the last nine games of the season, moving up to third spot and claiming a place in Europe.

Not surprisingly, the fans approved of Peter. They identified with his constant effort, relishing the fearsome tackling and limpet-like tenacity that nullified the creative skills of many an opposing star. His passing, while hardly from the top drawer, also passed muster, though even his most loyal supporters would acknowledge that his lack of pace and poor goal tally constituted weaknesses in the Nicholas game.

After making such a positive early impression, Peter was tipped for a long-term Highbury future, but following two steady campaigns, he found himself on the sidelines as the manager experimented with other players. Accordingly, the man who was to assemble a record 73 Welsh international caps - since out-stripped by Neville Southall - returned to Palace for £150,000 in October 1983.

BORN: Newport, Monmouthshire, 10.11.59. GAMES: 77 (3). GOALS: 3. HONOURS: 73 Wales caps (79-91).

OTHER CLUBS: Crystal Palace 77/8-80/1 (127, 7) and 83/4-84/5 (47, 7); Luton Town 84/5-86/7 (102, 1); Aberdeen 87/8 (39, 3); Chelsea 88/9-90/1 (80, 2); Watford 90/1-91/2 (40, 1).

1980/81 – 1982/83

VLADIMIR PETROVIC

The day Vladimir Petrovic walked out of Highbury for the last time, the pragmatists who had predicted his early demise proclaimed with smug satisfaction that they had told everyone so. The soccer purists, however, were more inclined to weep for the passing of one of the most talented footballers to don a Gunners shirt in the modern era.

Terry Neill paid £45,000 for Red Star Belgrade's midfield general in December 1982, and pitched him straight into action at home to Swansea. His nigh-perfect control, silky distribution and astute brain were evident at once, and allowances were duly made for his early failure to keep up with the furious First Division pace. There followed some matches in which he captivated crowds with breathtaking skill but, all too often, Vladimir would drift through games ineffectually, wandering around with the detached air of a man out for a quiet afternoon's aircraft-spotting.

It became clear that to deny him space was to stifle his effectiveness, which was further reduced by certain opponents who cashed in on his apparent aversion to stern challenges. Thus, as 1982/83 closed and just as the Yugoslav was beginning to pick up English, the Arsenal boss made up his mind that the Petrovic gamble had not come off. The decision was, perhaps, inevitable, but it's a sad reflection on the British game when a place can't be found for the likes of Vladimir Petrovic.

BORN: Yugoslavia, 1.7.55. GAMES: 19 (3). GOALS: 3. HONOURS: Yugoslavia caps.

OTHER CLUBS: Red Star Belgrade, Yugoslavia; Antwerp, Belgium.

1982/83

COLIN HILL

JOHN HAWLEY

RAPHAEL MEADE

When Arsenal freed Colin Hill to join Maritimo of Portugal in May 1986, it looked like the end of top-flight soccer or an essentially workaday defender. That he managed to regain his former status with Sheffield United and Leicester City, and that he won international caps for Northern Ireland - thanks to a parental qualification - speaks volumes for his determination.

Colin, who made his League debut for the Gunners at Norwich in April 1983, started the next season as David O'Leary's partner in the middle of the back four. He was competent but rarely dominant, and it was no surprise when manager Terry Neill sought an alternative in Tommy Caton. However, as befitted a former sprint champion, the resilient 20-year-old could offer considerable pace, and this served him well in the right-back role to which he was shifted for the remainder of the campaign.

The arrival of Viv Anderson during the following summer spelt the end of Colin's first-team tenure, and paved the way for his exit. His subsequent comeback to the big time offered much-needed inspiration to discarded youngsters everywhere.

BORN: Uxbridge, Middlesex, 12.11.63.
GAMES: 51. GOALS: 1. HONOURS: 21 Northern Ireland caps (90-).

OTHER CLUBS: Maritimo, Portugal; Colchester United 87/8-88/9 (69, 0); Sheffield United 89/90-91/2 (82, 1); Leicester City 91/2- (144, 0).

Hustling centre-forward John Hawley was something of a mystery man to most Gunners fans when he headed south from Roker Park in September 1981, but Arsenal boss Terry Neill knew exactly what he was getting for his £50,000. The two had worked together at Hull, where the Irishman had been manager, and Terry, anxious to replace the recently departed Frank Stapleton, reckoned the blond six-footer might surprise a few people with his goal-scoring prowess. At both Leeds and Sunderland, John had averaged close to a goal every two outings, so there seemed no good reason why he should not repeat the feat at Highbury.

In the event, while gaining a certain cachet with the North Bank for his fearless, helter-skelter style and constant effort, he never fitted into the Arsenal pattern. He contributed just three goals - all crisply taken, it should be said - and when Tony Woodcock was signed in the summer of 1982, John's North London future became bleak. Sure enough, a year later he was given a free transfer and left to play in Hong Kong.

BORN: Patrington, Yorkshire, 8.5.54.
GAMES: 15 (6). GOALS: 3.

OTHER CLUBS: Hull City 72/3-77/8 (114, 22); Leeds United 78/9-79/80 (33, 16); Sunderland 79/80-80/1 (25, 11); Orient on loan 82/3 (4, 1); Hull City on loan 82/3 (3, 1); Hong Kong; Bradford City 83/4-84/5 (67, 28); Scunthorpe United 85/6 (21, 7).

No striker could have wished for a more propitious start to his senior career than that enjoyed by Raphael Meade. The fleet-footed 18-year-old scored with the first kick of his debut, a September 1981 UEFA Cup encounter with Panathanaikos in Athens, after coming on as a substitute.

The eager Londoner, whose dashing style reminded many of a young Malcolm Macdonald, followed up by scoring the winner in his first League game, against Manchester City at Highbury, and it seemed only a matter of time before he claimed a regular place. However, Raphael's form was erratic, and as costly new marksmen were signed, he remained no more than a stand-in for the stars. Even a purple patch in December 1983, when he grabbed a hat-trick against Watford and netted twice against Spurs in the next game, could not improve his long-term status.

Later Raphael, whose ball skills never matched his finishing power, experienced problems off the pitch and in 1985 made a fresh start with Sporting Lisbon. A subsequent return to British football met with little success.

BORN: Islington, London, 22.11.62.
GAMES: 32 (19). GOALS: 16.

OTHER CLUBS: Sporting Lisbon, Portugal; Dundee United 88/9 (11, 4); Luton Town 88/9 (4, 0); Ipswich Town 89/90 (1, 0); Odense, Denmark; Plymouth Argyle 90/1 (5, 0); Brighton 91/2 (40, 9); Hong Kong; Brighton 94/5 (3, 0).

982/83 – 1984/85

1981/82 – 1982/83

1981/82 – 1984/85

ALAN SUNDERLAND

As long as there's an Arsenal, the name of Alan Sunderland will be honoured; his late, late winner against Manchester United in the 1979 FA Cup Final is enshrined for all time in the memory of any Gunners fan old enough to recall the events of that most dramatic of Wembley afternoons. Such immortality is an exalted compliment, granted to few, yet it would be unjust if the sharp-witted Yorkshireman's considerable all-round contribution to the Highbury cause were to be overshadowed totally by one fleeting moment of glory.

In fact, Alan became a crucial component of Terry Neill's team from the moment he was signed from Wolves for £240,000 in November 1977. At Molineux he had been employed mainly in midfield, and his early days in North London were spent in a deep, right-flank position where his speed, strength and adhesive ball skills made him invaluable both as forager and raider. But Alan found his most effective niche when he was switched to replace the injured Malcolm Macdonald alongside Frank Stapleton in attack, his bravery and aerial ability contributing richly to a formidable partnership.

The frizzy-haired front-runner was never a prolific scorer, yet he had a penchant for netting in the FA Cup. When he slid home Graham Rix's 89th-minute cross to settle that mighty clash with United, it was his sixth success of the 1978/79 competition, and his 13-second strike during a four-match marathon with Liverpool a year later took his tally to 15 goals in three FA campaigns. Sadly for Alan and Arsenal, he had but one winner's medal to show for his trio of Wembley finals, and was also a 1980 Cup Winners' Cup Final loser. No one, though, could question the wisdom of Terry Neill's investment. When the advent of Messrs Woodcock and Nicholas facilitated his free transfer to Ipswich in 1984, Alan headed for Suffolk with his place in Highbury folklore secure.

BORN: Mexborough, Yorkshire, 1.7.53.
GAMES: 277 (3). GOALS: 91.
HONOURS: FA Cup 78/9. 1 England cap (80).

OTHER CLUBS: Wolverhampton Wanderers 71/2-77/8 (158, 29); Ipswich Town 83/4-85/6 (58, 11); Derry City, Northern Ireland.

1977/78 – 1983/84

TONY WOODCOCK

1982/83 – 1985/86

In four seasons with Arsenal, Tony Woodcock established himself as the Gunners' leading goal-scorer of the eighties by a comfortable margin and almost doubled his total of England caps. Surely, not even the most demanding North Banker could complain that the curly-haired striker had not given magnificent value for money following his £500,000 move from FC Cologne in the summer of 1982? And yet, there persisted in the hearts and minds of many fans the niggling feeling that, somehow, there should have been more. After all, at Nottingham Forest Tony had been one of the most thrilling players in the land, and his German sojourn had done nothing to dent his image. For the North Londoners, he contributed some brilliant performances, and many more that were very fine, without *quite* attaining the consistency that would have placed him in the top bracket.

But whatever the reservations, there was no denying that when Tony was on song, he was one of the most lethal and entertaining marksmen in the First Division. His scorching pace, slick control and knack of worming past opponents in confined spaces fashioned count-less scoring opportunities, and his sharp reflexes in front of goal ensured that a fair proportion of them were accepted. Certainly, few went beg-ging on the Gunners' visit to Villa Park in October 1983, when Tony netted five times in a predatory display of the highest order.

He was no mere goal-hanger, however, often roaming to the left flank, where he enjoyed a fluent understanding with Kenny Sansom and Graham Rix, although some critics reckoned that he tended to take on one man too many before parting with the ball, and that he didn't do his share of tackling back. Such voices became more insistent as the Woodcock strike-rate dipped and after a 1985/86 campaign that was marred by injury, Tony rejoined Cologne for £140,000. A verdict on his Highbury stay? Satisfactory, but might have done better.

BORN: Nottingham, 6.12.55. GAMES: 164 (5). GOALS: 68. HONOURS: 42 England caps (78-86).

OTHER CLUBS: Nottingham Forest 73/4–79/80 (129, 36); Lincoln City on loan 75/6 (4, 1); Doncaster Rovers on loan 76/7 (6, 2); FC Cologne, West Germany, 79/80–81/2 and 86/7–87/8; Fortuna Dusseldorf, West Germany, 88/9.

CHRIS WHYTE

Chris Whyte, a tall, lean central defender with the loose, loping style of a Harlem Globetrotter, once looked every inch an England star on the rise. He made his Arsenal debut as a 20-year-old in October 1981, and took the eye with an impressive combination of composure, skill and strength. During the next 14 months he missed only one League game and won four under-21 caps, and his partnership with David O'Leary promised to form the heart of the Gunners' rearguard for the foreseeable future. But 'Huggy' - so dubbed after a character in the TV show, Starsky and Hutch - fell prey to inconsistency instead of consolidating on his encouraging start, and slipped agonisingly out of the reckoning.

Perversely, his all-round ability might have contributed to his untimely exit from Highbury on a free transfer in 1986. So comfortable was Chris on the ball that sometimes he tried to dribble out of dangerous situations with disastrous consequences. He loved to get forward, too - some saw him as a frustrated striker - and suffered from a tendency to be drawn out of position. After a spell in America, he revived his League career at West Bromwich, revealing new authority and maturity which precipitated a successful move to Leeds United, with whom he pocketed a title medal in 1992.

BORN: Islington, London, 2.9.61. GAMES: 108 (5). GOALS: 8.

OTHER CLUBS: Crystal Palace on loan 84/5 (13, 0); Los Angeles, USA (Indoor League); West Bromwich Albion 88/9-89/90 (84, 7). Leeds United 90/1-92/3 (113, 5); Birmingham City 93/4-95/6 (68, 1); Coventry City on loan 95/6 (1, 0); Charlton Athletic 95/6 (11, 0); Leyton Orient 96/7 (1, 0); Oxford United 96/7- (8, 0).

1981/82 – 1985/86

TOMMY CATON

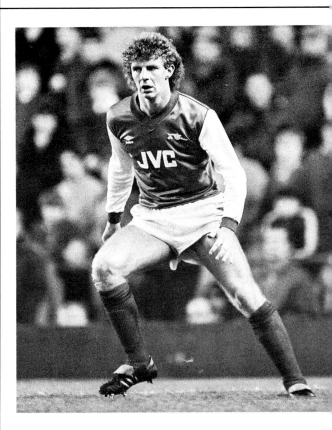

Tommy Caton arrived at Highbury with a glowing reputation; sadly, he didn't live up to it. The blond, curly-haired centre-half cost £500,000 from Manchester City in December 1983 after both Chris Whyte and Colin Hill had failed to emerge as a suitable long-term successor to Willie Young. The 21-year-old Merseysider was seen as an international stalwart of the future - indeed, he captained the England under-21 side in 1984 - but only rarely did he seem comfortable in the Gunners' rearguard.

Tall and strong, Tommy was adequate in the air and passed the ball neatly with his left foot, but he was short of pace, sometimes struggling to recover his position after forays upfield. His deficiencies were highlighted in a televised defeat at Old Trafford in November 1984, and subsequent barracking by a section of the Highbury crowd did little to boost his self-confidence.

After a creaky display at Southampton in December 1985, he was replaced by Martin Keown, and when Tony Adams entered the reckoning during the following season it was clear that Tommy had no future with Arsenal. As a result, he joined Oxford for £180,000 in 1987, helping them rise to the top flight, but later suffered relegation with Charlton Athletic. He died, tragically young, in 1993.

BORN: Liverpool, 16.10.62. GAMES: 95. GOALS: 3.

OTHER CLUBS: Manchester City 79/80-83/4 (165, 8); Oxford United 86/7-87/8 (53, 3); Charlton Athletic 88/9-90/1 (57, 5) DIED: Bampton, Oxfordshire, 30.4.93.

1983/84 – 1985/86

IAN ALLINSON

LEE CHAPMAN

Ian Allinson had no pretentions to grandeur – any such affectation would have been surprising, indeed, in a man signed on a free transfer from Colchester United – but the lively striker gave the Gunners nearly four years of redoubtable service, outshining more illustrious team-mates on many occasions. His acquisition by Terry Neill in October 1983 was unexpected, to say the least, but it was not long before Ian was justifying the manager's faith. A strong runner and industrious forager, he was particularly effective as a substitute, adding zest to many a lacklustre Gunners performance. He possessed more skill than he was credited with, too, controlling the ball deftly, crossing well and dispatching penalties with cool reliability.

His finest season was 1984/85, in which he enjoyed a spell of eight goals in 11 outings, while his greatest disappointment was omission from the 1987 Littlewoods Cup Final squad after scoring against Spurs in the semi-final replay. A measure of Ian's achievement is that he once kept Charlie Nicholas out of the side on merit for several games, and when he was freed to join Stoke in 1987 he could rejoice that he had exceeded the expectations of all but the most perceptive of soccer sages.

Little went right at Highbury for big, blond Lee Chapman as he became the latest in a line of strikers who strove unavailingly to fill the gap left by Frank Stapleton. A disappointing debut in August 1982 against Stoke City – from whom Arsenal manager Terry Neill had signed him for £500,000 only two weeks earlier – was followed by a spate of injuries, and just when vocal support might have lifted his performance, he was subjected to heavy criticism from impatient fans.

It should be said, however, that Lee was ill equipped to succeed Stapleton. Though he could never be faulted for lack of effort, he was an ungainly mover whose control and distribution were on the clumsy side; indeed, it was something of a mystery that so many balls were played to his feet instead of his head, with which he *was* dangerous.

There were few highlights during Lee's stay in North London – goals in either leg of the September 1982 UEFA Cup defeat by Spartak Moscow spring to mind – and it was not surprising when he was sold to Sunderland for a fifth of his purchase price in December 1983. Like his father, inside-forward Roy Chapman, Lee travelled widely during his career, eventually enjoying well-earned success with Leeds United.

BORN: Hitchin, Hertfordshire, 1.10.57. GAMES: 75 (30). GOALS: 23.

OTHER CLUBS: Colchester United 74/5-82/3 (308, 69); Stoke City 87/8 (9, 0); Luton Town 87/8-88/9 (32, 3); Colchester United 88/9-89/90 (38, 10).

BORN: Lincoln, 5.12.59. GAMES: 17 (11). GOALS: 6.

OTHER CLUBS: Stoke City 79/80-81/2 (99, 34); Plymouth Argyle on loan 78/9 (4, 0); Sunderland 83/4 (15, 3); Sheffield Wednesday 84/5-87/8 (149, 63); Niort, France 88/9; Nottingham Forest 88/9-89/90 (48, 15); Leeds United 89/90-92/3 (137, 62); Portsmouth 93/4 (5, 2); West Ham United 93/4-94/5 (40, 7); Southend United on loan 94/5 (1, 1); Ipswich Town 94/5-95/6 (21, 1); Leeds United on loan 95/6 (2, 0); Swansea City 95/6 (7, 4).

1983/84 – 1986/87

1982/83 – 1983/84

BRIAN TALBOT

The term 'midfield workhorse' might have been invented for Brian Talbot, but let no one delude themselves that the driving force of Bobby Robson's successful Ipswich Town side in the seventies was some sort of menial drudge. 'Noddy', as his team-mates knew him, was a skilled labourer who supplemented his renowned industry, strength and powers of motivation with a sound technique and intelligent approach which made him one of the Gunners' most influential players throughout his six-and-a-half seasons at Highbury.

Terry Neill signed Brian for £450,000 in January 1979, eight months after the chunky East Anglian had been the architect of his home-town team's FA Cup Final victory over the North Londoners. He slotted smoothly into the Arsenal engine room, his thrust and efficiency offering the ideal complement to the more artis-tic talents of Liam Brady and Graham Rix, and rendering irrelevant his slight deficiency in pace.

Within four months he had become the first man for a century to pick up FA Cup winners' medals with different clubs in successive campaigns. Brian took a major role in the triumph over Manchester United, arriving in the penalty box with typically perfect timing to open the scoring, and a year later was instrumental in securing yet another return to Wembley, heading the goal which decided the semi-final against Liverpool after three replays. His commitment against West Ham in the final was such that he collapsed with exhaustion after the 1-0 defeat, recovering in time to win the only England cap of his Highbury tenure, three weeks on in Australia.

Brian, for whom Watford paid £150,000 in July 1985, served as chairman of the Professional Footballers Association, and it was no surprise when one of soccer's more thoughtful characters moved into management. However, following the sad demise of Aldershot, he has not returned to the League scene.

BORN: Ipswich, 21.7.53. GAMES: 315 (11). GOALS: 49. HONOURS: FA Cup 78/9. 6 England caps (77-80).
OTHER CLUBS: Ipswich Town 73/4-78/9 (177, 25); Watford 85/6-86/7 (48, 8); Stoke City 86/7-87/8 (54, 5); West Bromwich Albion 87/8-89/90 (74, 5); Fulham 90/1 (5, 0); Aldershot 90/1-91/2 (11, 1).
MANAGER: West Bromwich Albion 88-91; Aldershot 91.

1978/79 – 1984/85

PAUL MARINER

1983/84 – 1985/86

Though hardly a candidate for the scrapheap, Paul Mariner was past his peak when Don Howe paid Ipswich Town £150,000 for the angular England centre-forward in February 1984. Arsenal were suffering from a shortage of goals and when manager Don Howe decided that a target man was needed to bring the best out of Tony Woodcock and Charlie Nicholas, he turned to a player who, for five years, had been one of the First Division's finest. Unfortunately, Paul was nearly 31 on arrival and was destined to experience only moderate success with the Gunners.

Yet his initial impact augured well. After scoring the winner at Nottingham Forest in his second game, he netted twice against his former club and finished the season with seven goals in 15 outings. The following campaign, however, proved more of a struggle, and after being supplanted by younger men for most of 1985/86, he accepted a free transfer to Portsmouth.

Arsenal fans were left to ponder on what Paul might have achieved had he moved to Highbury a few seasons earlier, say in 1981 when the sale of Frank Stapleton left a marked deficiency in the front line. Even in the twilight of his career, he was a majestic header of the ball, boasted a sure touch with either foot and packed a thumping shot. He remained strong, brave and unselfish, but his pace had declined and there was a distressing preponderance of indifferent displays.

Through it all, Paul maintained an admirable degree of professionalism, showing the versatility to stand in so effectively at centre-half when David O'Leary was injured at Luton in August 1985 that he retained the number five shirt for the next match. He was also capable of a spirited midfield contribution, as he proved against Aston Villa in a Milk Cup quarter-final replay in 1986, when he scored in a 2-1 defeat. By then, though, a disappointing Highbury sojourn was nearly at an end.

BORN: Bolton, Lancashire, 22.5.53.
GAMES: 60 (10). GOALS: 17.
HONOURS: 35 England caps (77-85).

OTHER CLUBS: Plymouth Argyle 73/4-76/7 (135, 56); Ipswich Town 76/7-83/4 (260, 96); Portsmouth 86/7-87/8 (56, 9); Naxxar Lions, Malta.

STEVE WILLIAMS

1984/85 – 1987/88

Steve Williams could control a football with utter certainty; if only he could have exercised similar mastery over his own temperament, he must have emerged as one of the foremost play-makers of his generation. Unfortunately, the impetuous, sometimes petulant Londoner spent so much time arguing with referees and niggling with opponents that his exquisite talents were seen in full flower with frustrating infrequency.

His days of grace were worth waiting for, however, and not for nothing did Highbury regulars declare that when Steve played well, then so did Arsenal. One of the most accurate distributors in Britain during the eighties, he could transform a meandering attack with one incisive touch. A speciality was floating the ball over several defenders to his target's feet, while he was also adept at sweeping passes to either wing. 'Willow', who was particularly effective when forming a right-flank triangle with Viv Anderson and David Rocastle, supplemented his creative skills with uncompromising firmness in the tackle, and was also unquenchably hungry for possession. If the ball wasn't delivered to his feet, he would often be seen glowering at less precise team-mates, a situation that led, occasionally, to unproductive histrionics.

Steve was signed by Don Howe, who paid Southampton £550,000 for his services in December 1984, but he performed rather fitfully until 1986/87, when the managerial reign of George Graham began. That term he played some of his classiest football and was a major influence as the Gunners lifted the Littlewoods Cup. But during the following campaign, he experienced differences with the strong-minded Scot and lost his place, missing the Wembley defeat by Luton Town which prised the trophy from Arsenal's grasp. The split was final, and in July 1988 Steve moved to Kenilworth Road for £300,000. The chance of a lifetime, of fulfilling his potential with one of soccer's greatest clubs, had passed him by.

BORN: Hammersmith, 12.7.58. GAMES 119 (2). GOALS: 5.
HONOURS: League Cup 86/7.
6 England caps (83-85).

OTHER CLUBS: Southampton 75/6-84/5 (278, 18); Luton Town 88/9-90/1 (40, 1); Exeter City 91/2-92/3 (48, 0).

STEWART ROBSON

1981/82 – 1986/87

The futility of forecasting a glittering future for promising young footballers is well documented, but in 1985, even the most cautious of Gunners fans might have risked the prediction that 20-year-old Stewart Robson had arrived in the Arsenal team to stay. Here was no flashy novice, the sort who dazzled today and fizzled out tomorrow; here was a versatile, ambitious young man whose compelling cocktail of skill and effort seemed destined to grace Highbury well into the nineties. Some pundits went further, speculating on his ultimate succession to the England role fulfilled by his illustrious namesake, Bryan, and although that was palpably reckless, it was easy to understand their enthusiasm.

Stewart had not long passed his 17th birthday when he made his League debut, playing at right-back against West Ham United at Upton Park in December 1981. In an impressively mature performance, he nullified the creative talents of the dangerous Alan Devonshire and revealed the confidence to overlap audaciously as the Gunners attacked.

It wasn't long before his all-round ability and application won him a place in midfield, where his development continued apace. Stewart kept the game simple, tackling venomously and wasting the ball rarely. Standing a quarter of an inch short of 6ft, he was competitive in the air – excelling as an occasional sweeper – and possessed a savage shot, as he showed when netting at home to Tottenham in April 1984. His progress was recognised by England under-21 caps and he was voted Arsenal's player of the year in 1985, but his North London days were numbered. After starting only five games under new boss George Graham, Stewart suffered a groin injury in September 1986, and on recovery four months later, he dumbfounded Highbury regulars by joining his boyhood favourites, West Ham, for £750,000. Sadly, the remainder of his career, with the Hammers and then Coventry City, was marred by fitness problems.

BORN: Billericay, Essex, 6.11.64. GAMES: 185 (1). GOALS: 21.

OTHER CLUBS: West Ham United 86/7-90/1 (68, 4); Coventry City 90/1-93/4 (57, 3).

GRAHAM RIX

For the young Graham Rix, playing alongside Liam Brady was a mixed blessing. It offered the bubble-haired Yorkshireman the priceless privilege of studying the midfield arts at the shoulder of the Irish master, but, inevitably, he suffered in comparison with the great man. No matter how brilliantly Graham performed, someone would say 'Yes, very good, but he's no Brady'. Of course he wasn't - for sheer creativity, Liam knew no contemporary peer in British football - but he *was* a gifted performer in his own right, and his record over 12 seasons was to earn him a distinguished niche in Gunners history.

Graham, who signed apprenticeship forms at Highbury in 1974 after slipping through Leeds United's net at an Elland Road trial, was a skinny teenager whom some believed might struggle to hold his own in the physically demanding world of professional football. Yet there was deceptive resilience in that slender frame, and any doubts were laid to rest by an abundance of natural talent. The Rix repertoire was impressive indeed: a beautiful passer who controlled the ball smoothly, he had a knack of drifting past his markers, and an occasional habit of delivering sudden, unexpectedly ferocious shots. That he was left-sided placed his abilities at an even greater premium - so many midfields lack balance because they are populated exclusively by right-footers - and he progressed to the status of first-team regular before his 20th birthday.

Those early years were to be packed with big occasions and featured several moments of high personal drama for Graham. Between 1978 and 1980 he appeared in three FA Cup Finals, playing a crucial role in the victory that sandwiched two defeats. With Arsenal and Manchester United level at two-apiece and extra-time looming, he sprinted down the left flank to receive a perfectly-weighted pass from Liam Brady, before floating the ball to the far post for Alan Sunderland to volley the winner. Then, the Gunners having thus qualified for the European Cup Winners' Cup, he supplied a similarly inviting cross for Paul Vaessen to shatter Juventus in the semi-final. However, the final, against Valencia in Brussels, was to end in tears after Graham missed decisively in a penalty shoot-out, and the fact that Liam - in his last game before leaving the club - had also failed from the spot was no consolation.

Graham now found himself as the North Londoners' play-maker-in-chief, which induced more constant involvement, lessening a previous tendency to drift into temporary isolation in his wide position. While he never dominated in the manner of his friend and mentor, he did well enough to earn England honours, and held his place as Ron Greenwood's team remained unbeaten during the 1982 World Cup Finals in Spain. At the outset of 1983/84, Terry Neill boosted his 25-year-old schemer by presenting him with the captaincy, perhaps in the belief that responsibility would engender the consistency that his game still lacked. Unfortunately, that November Graham suffered an Achilles tendon injury which caused lengthy absences over several campaigns, so a fair verdict could not be passed on the manager's manoeuvre.

His Arsenal career drew to a close as new Highbury boss George Graham made radical changes to the side, and in 1988 he was freed to join Caen of France. The outwardly languid Rix style, which in fact masked a good deal of strenuous effort, went down well across the Channel before he served Dundee, then joined Chelsea as a player-coach. But the Gunners saw his prime, and his considerable achievements with them should be judged on their own merits, not in relation to the deeds of a certain Dubliner.

BORN: Doncaster, 23.10.57. GAMES: 446 (17). GOALS: 51.
HONOURS: FA Cup 78/9.
17 England caps (80-84).
OTHER CLUBS: Brentford on loan 87/8 (6, 0); Caen, France; Le Havre, France; Dundee 92/3 (14, 2); Chelsea 94/5 (1, 0).

1976/77 – 1987/88

NIALL QUINN

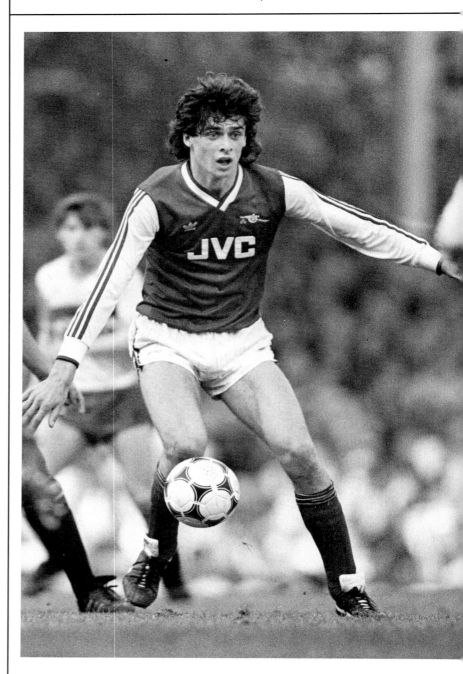

Niall Quinn will never be the world's most elegant centre-forward – in his early Arsenal days, a less graceful mover than the decidedly green Irish beanpole was difficult to imagine – but there wasn't a defender in the First Division who relished a confrontation with him. Ample evidence of the discomfiture Niall could cause was on view at Highbury when he made his senior bow, replacing the injured Tony Woodcock against Liverpool in December 1985. That day the 6ft 5in rookie scored in a 2-0 triumph, and gave Alan Hansen and Mark Lawrenson, that most majestic back-four duos, more problems than they expected to face from many an experienced star, let alone a toiling teenager whose most notable success to date had been on the Gaelic football fields of his homeland.

George Graham gave Niall his first settled senior run in 1986/87, but goals did not flow and for some months, woefully short of both pace and confidence, the newcomer seemed clumsier than ever. But while team-mates were profiting from the mayhem created by his towering physical presence, the manager was happy to persevere with him, and was vindicated by a steady improvement. Though Niall never scored heavily, it was his perfect far-post header in the White Hart Lane leg of the Littlewoods Cup semi-final that secured a replay against Spurs, and he richly deserved the subsequent reward of a Wembley winner's medal.

Ironically, just as his hard work was paying dividends in terms of more reliable control, neater distribution and increased tactical awareness, the advent of Alan Smith cost Niall his place. Though he ousted the Englishman for a brief midwinter spell in 1987/88, his Highbury future was clearly limited, and in March 1990 he joined Manchester City for £700,000. At Maine Road, the Eire international revelled in new-found responsibility, blossoming into a more accomplished all-round performer than his former critics would have dreamed possible.

BORN: Dublin, 6.10.66. GAMES: 81 (12).
GOALS: 20. HONOURS: League Cup 86/7.
61 Republic of Ireland caps (86-).

OTHER CLUBS: Manchester City 89/90-95/6 (203, 66); Sunderland 96/7- (11, 2).

1985/86 – 1989/90

VIV ANDERSON

1984/85– 1986/87

Few full-backs have entertained as flamboyantly as Viv Anderson. Whether sprinting into attack, that elastic stride carrying him past all but the speediest of opponents, or snaking out a long right leg to make a retrieving tackle when it seemed his winger had left him in a heap, the swashbuckling Midlander guaranteed value for money.

Yet the pace and talent that made him such an attractive performer, and the strength and aerial power that created such an impact at either end of the pitch, represented but part of Viv's worth to the Gunners and to every other club he has served. Allied to all that natural ability was a deep-seated hatred of losing and refusal to quit in the face of any odds; away from the action he was the soul of affability, but give him a rearguard action to fight and he snarled his defiance at the world.

Viv, who in his Nottingham Forest days became the first black footballer to win a full England cap, had slipped from the international scene by the time he joined Arsenal for £250,000 in July 1984. But after an uncharacteristically tentative start for his new club, he regained both his best form and his place in Bobby Robson's side, and by 1986/87 many respected judges saw him as the Gunners' most effective player. That term, in which Viv took a leading part in lifting the Littlewoods Cup, was to be his last in North London, his summer switch to Manchester United coming as a major disappointment to Arsenal fans. Although he was 31, the fee – which a tribunal decreed should equal his purchase price – was seen as inadequate, and there was bitterness similar to that caused by Frank Stapleton's move to Old Trafford six years earlier.

A perpetual chatterbox and leg-puller, Viv was missed almost as much for his vivacious personality as his professional skills, and if the Highbury dressing room became a more peaceful place for his absence, there is no doubt that it lost a lot of its sparkle.

BORN: Nottingham, 29.8.56. GAMES: 150. GOALS: 15. HONOURS: League Cup 86/7. 30 England caps (78–88).

OTHER CLUBS: Nottingham Forest 74/5–83/4 (328, 15); Manchester United 87/8–90/1 (54, 2); Sheffield Wednesday 90/1–92/3 (70, 8); Barnsley 93/4 (20, 3); Middlesbrough as player/assistant manager 94/5 (2, 0). MANAGER: Barnsley 93–94.

CHARLIE NICHOLAS

There have always been footballers whose special combination of artistry and personality can add thousands to a gate, elite entertainers whose gifts defy the glib pastime of pigeon-holing yet who fall into certain loose categories. Some, the likes of Alex James and George Best, would excel in any company, at any time; others - a young Charlie George springs to mind - are capable of scaling the heights, but only fitfully, when the situation is just right; the third and most perplexing group consists of extravagant talents who are doomed to be dazzling, yet ultimately dispensable adornments to their teams - and such a man was Charlie Nicholas.

Charlie was never cut out to be a messiah, but that was the role foisted on the immature 21-year-old when he joined Arsenal from Celtic for £650,000 in the summer of 1983. Harassed manager Terry Neill, eager to make up for a campaign in which a mid-table League position was hardly mitigated by semi-final defeats in the two major domestic cups, needed a performer of flair and quality to provide the necessary tonic. Who better than a man who had just netted more than 50 goals in a season, and who, it was presumed, could only improve?

On arrival in London, Charlie struck up an instant rapport with the North Bank that was never to wither throughout the fluctuations of fortune that lay ahead. He had gone a long way towards winning their affection by spurning Manchester United and Liverpool - reasoning, perhaps misguidedly, that the pressure for success would be less marked at Highbury than with the northern giants - and cemented his position in their hearts by sheer charisma. They were utterly charmed by the one-time car mechanic with the flowing dark hair and cheeky grin, and there was an indulgent acceptance, even approval, of the 'Champagne Charlie' hype that burgeoned out of all proportion.

The problem was that the Scottish star, while possessing scintillating skills that could light up the drabbest of games, was horribly inconsistent. After scoring twice on his second outing, at Wolverhampton, he didn't net again in the League until two spectacular efforts - a fierce drive and a delicate lob - against Spurs on Boxing Day. He could waltz around opponents with captivating audacity, yet sometimes retained possession too long, and his adherence to carefully prepared tactical plans tended to be less than total. Charlie - arguably a more potent force up front than in the deep position he filled so frequently - was at his best when the ball was played to his feet, but often he was asked to chase it, which he found frustrating. At times there was also a lack of steel in his game that did not sit well with the Arsenal style, and although his contribution over four-and-a-half years was by no means negative - after all, his two goals against Liverpool in the 1987 Littlewoods Cup Final secured the Gunners' first major trophy of the decade - it was hardly a shock when George Graham gave up the struggle to integrate his virtuosity into the team.

It should be stressed that when he was sold to Aberdeen for £400,000 in January 1988, Charlie had not spent all his time in England living up to his racy media image. Certainly he enjoyed life to the full, but, to be fair, he was a conscientious trainer who, away from football, spent much time on unsung charity work. In the end, he could not live up to expectations where it mattered, on the pitch, and that's an abiding sadness. Yet just five days before his departure, the North Bank, incensed by the latest in a woeful run of Arsenal performances, were calling for their hero with all the fervour they had shown on his first day. Few of Highbury's favourite sons have inspired such devotion.

BORN: Glasgow, 30.12.61. GAMES: 176 (8). GOALS: 54.
HONOURS: League Cup 86/7. 20 Scotland caps (83-89).

OTHER CLUBS: Celtic 80/1-82/3 (74, 48); Aberdeen 87/8-89/90 (78, 30); Celtic 90/1-94/5 (114, 37); Clyde 95/6 (31, 5).

1983/84 – 1987/88

DAVID O'LEARY

For more than a decade-and-a-half, Arsenal without David O'Leary would have been well-nigh unthinkable. A rising star in the seventies, the polished centrepiece of the side during the eighties, and the elder statesman of George Graham's thrusting new line-up of the early nineties, the imperturbable Irishman rejoiced in the unshakeable respect and affection of the Highbury faithful. Such devotion to long-serving stars is not uncommon in itself, but the warmth towards David extended beyond recognition of his perennial excellence at the heart of the Gunners' rearguard, and cannot be wholly explained, either, by his gentle, unassuming personality. In fact, it has much to do with his decision to remain in North London when his countrymen, Liam Brady and Frank Stapleton, opted for highly remunerative moves at the peak of their careers. Though their departures were understandable, both - and especially Frank's - provoked a measure of bitterness, and David's loyalty was rewarded by deep and lasting appreciation from the terraces.

His progress to the point where any top club might have coveted his services had been rapid after signing apprentice forms for Arsenal in 1973. He impressed immediately by frustrating the likes of John Radford and Ray Kennedy in practice matches, and was called up for his League debut at Burnley in August 1975, just three months after his 17th birthday. Despite his slender frame, David was deceptively strong and was blessed with a turn of speed not granted to many six-footers, seeming to eat up the ground with a long, loping stride that was destined to become so familiar. But it was his composure and cultured use of the ball that marked him out so vividly for an illustrious future. Only in the direst of straits would he opt for a hopeful upfield punt, preferring instead to play his way out of trouble before setting up an attack. David had a knack of taking the heat out of potentially dangerous situations before his goal was threatened and, unobtrusively but steadily, he grew into one of the First Division's most reliable back-four operators.

The Eire international's performances tended to be smoothly efficient rather than eye-catching, but some do linger in the memory. His form and bearing as the Gunners pipped Manchester United in the 1979 FA Cup Final was positively magisterial, and the penalty shoot-out defeat by Valencia in the ensuing season's European Cup Winners' Cup did scant justice to his flawless display against Argentinian maestro Mario Kempes.

David's stature at the club was recognised by a spell as captain in the early eighties, but as the decade wore on there were periods when he appeared to become stale. However, the start of the Graham regime brought renewed impetus and the O'Leary game was purring along as consistently as ever as the Littlewoods Cup was lifted in 1987. After an ankle injury sidelined him for much of 1987/88, he could not command a regular place throughout the Championship term that followed, but gave doughty service at right-back before excelling as a sweeper as the campaign reached its breathtaking climax.

There followed spells when team tactics dictated David's absence, though until the early months of 1992/93, his 20th and last season as a Gunner, he was in the side more often than out of it, breaking Arsenal's appearance record and playing a telling role in their continued success. Fittingly, that final term ended with David brandishing yet another trophy, the FA Cup, after coming on as a substitute in both Wembley encounters with Sheffield Wednesday. Two months later he was freed to join Leeds, though injury prevented the 35-year-old embarking on an Indian summer at Elland Road.

His most fervent fans rank him the equal of Liverpool's Alan Hansen, but that may be going a bit far; while the two were similar in many respects, the Scot was a truly peerless performer whose club place was never in jeopardy. Nevertheless, David O'Leary did more than enough to go down as one of British football's most accomplished modern-day defenders.

BORN: Stoke Newington, London, 2.5.58. GAMES: 678 (41). GOALS: 14.

OTHER CLUBS: Leeds United 93/4 (10, 0). HONOURS: League Championship 88/9, 90/1. FA Cup 78/9, 92/3. League Cup 86/7.
68 Republic of Ireland caps (76-93).

1975/76 – 1992/93

KENNY SANSOM

For all those who indulge in the meaningless but irresistible pastime of picking hypothetical teams of outstanding players from different eras, here is a tantalising question: who has been British football's finest left-back since the war? There is no shortage of candidates: Manchester United air crash victim Roger Byrne, 1966 World Cup hero Ray Wilson, converted winger Terry Cooper, masterful Scot Danny McGrain, and England stormtrooper Stuart Pearce . . . each one, in his own way, is worthy of the accolade. But the choice of many seasoned observers would fall on Kenny Sansom, who won more international caps than any of them and who served Arsenal with class and consistency for eight campaigns.

Of course, such selectorial fantasies are of supreme irrelevance, but even viewed in the most pragmatic terms, the acquisition of Kenny from Crystal Palace in August 1980 was one of Terry Neill's most inspired transactions as Arsenal manager. The deal itself was complicated, with £1 million striker Clive Allen – who never played a senior game for the Gunners – and reserve goalkeeper Paul Barron moving to Selhurst Park, but the upshot was that one of the brightest young defenders in the land was recruited to the Highbury cause.

Though already established in the England team, Kenny was by no means the finished product at the time of his arrival to replace the ageing Sammy Nelson. Devastatingly quick over short distances, enviably accurate at passing the ball with his left foot and astonishingly competitive in the air for a man of 5ft 6in, he was yet to attain a reliable positional sense. This meant that when his exhilarating touchline sorties broke down, he was not always in place to redeem the situation, thus placing instant pressure on his fellow defenders.

That did not stop supporters making him Arsenal's player of the year in 1981, however, and as his experience grew, so his reading of the game – knowing when to dash forward and when to hold back – improved immeasurably. Kenny was never one for the lunging tackle, invariably preferring finesse over force. He preferred to jockey his opponents away from the danger area and relied extensively on intelligent interceptions, a skill which proved particularly productive at international level.

As the eighties progressed, the polished number three became an ever more influential component of his club side and it was fitting that he should be leading the North Londoners when they won their first silverware for eight years, beating Liverpool in the 1987 Littlewoods Cup Final. But that summer a shadow appeared on the Sansom horizon in the shape of the newly purchased Nigel Winterburn, and the September boost of scoring his first goal for three years – the winner, on his birthday, at home to West Ham – did not set the tone for the remainder of 1987/88. During a troublesome season, he suffered a niggling groin injury, his captaincy passed to Tony Adams, and then the Gunners failed narrowly to retain their trophy, surrendering a Wembley lead to Luton just five minutes from full time.

Yet worse was to follow. George Graham dropped him for the new campaign and Kenny never made another senior appearance for the club. After four months in the reserves, he joined Newcastle United for £300,000, but failed to find happiness in the north and made a swift return to the capital with Queen's Park Rangers, later serving three further clubs before joining Watford as a coach. The anti-climactic departure from Highbury had hardly been in keeping with his magnificent service, but Kenny Sansom's honoured place in Arsenal history is not in doubt.

BORN: Camberwell, London, 26.9.58. GAMES: 394. GOALS: 6.
HONOURS: League Cup 86/7.
86 England caps (79-88).

OTHER CLUBS: Crystal Palace 74/5-79/80 (172, 3); Newcastle United 88/9 (20, 0); Queen's Park Rangers 89/90-90/1 (36, 0); Coventry City 90/1-92/3 (51, 0); Everton 92/3 (7, 1); Brentford 92/3 (8, 0); Watford 94/5 (1, 0).

1980/81 – 1987/88

GUS CAESAR

Gus Caesar's first taste of top-level soccer promised a sparkling future which, by the early nineties, seemed a world away. Playing at right-back at Old Trafford in December 1985, the 19-year-old debutant blotted Danish trickster Jesper Olsen out of the game, and although he stepped down when first-team regular Viv Anderson recovered fitness, Gus had served eloquent notice of his long-term ambitions.

By 1987, the Tottenham-born utility defender had made significant progress. That year he won three England under-21 caps and deputised in each of the Gunners' back-four positions, also showing aptitude as a one-on-one midfield marker. It seemed a standard introduction to eventual senior status for a dedicated athlete with the healthiest of attitudes to hard graft. But by the close of the decade, Gus - who during his Highbury career had broken an ankle three times - had drifted to the outer edge of the senior squad.

A propensity for making errors under pressure had become noticeable - a fumbled clearance that led to Luton's equaliser in the 1988 Littlewoods Cup Final was a case in point - and the arrival of new faces such as Andy Linighan and Colin Pates diminished his prospects still further. Distressingly, Gus found himself something of an aunt sally for barrackers and his football became an uphill struggle. He was given a free transfer in the summer of 1991.

BORN: Haringey, London, 5.3.66. GAMES: 30 (20). GOALS: 0.

OTHER CLUBS: Queen's Park Rangers on loan 90/1 (5, 0); Bristol City 91/2 (10, 0); Airdieonians 91/2-93/4 (57, 1); Colchester United 94/5-95/6 (62, 3).

1985/86 – 1990/91

COLIN PATES

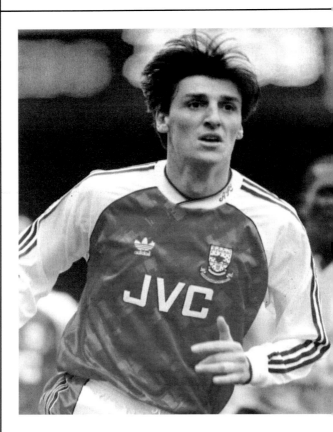

When George Graham paid £500,000 to Charlton Athletic for Colin Pates, he was taking out a low-risk, central-defensive insurance policy, complete with a couple of far-from-negligible bonuses. As well as offering reliably efficient cover for Messrs Adams, Bould, O'Leary and Linighan in the middle of the Gunners' rearguard, the left-sided Colin could double as a briskly competent midfielder. And even when he wasn't in the first team, which was most of the time, he was a paragon of professionalism who set an impeccable example to the club's youngsters.

Perhaps Colin, a Chelsea stalwart throughout the eighties, retained high ambition when he arrived at Highbury in January 1990; after all, he was still only 29. But, in truth, it seemed unlikely that he would be able to overcome the resident red-hot competition for a regular berth, and so it proved.

An astute, composed reader of the game, he was not one for extravagant flourishes, relying on fierce concentration and firm, decisive action to get the job done. His handful of senior outings permitted few highlights, though there was one, his only goal for the Gunners raising false hopes of glory by nosing them ahead, agonisingly briefly, in the European Cup defeat by Benfica at Highbury in November 1991.

In August 1993, Colin was freed to join Brighton, later becoming player-boss of Crawley after a knee injury had ended his League career.

BORN: Carshalton, Surrey, 10.8.61. GAMES: 16 (9). GOALS: 1.
OTHER CLUBS: Chelsea 79/80-88/9 (281, 10); Charlton Athletic 88/9-89/90 (38, 0); Brighton on loan 90/1 (17, 0); Brighton 93/4-94/5 (50, 0).

1989/90 – 1992/93

MARTIN HAYES

1985/86 – 1989/90

In one season of heady success, Martin Hayes topped the Highbury scoring charts, helped the Gunners lift their first major honour of the eighties, earned an England under-21 call-up . . . and set himself a standard he found impossible to maintain.

The tall, fair-haired striker, who could operate either in the centre of attack or in a more withdrawn left-flank position, made his debut when Graham Rix was dropped for the home encounter with Oxford United in November 1985. Martin got off to an encouraging start, laying on a goal for Tony Woodcock, but it was not until he settled into the side during 1986/87 that he began to excite widespread attention. Suddenly everyone wanted to know about the prolific speedster who was outstripping some of the First Division's paciest defenders.

Martin was skilful, too, as he proved with stunning solo efforts at Charlton in November 1986, and at Highbury against Leicester the following April, when he dribbled the ball from the half-way line before clipping it expertly past 'keeper Ian Andrews. That term he netted 24 League and Cup goals, 12 of them penalties, and was rewarded with a Littlewoods Cup winner's medal.

But in 1987/88, Martin flopped inexplicably, his talent still apparent but his self-belief seemingly in shreds. His one telling contribution was a close-range goal after joining the action as a substitute in the Littlewoods defeat by Luton at Wembley, and he slipped to the status of squad member. The next term brought little improvement, though he was called from the bench enough times to win a title medal, and his cool finish secured a crucial victory at Middlesbrough in May. By the summer of 1990, still only 24 but sinking ever lower in the pecking order, Martin accepted a £650,000 move to Celtic. He struggled to adapt to Scottish football, however, and after making little impression during a spell on loan to Wimbledon, he saw out his professional days with Swansea City.

BORN: Walthamstow, London, 21.3.66.
GAMES: 92 (40). GOALS: 34.
HONOURS: League Championship 88/9.
League Cup 86/7.

OTHER CLUBS: Celtic 90/1 (7, 0);
Wimbledon on loan 91/2 (2, 0); Swansea City
92/3-94/5 (61, 8).

PAUL DAVIS

One fleeting, flowing sequence of action offered Arsenal fans sorely-needed, if all-too-temporary, relief on an evening of Highbury torture in December 1990. The Gunners, who had yet to lose a game in any competition that term, were in the process of suffering their heaviest home defeat for more than 60 years - 6-2 against Manchester United in the Rumbelows League Cup - when Paul Davis trespassed into the Red Devils' limelight with a scintillating illustration of his midfield art. Breaking up an attack on the edge of his own penalty area, he drifted elegantly past an opponent, carried the ball 40 yards upfield, and then swept a perfectly weighted pass to free Lee Dixon for a raid down the right. That move, like Arsenal on the night, was doomed to failure, but it encapsulated the immense all-round value of the nimble schemer, whose achievements rarely *quite* matched his bountiful natural ability.

Paul, who turned professional in 1979, made his League debut at White Hart Lane the following April, impressing instantly with his slick control and imaginative distribution. Seasoned campaigners, who had watched numerous promising youngsters fall by the wayside, tipped the quiet Londoner for an international future, and there was plenty of evidence to support their case. Paul's left foot was an instrument of precision which, on his day, he could use with infinite variety and cunning, though he found consistency harder to attain.

In the early and middle eighties, he established a first-team niche and won England under-21 honours without stepping up the extra gear necessary to assert himself among the elite talents of the day. During 1986/87, however, Paul exerted a major influence as the Littlewoods Cup was won, and new manager George Graham demonstrated confidence in the play-maker's growing maturity by handing him the captaincy for a brief spell when Kenny Sansom was unfit.

But serious setbacks were lying in wait, and it was cruel luck that they should remove Paul for most of 1988/89, the term that saw the Championship return to Highbury. First came a nine-match suspension for punching Southampton's Glenn Cockerill and breaking his jaw, a wholly uncharacteristic outburst; then he suffered several debilitating injuries that forced him to mark time, though he did make one vivid contribution to the title effort in March, scoring one of his all-too-rare goals with a diving header at home to Charlton.

Come the start of 1990/91, Paul was fit and eager to renew the impetus of his stuttering career, and he succeeded, at times so compellingly that there were calls for a first full cap. In September he graced a drab, goalless North London derby at Highbury, outshining the much-lauded Paul Gascoigne and inspiring *The Independent* newspaper's typically apt headline: 'Davis the visionary in land of the blind'.

He developed a fruitful understanding with Michael Thomas, stood in once more as skipper during Tony Adams' enforced midwinter break, and appeared, at last, to be reaching the elusive peak of his powers. Then, out of the blue, there were mutterings about so-called defensive inadequacies and the team's most perceptive prompter was dropped. Soon he was back, however, as the Gunners strove for an unprecedented second League and FA Cup double, and although he was in his 30th year, it was clear that Paul remained a potent creative force.

Unfortunately, Graham chose thereafter to use him only fitfully. Clearly there were differences between the two men concerning work-rate and Paul was condemned to long periods of inaction. There was to be one more sustained Davis contribution to the Arsenal cause, though, when he was recalled for the entire Cup Winners' Cup campaign of 1993/94. Faced with the more measured requirements of European competition, Paul excelled, underlining his sheer class once more. It was a fitting last major hurrah before his free transfer to Brentford in September 1995.

BORN: London, 9.12.61. GAMES: 414 (31). GOALS: 37. HONOURS: European Cup Winners' Cup 93/4; League Championship 88/9, 90/1. FA Cup 92/3. League Cup 86/7, 92/3.

OTHER CLUBS: Brentford 95/6 (5, 0).

1979/80 – 1994/95

JOHN LUKIC

The warmth and esteem in which John Lukic was held by Highbury regulars had tended to be mainly of the unspoken variety until manager George Graham confirmed, in March 1990, that he was seeking to sign England international David Seaman. Then, during several home games, there were chants in praise of the likeable, lanky custodian, and on one touching occasion a group of his fans held a small protest demonstration outside the ground. The display of loyalty was understandable and in no way a reflection on the even more outstanding merits of his eventual replacement. John had played a dependable part in lifting two major trophies, the Littlewoods Cup in 1987 and the Championship two years later, all the while receiving few public plaudits but building up a store of much-deserved goodwill.

Terry Neill had paid Leeds United £75,000 for the 22-year-old son of Yugoslavian parents in July 1983, seeing him as an able long-term successor to Pat Jennings. After learning at the Irishman's shoulder for 18 months, John became first choice for the remainder of the decade, establishing himself as one of the leading all-round goalkeepers in the top flight. A magnificent shot-stopper whose prodigious 'route one' goal kicks were a potent attacking weapon, he dealt efficiently with the majority of crosses, although like most of his contemporaries he experienced the occasional day when nothing seemed to stick.

When it became clear he had no future in North London, John returned to Leeds in May 1990 for £1 million, having given the Gunners seven years of irreproachable service and leaving them with a handsome profit. The change did him good, and back at Elland Road, where he had once seen off the challenge of the young Seaman, he showed the best form of his career to date. None of his friends and admirers at Highbury begrudged him his renewed success, which included a second title medal in 1991/92.

In 1996 John was welcomed back by Arsenal as David's deputy, and he proved largely dependable during two first-team stints.

BORN: Chesterfield, Derbyshire, 11.12.60.
GAMES: 293. GOALS: 0.
HONOURS: League Championship 88/9.
League Cup 86/7.

OTHER CLUBS: Leeds United 79/80–82/3 (146, 0) and 90/1–95/6 (209, 0).

1983/84 – 1989/90 & 1996/97

KEVIN RICHARDSON

1987/88 – 1989/90

Kevin Richardson was once described as 'the most consistently high–class ordinary player in the First Division', which summed up neatly, if a touch uncharitably, the Geordie midfielder's three seasons of Highbury endeavour. Indeed, there had been few fanfares in August 1987 when George Graham paid Watford £200,000 for the 5ft 7in workhorse, who at 24 was already the veteran of a Championship success with Everton two years earlier. Though renowned for his enthusiasm and combativeness, Kevin was hardly the sort of polished performer who might have been expected to join Arsenal but, neither for the first nor last time, the Gunners' manager had made an extraordinarily shrewd purchase.

For most of 1987/88 the newcomer wore the number-11 shirt to which Graham Rix was gradually losing his claim, and did the competent job expected of him, tackling waspishly, denying opponents the space to play, and buzzing industriously to all corners of the pitch. But come the following season, with Paul Davis sidelined by suspension and injury, Kevin appeared to take on more responsibility, helping to ease the burden of the creative but inexperienced Michael Thomas, and chipping in with constructive contributions of his own. Though there was always the chance of an inept miskick to the feet of an opponent, the former Evertonian *was* capable of perceptive, penetrating passes, and played a steady all–round part in the title triumph.

After a third term of yeoman service, player and boss had a difference of opinion, and the Richardson sojourn at Highbury ended in a £750,000 move to Real Sociedad. But despite the discord, both Kevin and the North Londoners had reason to bless their association. He had added lustre to his career and became one of the few players to win Championship medals with two clubs, and they had made £550,000 profit from a man who had helped them win English football's top domestic prize. Later, Kevin excelled for Aston Villa and continued to confound the purists by winning a full England cap.

BORN: Newcastle, 4.12.62. GAMES: 110 (11). GOALS: 8. HONOURS: League Championship 88/9. 1 England cap (94).

OTHER CLUBS: Everton 81/2-86/7 (109, 16); Watford 86/7 (39, 2); Real Sociedad, Spain, 90/1; Aston Villa 91/2-94/5 (143, 13); Coventry City 94/5- (74, 0).

DAVID ROCASTLE

The dancing feet of David Rocastle offered persuasive argument that their multi-talented owner was the most thrilling Arsenal footballer of the eighties. The pity was that as the Gunners shaped up to become one of the new decade's dominant forces, the man whose total of England caps reached double figures before his 23rd birthday had lost the dazzling momentum that had established his reputation.

It was clear from David's earliest senior showings in 1985/86, the final term of Don Howe's Highbury reign, that he had the makings of an irresistible performer. Whether pushed forward as an orthodox flankman or operating on the right side of midfield, he possessed the priceless ability to stir a crowd. Watching David weave past a posse of flabbergasted defenders with the ball apparently stitched to his foot, it seemed reasonable to wonder whether rival fans might be shamed into abandoning their churlish chants of 'boring, boring Arsenal'. That proved a naive notion, of course, but there was no denying that a stimulating new entertainer was abroad in North London.

David's precocious gifts were recognised by the supporters' player of the year award in 1986, and at Wembley the following spring he collected his first major honour, playing an enterprising part in the Littlewoods Cup defeat of Liverpool. Over the next two campaigns, 'Rocky' did not miss a League game and was seen by many as the jewel in George Graham's 1988/89 Championship crown. At the end of that season, he was hailed as Barclay's Young Eagle of the Year, and his place in the England side was looking increasingly secure. It was easy to see why: his beautifully balanced dribbling skills were supplemented by startling acceleration and a savage shot, and his penchant for hammering low crosses into crowded penalty areas induced chaos in the coolest defence.

Not surprisingly, such a dangerous player came in for plenty of physical punishment, but David, who boasted his own line in cleanly-timed whiplash tackles, was ever-ready to bite back when provoked. Such a steely streak is admirable when controlled, but an inability to walk away from trouble can bring serious consequences, as he discovered when sent off for retaliation in an ill-tempered match at Old Trafford in January 1987. However, by the summer of 1989 that unsavoury incident had long been consigned to history and – a title medal safely secured and the World Cup in prospect – all seemed right with the Rocastle world.

Yet 1989/90 was to bring frustration and anti-climax. As the Gunners' chances of retaining their Championship receded, so David's form declined. The instinct for knowing when to release the ball seemed to desert him, and passes that once had been delivered with exquisite weight and accuracy now tended to go astray. Suddenly no longer the same devastating creator, he could not rely on a regular first-team place, and was omitted from Bobby Robson's World Cup party. He began the 1990/91 campaign back in the Arsenal side, but with competition for places growing ever more fierce, he was dropped in November. Further thwarted by a broken toe in his comeback game, he was left to scrap for his place again and managed just enough outings to claim a title medal.

Season 1991/92 saw him back in favour, his talent glowing so incandescently in a new central midfield role that he earned an England recall, and seemed to have put an aggravating mid-career blip behind him. But, to the dismay of many Gunners loyalists, he was sold to Leeds for £2 million in the summer of 1992. In truth, 'Rocky' was a gem who lost his lustre at Elland Road and never fully recovered it elsewhere. But the feeling persists that George Graham might – indeed, should – have made considerably more of David Rocastle at a time when glorious ability such as his was in woefully short supply at Highbury.

BORN: Lewisham, London, 2.5.67. GAMES: 258 (17). GOALS: 34.
HONOURS: League Championship 88/9, 90/1. League Cup 86/7.
11 England caps (88-92).

OTHER CLUBS: Leeds United 92/3-93/4 (25, 2); Manchester City 93/4 (21, 2);
Chelsea 94/5- (29, 0); Norwich City on loan 96/7 (11, 1).

1985/86 – 1991/92

BRIAN MARWOOD

Brian Marwood's crucially important contribution to Arsenal's 1989 Championship victory reflects untold credit not only on the effervescent winger himself, but also on the keen acumen of George Graham. All the Gunners' competitors knew where to find Brian, and what his capabilities were, but it was the Highbury boss who parted with £600,000 to sign the 28-year-old flankman from Sheffield Wednesday in March 1988. Thus equipped with a superb crosser of the ball to supply front-runner Alan Smith with ammunition, the North Londoners topped the First Division's scoring charts and enjoyed their most successful campaign for 18 years.

Brian, a perky character who rejoiced in the affection of the North Bank, was ideally equipped for his role of provider-in-chief. He possessed the suprisingly rare ability to dispatch the ball accurately from touchline to goal area with either foot, and the intelligence to vary his delivery. The diminutive north-easterner boasted splendid control and revelled in wrong-footing opponents with a dip of his shoulder before making his centre in the extra time and space his manoeuvre created. Also, he was an emphatic finisher, who netted in each of the opening five games of 1988/89, and offered a reliable service from the penalty spot.

Such was his impact at the time that terrace cries of 'Marwood for England' were answered in the affirmative by Bobby Robson, who awarded Brian his sole cap as a substitute for team-mate Michael Thomas against Saudi Arabia in Riyadh. Sadly, injuries were the bane of his career, and he was sidelined both for the climax of the title season and much of the next, before joining Sheffield United for £350,000 in September 1990. An articulate man who went on to chair the Professional Footballers Association, Brian was arguably the shrewdest short-term buy in Arsenal's post-war history.

BORN: Seaham, County Durham, 5.2.60.
GAMES: 60. GOALS: 17. HONOURS:
League Championship 88/9.
1 England cap (88).

OTHER CLUBS: Hull City 79/80-83/4
(158, 51); Sheffield Wednesday 84/5-87/8 (128, 27); Sheffield United 90/1-91/2 (22, 3); Middlesbrough on loan 91/2 (3, 0); Swindon Town 92/3 (11, 1); Barnet 93/4 (23, 0).

1987/88 – 1989/90

PERRY GROVES

1986/87 – 1992/93

If only the Scouse comedians who dubbed David Fairclough 'The Bionic Carrot' had been able to see into the future, surely they must have reserved that colourful, affectionate tag for Perry Groves. Admittedly it suited Liverpool's goal-scoring substitute well enough, but in respect of the Gunners' perennially under-praised utility forward, it would have been supremely apt. Indeed, witnessing Perry scamper frantically into attack, his red, close-cropped bullet head unmistakable from every corner of the most palatial stadium, the mind's-eye comparison with a vivid, high-velocity vegetable was irresistible.

Not that he needed a nickname to make an impact. After George Graham paid Colchester £40,000 to make the fast, fiery Londoner his first signing as Arsenal manager in September 1986, Perry served the Highbury cause with honesty, spirit, and yes, more skill than many sneering critics gave him credit for. Admittedly, his control could have been better and there were times when he ran impetuously into trouble instead of parting with the ball. But at his best he could light up a game with a swift, incisive raid – the left-flank dash past several Liverpool defenders to lay on the winner for Charlie Nicholas in the 1987 Littlewoods Cup Final was a perfect example – and he had the strength to retain possession under heavy pressure. Even when Perry was off form, he was never less than combative, and was always ready to chase causes that a more thoughtful player might have given up as lost.

He could operate in any front-running role – being most effective on the left – though his finishing was once described, with some accuracy, as 'usually wild but spasmodically deadly'. Long-throw expert Perry, a nephew of former Arsenal captain Vic Groves, never quite managed to cement a long-term regular place, making no less than 83 appearances as a substitute, but he was an important squad member during the Gunners' most successful post-war era. He was sold to Southampton for £750,000 in August 1992, only for injury to force him out of full-time football before he could make his mark as a Saint.

BORN: London, 19.4.65. GAMES: 120 (83). GOALS: 28. HONOURS: League Championship 88/9, 90/1. League Cup 86/7.

OTHER CLUBS: Colchester United 81/2-86/7 (156, 26); Southampton 92/3 (15, 2).

LEE DIXON

The name of Lee Dixon has become woven inextricably into the very fabric of Arsenal FC; no matter what the future holds for the indomitable blond Mancunian, in his 34th year at the time of writing, his niche in Highbury folklore is assured.

Yet it has been a hard-won eminence, due principally, of course, to season after season of excellence as the Gunners' right-back, but thanks also to a doughty single-mindedness that typifies the Arsenal ethos.

Like Tony Adams, Lee has suffered periods of fatuous vilification, and though he has experienced occasional slumps in form - there was one horribly shaky spell during 1991/92 - he has risen above the abuse with consummate professionalism, invariably regaining the level of performance which earned him 21 England caps during the early nineties.

The calm resolution which has been Lee's hallmark was evident throughout the steady, but unerringly sure rise he enjoyed after taking the only downward step of his career, a move from Burnley to Chester City in 1984. His upwardly-mobile travels since arriving at Fourth Division Sealand Road on a free transfer took in Bury of the Third (fee: £3,500) and Stoke City of the Second (£40,000), before George Graham elevated him to a place among the elite when he made him an Arsenal player at a cost of £400,000 in January 1988.

A mere 16 months later Lee had won a Championship medal and before another season had passed he was an England international; there followed another title gong, then FA Cup and European glory to complete a dozen years of spiralling soccer success.

His North London tenure began with a handful of senior outings in the spring of 1988, after which he slotted confidently into the side for the following campaign. He had been a winger as a youngster at Turf Moor, and his instinct for getting forward dovetailed perfectly with the prominent attacking profile the Highbury boss demanded of his full-backs. Lee took the eye with his pace, especially in sharp bursts, and, crucially, he matched fleetness of foot with quickness of thought. His ability to knock accurate early crosses to front-runner Alan Smith became a telling ingredient in countless Arsenal raids, and his sure control with either foot was evident whether in his own penalty box or the opposition's.

In fact, such was his comfort in possession that, in his early days as a Gunner, there were moments when an audacious back-pass to his 'keeper - perhaps a first-time lob or a subtle volley - had his own supporters gasping at such apparent foolhardiness. But as they became familiar with the cool customer in the number-two shirt, they realised that there was was no crisper, more reliable striker of the ball at the club, and sharp intakes of breath on the terraces became increasingly rare.

Lee's abundant all-round talent should not detract from the more prosaic, but essential attributes which have enabled him to discharge his defensive duties so efficiently. A brisk but by no means thunderous tackler, he has excelled at jockeying forwards into unpromising situations before nicking the ball away, an approach that did much to blunt the effectiveness of John Barnes as Liverpool surrendered the title on that unforgettable night at Anfield in May 1989.

Undoubtedly, however, Lee has been at his most compelling when surging into advanced positions, parading his wares as one of the most accomplished exponents of creative full-back play in the modern game. Not surprisingly, he has proved outstanding as a wing-back under Arsene Wenger and, apparently refreshed by the positive emphasis demanded by the role, he seemed to acquire a new lease of life.

Inevitably, he had slowed slightly, slipping out of the England reckoning as he was over-taken by young bucks such as Rob Jones and Gary Neville. But a combination of ability, character and accumulated nous meant that Lee Dixon remained one of the hardest-to-outwit defenders in the Premiership.

BORN: Manchester, 17.3.64. GAMES: 415 (4). GOALS: 21.
HONOURS: European Cup Winners' Cup 93/4; League Championship 88/9, 90/1; FA Cup 92/3. 21 England caps (90-93).

OTHER CLUBS: Burnley 82/3-83/4 (4, 0); Chester City 83/4-84/5 (57, 1); Bury 85/6 (45, 6); Stoke City 86/7-87/8 (71, 5).

1987/88 —

ALAN SMITH

Some players sail through their careers, their reputations gorged on a surfeit of praise; others, in reality equally worthwhile but not cast in the heroic mould, are doomed to be under-rated. Alan Smith, one of the most effective all-round centre-forwards the Gunners have ever had, falls firmly into the second category.

The rangy West Midlander represented one of George Graham's most astute excursions into the transfer market – high praise in itself – yet there was a period when he was accused of being an £800,000 flop. Alan's time of travail followed his arrival at Highbury, which was an unusually protracted affair. He was signed from Leicester in March 1987, but with the deadline for deals having passed, the North Londoners allowed their expensive acquisition to return to Filbert Street on loan for the remainder of that season.

Come August, he was slow to settle as the Gunners' chief marksman and midwinter found him in the grip of a goal famine. After being displaced briefly by the young Niall Quinn, Alan fought back with characteristic determination, working hard to improve his first touch on the ball. He scored with a sharp drive in the Littlewoods Cup Final defeat by Luton, and by the start of 1988/89 was ready to prove his critics wrong.

Throughout that arduous, but ultimately glorious campaign, Alan was a revelation. Newly adept at controlling long passes out of defence and retaining possession before laying the ball off accurately, he became the smooth, reliable fulcrum of the Arsenal attack, his perpetual movement – whether roaming to the flanks or foraging inside his own half – making him an ideal and ever-available target man. The industrious six-footer netted his share of the rousing goals expected of a spearhead, being equally potent with head and feet, but he relied more on intelligence than aggression, and frequently created mayhem with sweet flicks in the subtle style of sixties Spurs star Alan Gilzean.

The Smith bandwagon started to roll at the outset of that title term – he struck three times at Wimbledon on the opening day – and maintained its momentum right through to the titanic showdown with Liverpool. That night at Anfield, Alan's perfectly-timed run past a gaggle of static Reds enabled him to meet a Nigel Winterburn free-kick unchallenged, and nudge the ball past Bruce Grobbelaar for the opening goal; then, as the final seconds were ticking away, his calm and precise service to Michael Thomas set up the decisive strike. Nine months earlier, many fans had been unconvinced of his suit-ability to lead the Arsenal attack; by the end of the season, having topped the First Division scoring list with 23 goals and become an England player, he had nothing left to prove.

As the Gunners experienced anti-climax in 1989/90, Alan's strike-rate declined, undoubtedly affected by the frequent absences of injury-stricken winger Brian Marwood, on whose crosses he thrived. But by then he was a mature footballer who involved himself in the build-up of almost every attack, and could not be judged merely on his goal tally. Come 1990/91 he was integrating fluently with Messrs Merson, Campbell and Limpar, and that season's title victory had much to do with his understated excellence, not to mention another 22 goals.

Over the next four campaigns Alan laboured in the deep shadow cast by newly-arrived Ian Wright and, though his overall input remained immense, he became little more than an occasional scorer. However, there *was* one moment of pure bliss, one strike of incalculable import: the 25-yard left-foot volley that sunk Parma to secure the Cup Winners' Cup in 1994.

Though he was a regular choice no longer, Alan's injury-induced retirement in the spring of 1995 was a blow which a club in transition could ill afford. He was never one to hog the headlines; maybe he was too unselfish for his own good. But let nobody doubt that Alan Smith was a centre-forward of the highest class.

BORN: Bromsgrove, Worcestershire, 21.11.62. GAMES: 316 (29). GOALS: 115. HONOURS: European Cup Winners' Cup 93/4; League Championship 88/9, 90/1; FA Cup 92/3; 13 England caps (88-92).

OTHER CLUBS: Leicester City 82/3-86/7 (200, 76).

1987/88 – 1994/95

MICHAEL THOMAS

Michael Thomas could play until he was 50 and lift more trophies than Steve Davis, yet still he would never match the moment when he won the Championship for Arsenal at Anfield in the spring of 1989. Indeed, the melodramatic circumstances of that deathless deed would stretch the credibility of comic-strip fiction's most gullible addict. The Gunners needed victory by two goals to take the title and prevent Liverpool from winning the League and FA Cup double; after nearly two minutes of injury time, they were just one up and apparently doomed to glorious failure when Alan Smith laid the ball into the path of midfielder Michael, some 30 yards from goal. The loose-limbed Londoner took a lucky rebound from Steve Nicol and bore down on Bruce Grobbelaar; defenders converged for one desperate final challenge and the extrovert 'keeper spread himself at the attacker's feet. But, as a worldwide TV audience gaped in disbelief, Michael slipped the ball coolly into the corner of the net before launching himself into an ecstatic celebratory somersault.

Truly it was the most stunning strike in League history, and for once no superlative was unjustified. Yet no matter how significant that goal was, it should not overshadow completely its scorer's overall contribution to the rise of George Graham's new Arsenal. It is easy to forget, now, that although the former captain of England's schoolboy, youth and under-21 teams was to progress quickly - perhaps too quickly - to full international status in his midfield role, he played most of his early games for the Gunners at right-back. Soon after making his League bow with Portsmouth during a brief loan stint at Fratton Park, Michael was called up as a deputy for Viv Anderson in February 1987, then drafted in for Kenny Sansom on the left before capping his first senior campaign with a substitute appearance in that term's Littlewoods Cup Final victory over Liverpool.

With Viv having departed to Old Trafford, the versatile 20-year-old - he could also step in as a central defender - spent the first five months of 1987/88 in the number-two shirt before moving forward to become both a worker and creator at the side's hub. Michael impressed mightily at his new task, shuttling athletically up and down the pitch, and delighting at times with deft, almost nonchalant distribution. The supporters voted him player of the year and he began 1988/89 in such persuasive style that Bobby Robson could not resist selecting him for top-level duty. Suddenly, Michael seemed to lose his way; the industry remained, but where once his ball-work had been crisp, now it was clumsy, and he retained his place in the Arsenal team only because of injury to Paul Davis. Perhaps he had travelled too far, too soon, but he battled on diligently, reaping sensational reward for his persistence in that fairytale climax to the Championship race.

Thereafter Michael appeared to stabilise his career, emerging as a more mature, consistent operator, winning a brief England recall and contributing tellingly to the Gunners' second League crown in three years. Though he could hardly be described as prolific, he chipped in with some lovely goals, too, a particular gem coming at home to Manchester City in October 1989, when he robbed an opponent near the half-way line, waltzed past another and played a slick one-two with Alan Smith before stroking the ball home from just inside the penalty box.

But just as he seemed set to become a Highbury stalwart into the mid-nineties, differences surfaced between Michael and his manager. He was dropped and, to the disapproval of many fans, was sold to Liverpool for £1.5 million in December 1991. After helping the Reds to win that term's FA Cup, he suffered a plague of injuries which did not abate until mid-decade, when he recovered his best form. Then all he needed, if the fixtures computer would oblige in the not-too-distant future, was a last-match showdown . . . against Arsenal.

BORN: Lambeth, London, 24.8.67. GAMES: 186 (20). GOALS: 30.
HONOURS: League Championship 88/9, 90/1; League Cup 86/7.
2 England caps (88-89).

OTHER CLUBS: Portsmouth on loan 86/7 (3, 0); Liverpool 91/2- (112, 8).

1986/87 – 1991/92

TONY ADAMS

Has English football known a centre-half in modern times who combined guts and nous to greater effect than Tony Adams? Has any stopper been more mentally and physically resilient or able to inspire his team-mates more passionately than the Arsenal skipper? The answer is 'no' on both counts, and while crass pundits and fans have revelled periodically in heaping scorn on Tony's head, and hugely harrowing personal crises have hardly been conducive to life as a professional athlete, there is not a manager in the Premiership who wouldn't leap at the chance of naming the 6ft 3in Essex man in his side.

Indeed, if one of the most telling measures of a footballer's stature is the esteem in which he is held by his boss, then Tony is a veritable giant. George Graham extolled the Adams virtues in a manner reminiscent of Bill Shankly when that great man was painting a picture in words of his sixties Liverpool skipper, the mountainous Ron Yeats. Borrowing a phrase from that most quoted of soccer sages, George referred to his team-leader as 'my colossus', and when exceptional circumstances put his loyalty to the test in December 1990, it was not found wanting. After Tony was jailed for drink-driving, the Highbury boss left the world in no doubt that he, and Arsenal, would stand by their man; thus, on his release, the 24-year-old England defender was reinstated immediately.

Anyone who has witnessed Tony exuding authority at the heart of the Gunners' rearguard will not be surprised by such unreserved enthusiasm from a renowned disciplinarian. Adams' aerial dominance and his willingness to hurl himself into the path of anything threatening the North Londoners' goal would be enough, probably, to guarantee his place in the side, yet those sterling attributes merely begin to tell the full tale of his value. Over the years, he has become ever more comfortable on the ball and his reading of the game has improved immeasurably. Then there have been crucial goals in big games, notably the trademark headers that beat Spurs in the 1993 FA Cup semi-final and Torino on the way to European glory the following term. But most important of all, Tony Adams has been a motivator supreme, a rock of a man who became the very symbol of his club's ambition, a winner first and last.

Right from his earliest first-team days – he made his debut at 17, in November 1983 – there had been murmurings about ponderous movement and indifferent distribution, giving rise in the late eighties to the 'donkey' tag coined so asininely by a tabloid newspaper and which stuck. His tormentors didn't realise it but they were merely toughening his resolve and he answered them by holding aloft the Championship trophy in May 1989. Perversely, the experience of personal abuse proved valuable, no doubt, in enabling him to cope with even less savoury insults following his incarceration in mid 1990/91, his response being a succession of towering performances on the road to another League title.

However, in fairness to Tony's more reasonable critics, it should be admitted that he is *not* the complete all-rounder, sometimes diving in with challenges when he might be better advised to stand off and, despite a marked advance, he will never emulate the touch and poise of a David O'Leary. But the man who was capped by England at the age of 20, was voted young player of the year in 1987, and succeeded Kenny Sansom as club captain during 1987/88, looked ever more impressive during the early nineties, his game showing more refinement without losing its cutting edge.

In David Platt's absence, he skippered England in 1994, by which time he had overcome a blip in his international progress caused, perhaps, by premature selection. But of infinitely more concern to Highbury regulars was their man's undiminished dedication to the Arsenal cause, even after admitting to alcoholism in 1996. He faced his latest problems squarely and emerged as a leaner, less mean, scarcely less effective performer than the snarling warrior of yesteryear. Has any public figure shown more dignity in fighting back from addiction than Tony Adams, who discarded his macho mask and reassessed his values so movingly? No – and that stands as his greatest achievement of all.

BORN: Romford, Essex, 10.10.66. GAMES: 504 (6). GOALS: 39.
HONOURS: European Cup Winners' Cup 93/4; League Championship 88/9, 90/1; FA Cup 92/3; League Cup 86/7, 92/3. 47 England caps (87–).

1983/84 –

NIGEL WINTERBURN

As Arsenal challenged boldly for honours during George Graham's managerial pomp, the adventurous exploits of Nigel Winterburn offered vivid evidence of the changing face of football tactics. Not that overlapping defenders had been newly invented but, with or without the security of a sweeper system behind him, the dapper left-back made far more frequent forays into enemy territory than had his predecessors in a more orthodox age.

Indeed, in some games, such as the December 1990 clash with Sheffield United, Nigel became the Gunners' most prominent and effective attacker. That day at Highbury, the Blades seized an early initiative, neutralising their hosts' front-runners and midfielders by constant harrying, and reached half-time with a deserved 1-0 lead. After the break, Nigel pushed forward incessantly and transformed the match, his crosses leading to three goals in a 4-1 victory.

Of course, to employ such methods demands superior players, and the consistent, highly-motivated Midlander falls firmly into that category. He has the skill and pace of many a winger, though his raids would be even more threatening if he cut inside more frequently. He can finish, too, as he proved with long-range goals against Norwich and his former club, Wimbledon, on the last lap of the 1988/89 Championship race, though it must be admitted that more recently the Winterburn shot has been distinctly erratic and, consequently perhaps, increasingly rare.

But that is the merest quibble; Nigel has retained his most precious constructive asset, the accuracy of his left-foot distribution, whether whipping wicked centres from byline to goalmouth, or prising open a locked defence with a penetrating through-ball. The latter knack was displayed to invaluable effect in the FA Cup fifth-round tie at Shrewsbury in February 1991 when, after ploughing through 40 yards of Gay Meadow mud, the determined number-three unleashed a raking, long-distance pass to set up Michael Thomas for the winner.

Importantly, Nigel's commitment to going forward does not mean he neglects his defensive duties. He has the stamina to recover his ground rapidly if he loses possession, is a competent tackler, and is adept at blocking opponents by neat positional play.

His long-lasting success is a testimony to his self-belief after being released by Birmingham, whom he had joined as an apprentice. Four years with Wimbledon, during which he won England under-21 recognition, established his credentials, but there was no automatic senior slot waiting for him after his £400,000 move to Arsenal in May 1987. Nigel spent much of his first year at Highbury in the reserves before breaking through early in 1988, sometimes in place of the injured Kenny Sansom on the left, but serving also on the right.

Soon it became evident that George Graham had spent wisely, yet the newcomer's most dramatic moment that term saw him fail to convert a crucial penalty at Wembley. Had his low shot beaten Luton 'keeper Andy Dibble, the Gunners would have been 3-1 up with only eight minutes left to play, and, surely, the Littlewoods Cup would have been retained; instead, the Hatters recovered to claim an unlikely triumph. However, there was to be no shortage of trophies at Highbury over the next six years, during which Nigel emphasised his all-round quality with near-metronomic consistency. Indeed, but for the formidable Stuart Pearce, the ex-Don must have garnered considerably more than his two full caps.

Supplanting such a polished performer as Kenny Sansom, who was sold soon after his successor had settled into the Arsenal team, was a truly daunting challenge which Nigel met with distinction. By 1996/97, at 33, he remained sprightly enough to hold his own in most company, even seeming to reverse the ageing process by eliminating slight signs of vulnerability which had crept into his game during the previous term. Clearly, it would take an exceptional player to dislodge Nigel Winterburn.

BORN: Nuneaton, Warwickshire, 11.12.63. GAMES: 449 (1). GOALS: 10.
HONOURS: European Cup Winners' Cup 93/4; League Championship 88/9, 90/1; FA Cup 92/3; League Cup 92/3. 2 England caps (89-93).
OTHER CLUBS: Wimbledon 83/4-86/7 (165, 8).

1987/88 –

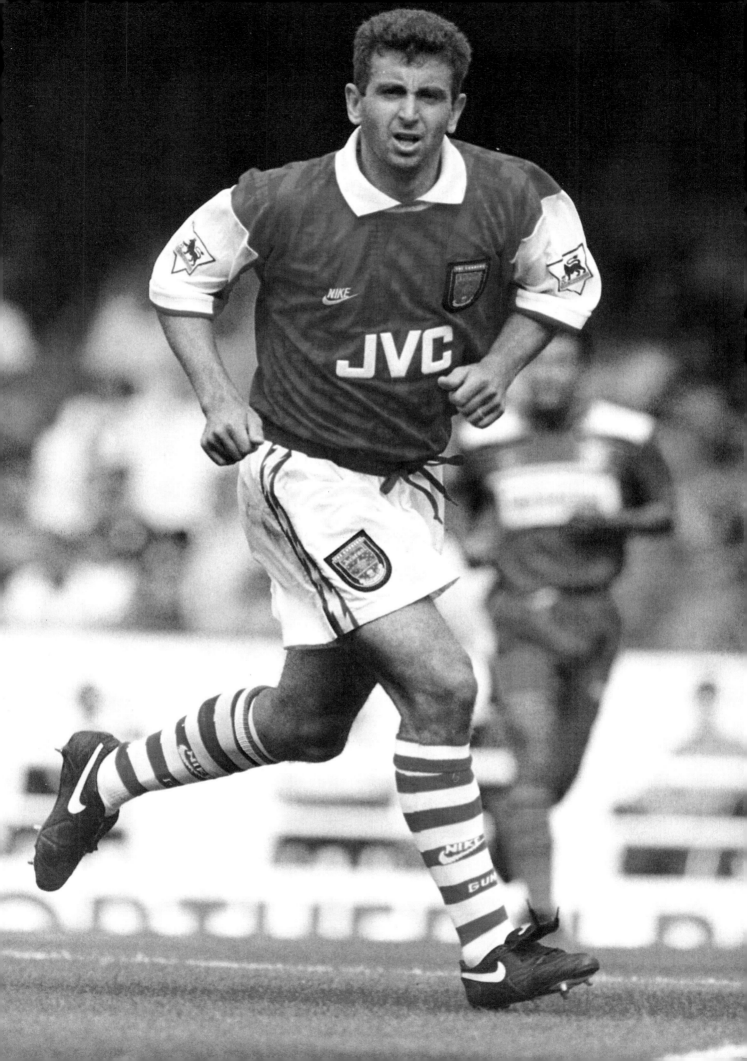

STEVE BOULD

Unobtrusive excellence, even over lengthy periods, is not the stuff of which popular heroes are made. Take the case of Steve Bould. As Arsenal won the Championship twice in three years, the lean, lantern-jawed stopper was, for the most part, a study in streetwise magnificence, an inelegant but unremittingly effective monument to consistency. Yet when it came to public recognition, he was not so much unsung as ignored.

Eventually a shaft of limelight filtered in Steve's direction following his man-of-the-match show in the 1994 Cup Winners' Cup Final victory over Parma and his belated England call-up a week later. Until then, even when his name cropped up among devoted Gunners fans, invariably it was for the purposes of unfavourable comparison with more fashionable players whom, it was contended, were more cultured or constructive, or easier on the eye. In professional circles, however, especially at Highbury, there were no such reservations. Among his peers Steve has long been respected as a key component of a famously mean rearguard, a man whose approach is devoid of frills but devastatingly effective, and without whom the side would be infinitely more vulnerable.

Arsenal recruited the 6ft 3in centre-half from Stoke City, his hometown club, in the summer of 1988, a transfer tribunal setting the fee at £390,000. When the new season got under way, Steve lost little time in justifying the Victoria Ground case for more cash, his aggression and power offering a daunting prospect to all who would seek a way through the North Londoners' defence. The manager varied his line-up as tactics demanded, but when it became clear that David O'Leary could no longer count on automatic selection, there were howls of outrage from fans of the talented and long-serving Irishman.

Inevitably, the critics focused their discontent on the newcomer, claiming that his tackling was crude and that he conceded needless free-kicks in dangerous situations. They also slammed his passing ability and complained that he could not match their hero's pace. Even after he had made 30 appearances in the 1988/89 Championship campaign, his work tended to be damned by faint praise, and few bemoaned his absence when fitness eluded him during much of the subsequent term.

But, for those who needed it, incontrovertible evidence of his true value was on the way. Undeterred by the arrival in the 1990 close season of £1.2 million Andy Linighan, whom many predicted would remove the former Potter permanently from the first-team reckoning, Steve rose to new heights. In retaining his place, not only did he display the stern efficiency that had become his hallmark, but also revealed the fruits of hard work on all aspects of his game. Where once he had been content to hoof his clearances in the general direction of Alan Smith's head, the new, improved Bould was ready and able, when commonsense allowed, to trap the ball and push it confidently to an unmarked colleague. Never was his progress more evident than during the midwinter absence of Tony Adams, his regular partner in the middle of Arsenal's back four. Steve revelled in the extra responsibility, and a measure of his influence was the way the defence rocked when injury forced him to leave the action in the February encounter with Chelsea in which the Gunners finally surrendered their unbeaten League record. In attack, while rarely finding a place on the scoresheet himself, Steve has been an important weapon in the Arsenal armoury, being particularly dangerous on the near post at set pieces.

The longer he has played at the top level, the more of a bargain he has proved to be. Of course, he will have to go one day and there were a few indications of declining powers during his injury-disrupted 1995/96 campaign. But new boss Arsene Wenger was too wise to write him off, realising that it would take one mighty fine performer to replace Steve Bould. Messrs Linighan, Pates, Keown and Marshall would all testify to that.

BORN: Stoke-on-Trent, Staffordshire, 16.11.62. GAMES: 299 (12). GOALS: 8.
HONOURS: European Cup Winners' Cup 93/4; League Championship 88/9, 90/1.
2 England caps (94).

OTHER CLUBS: Stoke City 81/2-87/8 (183, 6); Torquay United on loan 82/3 (9, 0).

1988/89 —

PAUL MERSON

The smile said it all – the one which habitually adorned the face of Paul Merson during 1996/97, the one which proclaimed the simple joy of living, and of playing football with all the immense flair and imagination at his disposal.

What twists and turns remain in the turbulent, often tortured tale of the gifted Londoner, none can say. But for now, at least, here is a performer who can illuminate any stage with flashes of breathtaking inspiration, one who has emerged from the darkness that engulfed him off the pitch, threatening his Highbury future, his career, even his life.

That Paul has stepped back from the abyss of drugs, drink and gambling to resume his soccer duties is wondrous to record. At the time of writing, with more than two years of successful rehabilitation behind him, hope is burning bright, though the road to redemption remains long and strewn with pitfalls.

As a young striker, Paul had exhibited a mixture of bountiful promise and worrying inconsistency. He made his senior Arsenal debut in November 1986 but it was for Brentford that he played his first full League game, during a loan spell in spring '87. On his return from Griffin Park he was drafted straight into top-flight action, scoring three times in five starts before the end of the campaign. Paul extended his experience with intermittent appearances thereafter, before establishing himself with verve and enterprise as the title was won in 1988/89.

By then the Merson momentum was gathering at breakneck pace. He was the PFA's young player of the year in 1989 and under-21 caps began to pile up. It was easy to see why: Paul was not only quick and eager, strong and skilful; he was also capable of the unexpected and the spectacular. But predictions of early elevation to stardom proved premature. After a bright start to 1989/90, the precocious swashbuckler's form declined alarmingly in the winter, pressure built up, and he was dropped.

Happily, a renaissance was imminent. Paul began the next season in determined mood and soon he was doing justice once more to his abundant talent. Goals began to accumulate, though his contribution went way beyond finding the net. Whether roaming freely, probing for openings and exchanging quickfire passes with Alan Smith and Anders Limpar, or lying deeper and either running at defences or undoing them with searching, diagonal passes, he was a key figure in another Championship triumph.

By late 1991/92 Paul was irresistible. He won a deserved full England call-up and seemed on the threshold of a thrilling prime. But then the script went awry. In 1992/93 his form became erratic for reasons which would become shockingly evident. During the next campaign he began to gain weight alarmingly and his displays became ever more wayward. Clearly hard work and a new direction were needed urgently, but it was not until November '94 that the scale of his predicament was revealed.

That midwinter was bleak, indeed, for Paul as he underwent intensive therapy for his addictions. Many believed he was finished, but he emerged from his ordeal – at least, that stage of it – to return to League service in the February, thereafter retaining his place for more than 100 successive games until sidelined by a hernia in spring '97. He was accorded a rapturous homecoming by the Gooners, who have always warmed to him, even when he has been found wanting. Yes, they adore his mercurial brilliance but, beyond that, they love about their 'Merse' a certain impudence which is often as apparent on his face as in his game.

To his credit he has striven ceaselessly under both Bruce Rioch and Arsene Wenger, whether operating wide on either flank or in a roving midfield role. At first Merson Mk II played merely responsibly and sensibly, but has since gone on to light up Highbury as of old and he earned a recall to the England squad in autumn '96. Paul owes a mammoth debt of gratitude to Arsenal and their supporters which, at 29, he is young enough to repay. His salvation, or otherwise, is in his own hands.

BORN: Brent, London, 20.3.68. GAMES: 378 (44). GOALS: 99.
HONOURS: European Cup Winners' Cup 93/4; League Championship 88/9, 90/1; FA Cup 92/3; League Cup 92/3. 15 England caps (91–).

OTHER CLUBS: Brentford on loan 86/7 (7, 0).

1986/87 –

ANDERS LIMPAR

Legions of Arsenal fans, bewitched by Anders Limpar's coruscating contribution to the 1991 title triumph, reckoned that the Swedish imp was heaven sent; George Graham might have contended that managerial expertise had something to do with the mercurial entertainer's arrival in North London in the summer of 1990. Either way, the £1.3 million signing from unfashionable Italian club Cremonese brought a much-needed new dimension to a Gunners side that was irreproachably industrious and efficient, but distinctly lacking in audacity and the capacity to surprise. Thus there were heavy hearts among Highbury regulars when the relationship between player and boss deteriorated distressingly, culminating in Anders' £1.6 million sale to Everton in March 1994.

The Swede had made an instant impact on the English game that had exceeded most expectations. Few knew more about him than vague newspaper descriptions of a ball-juggling midfielder, and most supporters were prepared to reserve judgement while the 25-year-old international settled in. Their patience, though admirable, was not to be needed, as Anders offered ample swift explanation of George's tenacity in pursuing his talented quarry for 18 months before completing the deal.

Operating on Arsenal's left flank – he played on the right for his country, and Cremonese had employed him in the centre – the newcomer exhibited all the thrilling skills and mesmeric charm of an old-fashioned winger, threw in the zest and persistence of the most dynamic prompter, and completed a captivating cocktail with lethal shooting power. He possessed the god-given knack of turning games that were apparently deadlocked, such as a dour November encounter at Coventry which was goalless until he plundered the points with a brace of unstoppable edge-of-the-box strikes in the dying minutes.

The rapier-like Anders presented a bewildering set of problems for defenders. Invariably in total control of the ball – which he had a habit of rolling forward ominously with the sole of his boot before launching into a twisting, tormenting dribble – he could pass incisively with either foot, wreak havoc with smooth changes of direction, and conjure openings where none seemed to exist.

On the debit side was a tendency to produce his best form only in spasms, and sometimes he was guilty of reacting petulantly to the robust attentions of bemused markers. More combustible in the Italian tradition than stoical in typically Scandinavian manner, Anders attracted criticism for protracted protests to referees – his English is perfect – and some opponents felt aggrieved by dramatic penalty-area tumbles.

Such occasional misunderstandings, inevitable for an overseas player in his first British campaign, did nothing to mar his exhilarating early achievements, but during the following term the script began to go awry. Limpar and Graham became involved in embarrassing public acrimony over Anders' release for internationals and the peace between them seemed uneasy ever after. Come 1992/93, George was accusing the Swede of lack of application and the wingman's confidence appeared to drain away. He was in and out of the side and, even when selected, he seemed something of an outsider, as though colleagues were unwilling to entrust the ball to his custody. Such a situation could not continue and the inevitable parting of the ways occurred.

Here was an artist who could offer lyrical moments of pure joy – the likes of his 45-yard lobbed goal at home to Liverpool in April 1992 – but who could frustrate appallingly. Though George Graham's decision to sell was understandable in the circumstances, the English game owes it to the fans to accommodate such talents as Anders Limpar wherever possible. The alternative is too dull to contemplate.

BORN: Solna, Sweden, 24.9.65. GAMES: 95 (20). GOALS: 20.
HONOURS: League Championship 90/1. 52 Sweden caps.
OTHER CLUBS: Orgryte, Sweden; Young Boys, Switzerland 88/9; Cremonese, Italy, 89/90; Everton 93/4-96/7 (66, 5); Birmingham City 96/7 (4, 0).

1990/91 – 1993/94

MARTIN KEOWN

1985/86 & 1992/93 –

Scuttling awkwardly around the pitch like some crabby truant-catcher in grim pursuit of his victim, Martin Keown does not cut an heroic figure. Indeed, there is something about his very presence, a kind of reverse charisma, which makes the versatile, deceptively athletic Oxonian an inviting target for those who would ridicule all things Arsenal. Yet while he is clearly not a born entertainer – no one would argue with that – the much-maligned Martin *is* an impeccable professional whose standard of effectiveness and reliability rarely falters.

His most frequent berth has been in central defence, where his enviable pace, incisive tackle and ability to spring from a standing start have outweighed a sometimes maddening lack of passing ambition, though doubtless managerial instructions have had some bearing on this. Martin has excelled, too, as a man-marker in midfield, his knack of neutralising attractive opponents contributing to his joyless image.

In view of today's curmudgeonly perception of Martin, it is fascinating to recall how he was viewed after breaking into Arsenal's side as a teenager in 1985/86. Then he was lauded as a neat and constructive operator and tipped as a long-term partner for David O'Leary. But after only half a season of senior action, he refused to accept the contract offered by George Graham and joined Aston Villa in a £125,000 deal.

Thereafter Martin served Everton, winning an England call-up in the process, before becoming the first player since the war to re-sign for the Gunners, his Highbury return costing £2 million in February 1993. Since then he has missed out on three knockout triumphs – being cup-tied for the 1992/93 'double' and injured when the Cup Winners' Cup was lifted a year later – and has not always remained an automatic choice.

Martin has never been absent from the line-up for long, though, and the mid nineties found him in regular demand, most recently on the right of the back three. Under both Rioch and Wenger, the old Keown solidity remained mostly intact, but was garnished with moments of invention which the crowd adored and which helped to secure an England recall. There was even the occasional nutmeg. Whatever next?

BORN: Oxford, 24.7.66.
GAMES: 189 (26). GOALS: 3.
HONOURS: 12 England caps (92-).

OTHER CLUBS: Brighton and Hove Albion on loan 84/5-85/6 (23, 1); Aston Villa 86/7-88/9 (112, 3); Everton 89/90-92/3 (96, 0).

ANDY LINIGHAN

1990/91 – 1996/97

One incandescent moment of deathless drama transformed Andy Linighan from spare part to Highbury folk hero and won the FA Cup for Arsenal. Sadly for the quietly competent centre-half, it was not enough to secure a regular first-team spot. He had pace and courage, skill and aerial power, but he would never have the 'devil' of Messrs Bould and Adams.

Andy's sudden impact came at the last gasp of extra-time in the Wembley replay against Sheffield Wednesday in 1993: the scores were level, a penalty shoot-out seemingly inevitable, when the stand-in stopper - he was deputising for the injured Bould - hurtled forward to meet Paul Merson's corner with a bullet header that claimed the spoils. The instant was all the more vivid because of Andy's blood-spattered face, the legacy of a first-half crack from Mark Bright's elbow. In truth, the gleeful north-easterner's gory grin at the final whistle offered the happiest memory of a dismal game, but that was not going to detract from the headiest achievement of a career which had lost impetus following his £1.2 million move from Norwich in July 1990.

Having commanded such a hefty fee, the tall, upright newcomer must have expected an early baptism, yet it was December before he started a League game. Chief obstacle was the inspired Bould, and with the likes of Adams and O'Leary also on the scene, poor Andy could be excused if he became frustrated. With the Canaries, he had gained four England 'B' caps and attracted plaudits aplenty for his all-round game. Now it was expected that he would prosper on the grander stage, but he could not match Bould's abrasive edge and it took the unavailability of Adams to give him a settled run. Once in the side, Andy seemed edgy. Though he was generally efficient, his distribution was uncharacteristically erratic and he was dropped after several outings. Given a second chance, he began to settle before injury halted his progress.

There followed further irregular calls to arms, but even after his Wembley boost, Andy was to remain a distinguished reserve until he was allowed to join Crystal Palace in January 1997. As a Gunner he had excelled only spasmodically, though clearly he could have thrived at a level only slightly less exalted. And whatever his shortcomings, Andy Linighan had known the sweetest of moments.

BORN: Hartlepool, County Durham, 18.6.62.
GAMES: 134 (21). GOALS: 8.
HONOURS: FA Cup 92/3; League Cup 92/3.

OTHER CLUBS: Hartlepool United 80/1-83/4 (110, 4); Leeds United 84/5-85/6 (66, 3); Oldham Athletic 85/6-87/8 (87, 6); Norwich City 87/8-89/90 (86, 8); Crystal Palace 96/7- (19, 2).

PAL LYDERSEN

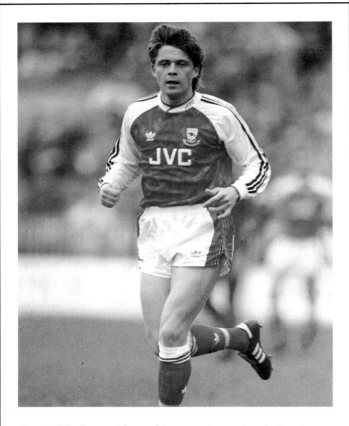

Poor Pal Lydersen. After making scant impression during three and a half largely anonymous years as a Gunner, he was consigned to Highbury history as one of several mysterious question-marks against George Graham's transfer judgement – only to be dragged back into the limelight a few months later in wholly unsavoury circumstances.

When news of the 'bung' scandal broke, the purchase of Pal seemed a mystery no more, but that can have been little comfort to the Norwegian international utility man, an innocent bystander as details of the alleged chicanery unfolded.

Few Arsenal fans had heard of Pal when he was signed for £500,000 from IK Start in November 1991, but when he enjoyed a brief senior run later that term as a right-back deputy for Lee Dixon, most observers were mildly impressed. He was quick for a six-footer and capable in the air, but what took the eye was a quality of distribution that, it must be hoped, was the envy of his midfield colleagues. His short game was neat and crisp, while he could dispatch 60-yard passes, confidently and accurately.

The problem was that his defensive qualities left much to be desired and, faced with the daunting prospect of unseating either Dixon or Nigel Winterburn and unable to win a midfield slot, he slipped out of contention, eventually being freed to rejoin his hometown club in the spring of 1995. Soon came the allegations that Graham had made a personal profit from buying Pal, thus ensuring that the name of Lydersen will be long remembered at Highbury, but for a sad, sad reason.

BORN: Kristiansand, Norway, 10.9.65.
GAMES: 13 (3). GOALS: 0.
Honours: 17 Norway caps.
OTHER CLUBS: IK Start, Norway.

1991/92 – 1992/93

ANDY COLE

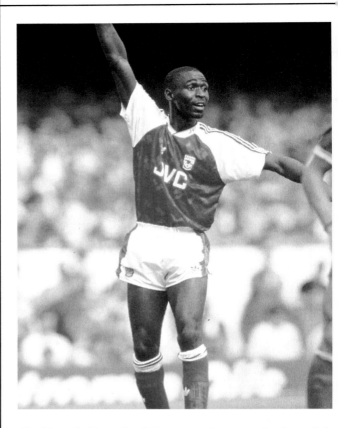

Decisions, decisions. Football managers have to make them all the time and, occasionally, even the canniest boss can drop a clanger. Consider the dilemma facing George Graham in the summer of 1992. Andy Cole was a young striker of immense promise, but with only six minutes of first-team football to his credit. Also on the Highbury books, immeasurably more experienced and well entrenched, were the likes of Ian Wright, Alan Smith, Paul Merson and Kevin Campbell.

What could Graham do? Hang on to the increasingly frustrated Cole, knowing that there was no immediate breakthrough in prospect, or let him seek his fortune elsewhere, with the Gunners pocketing a tidy sum in the process?

With the convenience of hindsight, countless pundits have insisted that Arsenal should have kept Cole and sold Campbell, but that is to ignore the facts at the time. True, Andy was quick, brave and an instinctive finisher, but his strike-rate in the reserves was nowhere near as impressive as Kevin's. Also, Campbell had helped to win the title in 1991 and, though he was destined to disappoint, he was deemed too valuable to release at that stage.

Accordingly, the self-confident Cole was sold to Bristol City for £500,000, plus a percentage of any sell-on price. His subsequent form, particularly for Newcastle – the jury is still out following his record-breaking move to Manchester United – appeared to make a nonsense of Graham's judgement. A mistake? Perhaps, but an understandable one.

BORN: Nottingham, 15.10.71. GAMES: 0 (1). GOALS: 0.
HONOURS: 1 England cap (95).
OTHER CLUBS: Fulham on loan 91/2 (13, 3); Bristol City 91/2–92/3 (41, 20); Newcastle United 92/3–94/5 (70, 55); Manchester United 94/5– (72, 29).

1990/91

KEVIN CAMPBELL

1987/88 – 1994/95

The poignant case of Kevin Campbell offers vivid proof that youthful promise, no matter how vibrant, can dissolve demoralisingly into frustrating mediocrity.

As a teenage marksman, the muscular Londoner was a veritable prodigy. He shattered club scoring records at youth level, netted 94 times in 89 reserve outings and then exploded on to the senior scene with a series of raw but periodically thrilling contributions in the late eighties.

When his eight strikes in a ten-game spell in the spring of 1991 proved a crucial factor in Arsenal's title triumph, it seemed that Kevin's apprenticeship was complete.

It wasn't just his goals which had elated Gooners drooling over their 'new Malcolm Macdonald', they loved everything about his exhilarating game. Brimming with zest and boasting fearful power and pace, Kevin could charge past defenders, brushing them aside like so much matchwood before finishing venomously. True, the Campbell control was no more than adequate, but that was expected to improve with the hard work he was always willing to put in. Here, it seemed, was a player with limitless, almost frightening potential.

But then, imperceptibly at first, it all began to go horribly wrong. Though Kevin managed a respectable 13 League goals in 1991/92, he appeared less forceful than before, perhaps being a little in awe of the ebullient new signing, Ian Wright. This trend continued alarmingly into the following term, when the younger man's profligacy in front of goal began to make him a scapegoat for over-critical fans.

Season 1993/94 signalled some improvement, with important goals in the Cup Winners' Cup campaign, but then 1994/95 saw poor Kevin hit rock bottom. His confidence, never the hardiest, now withered pitiably. He remained wholehearted but his work looked crude and predictable; chances would be snatched at and missed, his touch let him down repeatedly and frequently his reading of the game was woeful.

It seemed that Kevin was stuck on a plateau from which he was not going to rise; it was time to go. In the summer of 1995 a £2.5 million deal took him to Nottingham Forest where, all his friends at Highbury hoped fervently, he might recover some of that early impetus.

BORN: Lambeth, London, 4.2.70. GAMES: 164 (62). GOALS: 59. HONOURS: European Cup Winners' Cup 93/4; League Championship 90/1; FA Cup 92/3; League Cup 92/3.

OTHER CLUBS: Leyton Orient on loan 88/9 (16, 9); Leicester City on loan 89/90 (11, 5). Nottingham Forest 95/6- (38, 9).

PAUL GORMAN

RAY HANKIN

DAVID MADDEN

JOHN KAY

DANNY O'SHEA

DAVID CORK

PAUL GORMAN 1981/82 - 1983/84

Midfielder. BORN: Dublin, 6.8.63. GAMES: 5(1).
GOALS: 0. OTHER CLUBS: Birmingham City 84/5 (6,0); Carlisle
United 84/5-89/90 (148, 7); Shelbourne, Republic of Ireland, on loan
89/90; Shrewsbury Town 90/1- (30, 0).

RAY HANKIN 1981/82

Striker. BORN: Wallsend, Tyneside, 2.2.56. GAMES: 0 (2). GOALS: 0.
OTHER CLUBS: Burnley 72/3-76/7 (112, 37); Leeds United 76/7-
79/80 (83, 32); Vancouver Whitecaps, Canada; Middlesbrough 82/3 (21,
1); Peterborough United 83/4-84/5 (33, 8); Wolverhampton Wanderers
84/5 (10, 1).

JOHN KAY 1982/83 - 1983/84

Full-back. BORN: Sunderland, 29.1.64. GAMES: 13 (1). GOALS: 0.
OTHER CLUBS: Wimbledon 84/5-86/7 (63, 2); Middlesbrough on
loan 84/5 (8, 0); Sunderland 87/8-93/4 (199, 0); Shrewsbury Town on
loan 95/6 (8, 0); Scarborough 96/7- (34, 0).

DANNY O'SHEA 1982/83

Midfielder. BORN: Kennington, London, 26.3.63. GAMES: 9.
GOALS: 0. OTHER CLUBS: Charlton Athletic 84/5 (9, 0); Exeter
City 84/5 (45, 2); Southend United 85/6-88/9 (118, 12); Cambridge
United 89/90-94/5 (203, 1); Northampton Town 94/5- (80, 1).

DAVID CORK 1983/84

Forward. BORN: Doncaster, Yorkshire, 28.10.62. GAMES: 6 (2).
GOALS: 1. OTHER CLUBS: Huddersfield Town 85/6-87/8 (110, 25);
West Bromwich Albion on loan 88/9 (4, 0); Scunthorpe United 88/9
(15, 0); Darlington 90/1 (33, 8).

DAVID MADDEN 1983/84

Midfielder. BORN: Stepney, London, 6.1.63. GAMES: 2. GOALS:
0. OTHER CLUBS: Bournemouth on loan 82/3 (5, 0); Charlton
Athletic 84/5 (20, 1); Los Angeles, USA; Reading 87/8 (9, 1);
Crystal Palace 88/9-89/90 (27, 5); Birmingham City on loan 89/90
(5, 1); Maidstone United 90/1 (10, 0).

BRIAN SPARROW 1983/84

Utility. BORN: Bethnal Green, London, 24.6.62. GAMES: 2.
GOALS: 0. OTHER CLUBS: Wimbledon on loan 82/3 (17, 1);
Millwall on loan 83/4 (5, 2); Gillingham on loan 83/84 (5, 1);
Crystal Palace 84/5-86/7 (63, 2).

BRIAN SPARROW

RHYS WILMOT

LEE HARPER

KWAME AMPADU

GAVIN McGOWAN

RHYS WILMOT 1985/86 – 1986/87

Goalkeeper. BORN: Newport, South Wales, 21.2.62. GAMES: 9.
GOALS: 0. OTHER CLUBS: Hereford United on loan 82/3 (9, 0);
Orient on loan 84/5 (46, 0); Swansea City on loan 88/9 (16, 0);
Plymouth Argyle on loan 88/9 (17, 0); Plymouth Argyle 89/90–91/2
(116, 0); Grimsby town 92/3; Crystal Palace 94/5 (6, 0); Torquay
United 96/7 (34, 0).

KWAME AMPADU 1989/90

Midfielder. BORN: Bradford, Yorkshire, 20.11.70. GAMES: 0 (2).
GOALS: 1. OTHER CLUBS: Plymouth Argyle on loan 90/1 (6, 1);
West Bromwich Albion on loan 90/1 (7, 0); West Bromwich Albion
91/2–93/4 (42, 3); Swansea City 93/4– (128, 11).

SIGGI JONSSON 1989/90 – 1990/91

Midfielder. BORN: Iceland, 27.9.66. GAMES: 3 (6). GOALS: 1.
HONOURS: Iceland caps. OTHER CLUBS: Akranes, Iceland;
Sheffield Wednesday 84/5–88/9 (67, 4); Barnsley on loan 85/6 (5, 0).

LEE HARPER 1996/97 –

Goalkeeper. BORN: London, 30.10.71. GAMES: 1. GOALS: 0.

GAVIN McGOWAN 1992/93 –

Defender. BORN: Blackheath, Kent, 16.1.76. GAMES: 4 (2). GOALS:
0. OTHER CLUBS: Luton on loan 96/7 (2, 0).

MATTHEW ROSE 1995/96 – 1996/97

Defender. BORN: Dartford, Kent, 24.9.75. GAMES: 2 (3). GOALS: 0.

NICOLAS ANELKA 1996/97 –

Forward. BORN: Paris, 14.3.79. GAMES: 0 (4). GOALS: 0.
OTHER CLUBS: Paris St-Germain, France, 95/6–96/7.

SIGGI JONSSON

NICOLAS ANELKA

MATTHEW ROSE

JIMMY CARTER

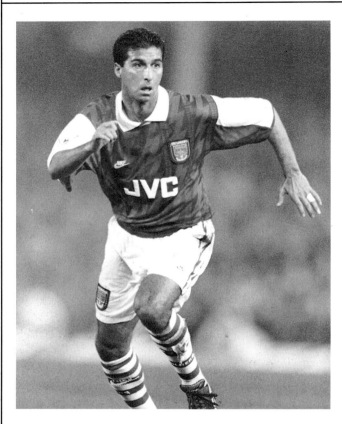

Jimmy Carter's £500,000 move from Liverpool to Arsenal in October 1991 prompted a sharp question from puzzled Arsenal fans: 'If he's not good enough for them, why is he good enough for us?' Sadly, it wasn't long before their scepticism was justified; clearly, the fast but frustrating flankman wasn't good enough for either. Bedding in at Highbury was never going to be easy for the lithe Londoner, who had looked so impressive for Millwall before flopping at Anfield. He arrived at a time when the Gunners' defence of their League title was floundering, and only instant brilliance would have satisfied the more restive elements in the crowd. What they got from Jimmy was an apparent shortage of ideas and a failure to capitalise on his undoubted pace and skill.

From his position on the touchline he was not insulated from the more unkind comments and his already fragile confidence appeared to hit the depths. To be fair, he would have needed prodigious resolve to have prospered in a role illuminated so frequently by Anders Limpar; sadly, that was a quality Jimmy seemed not to possess.

The nearest he came to glory was a disallowed injury-time goal against Wrexham in January 1992. If that had stood he would have averted Arsenal's deepest modern FA Cup humiliation and the fans would have had something, at least, to remember him by. As it was, when he was freed to join Portsmouth in May 1995, he left them with nothing. Away from the Premiership spotlight, he recaptured some of the elan that had lit up his Millwall days. Jimmy Carter had returned to his true level.

BORN: Hammersmith, London, 9.11.65.
GAMES: 21 (8). GOALS: 2.
OTHER CLUBS: Millwall 86/7-90/1 (110, 10); Liverpool 90/1 (5, 0); Oxford United on loan 93/4 (5, 0) and 94/5 (4, 0); Portsmouth 95/6- (62, 5).

1991/92 – 1994/95

NEIL HEANEY

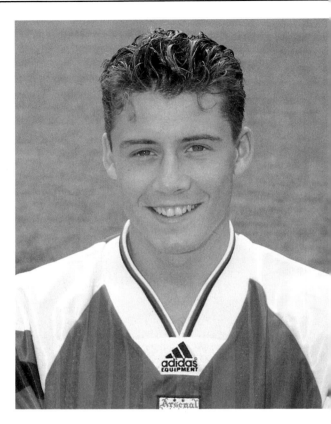

Neil Heaney was a young flankman of enviable all-round talent, but who needed the knowhow only first-team experience would have brought. Perversely, a settled run at senior level was always likely to elude the rather inconsistent rookie during the early nineties, a period when constant trophy-seeking discouraged George Graham from experimentation.

The personable Teessider had been something of a prodigy, helping the Gunners win the FA Youth Cup in 1988 while still on schoolboy forms. His splendid progress continued as he earned four England under-21 caps despite then having only one senior appearance for Arsenal to his credit - when he came off the bench as a substitute for Anders Limpar at Sheffield United in April 1992 - and expectations soared.

Indeed, Neil had much to offer. He could master the ball with either foot and thus was able to operate down either touchline; he carried a ferocious shot, was quick, strong and industrious, and was more adept at aerial combat than most wingers.

True, he needed to think more about his game, perhaps tone down his helter-skelter approach slightly, but many Highbury regulars agreed that the rudiments of a fine player were in place. However, they were to be deprived of witnessing the next stage of his development when the manager sold him to Southampton for £300,000 in March 1994. A further move followed, to Manchester City, and it seemed likely that Maine Road would play host to the make-or-break years of Neil Heaney's career.

BORN: Middlesbrough, Yorkshire, 3.11.71.
GAMES: 4 (4). GOALS: 0.
OTHER CLUBS: Hartlepool United on loan 90/1 (3, 0); Cambridge United on loan 91/2 (13, 2); Southampton 93/4-96/7 (61, 5); Manchester City 96/7- (15, 1).

1991/92 – 1993/94

PAUL DICKOV

MARK FLATTS

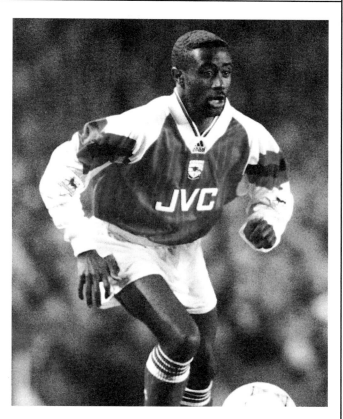

Play him or sell him: that was the acute dilemma facing Arsenal over ebullient young marksman Paul Dickov in 1996. Reluctantly, but understandably in view of the fierce competition for striking places at Highbury, they took the latter course. Quick and skilful, brave and bursting with brio, the tiny, scurrying Scottish under-21 international had been on the fringe of the senior side for three years, invariably impressing whenever he was given a chance. There were sharply-taken goals against Crystal Palace and Spurs at the tail-end of 1992/93, a smart brace in the 2-0 League Cup victory over Oldham at Highbury in November 1994 and, best of all, an effervescent display and an opportunist's goal when called on as a second-half substitute at home to Sheffield Wednesday a year later.

Following that last-mentioned strike, one newspaper headline proclaimed 'King Dickov', the accompanying report extolling his all-round virtues and transparent desire for success, but still his frustration did not abate. With Wright, Bergkamp and Merson all fixtures in the team, and with Hartson lurking, Paul was consigned once more to the reserves and the question-mark over his future loomed ever larger.

Clearly, the 5ft 6in front-man could have done with a few extra inches, but he lacked nothing else and the history of the game is littered with players of similar stature who have scaled the soccer heights. However, with his 24th birthday looming, and with no sign of an extended first-team run on the horizon, it became inevitable that if Paul Dickov was destined for stardom, he would have to achieve it away from Highbury. A £1 million move to Manchester City in August 1996 gave him the opportunity he so richly deserved.

BORN: Glasgow, 1.11.72. GAMES: 8 (17). GOALS: 6.
OTHER CLUBS: Luton Town on loan 93/4 (15, 1); Brighton on loan 93/4 (8, 5); Manchester City 96/7- (29, 5).

Players with far less ability than Mark Flatts have achieved infinitely more. At this stage of the bounteously gifted Londoner's possible footballing lifespan, that need not be an epitaph; but there is a growing likelihood that, unless the former England youth international gets to grips with his game in the near future, his vast potential will remain frustratingly untapped.

More of a traditional winger than a modern midfielder, Mark has the capacity to destroy a defence with two-footed trickery and a sudden turn of pace that is deceptive in one who moves with such easy fluidity. Manchester City were his victims at Maine Road in January 1993 when, deputising for the injured Anders Limpar on the left flank, he tormented poor Terry Phelan all afternoon before jinking past two opponents to lay on the only goal of the game for Paul Merson.

On other days, though, Mark would irritate Arsenal fans and management alike by his failure to supply a telling final ball, or to get a shot on goal after reaching a promising position. Also, he never relished tackling back, which is seen as a huge minus on any footballer's balance sheet at Highbury, and he could squander possession with apparent nonchalance, a defect which no coach could tolerate for long.

After bright form in 1992/93, Mark never contributed more than flashes of flair, merely hinting at brilliance rather than achieving it. Inevitably, he slipped down the Arsenal pecking order and was freed in 1996. Clearly, he had the talent to redeem the situation, but did he have the will? And, most pertinently of all by 1997, which club would give him the chance?

BORN: Islington, London, 14.10.72. GAMES: 10 (8). GOALS: 0.
OTHER CLUBS: Cambridge United on loan 93/4 (5, 1); Brighton on loan 93/4 (10, 1); Bristol City on loan 94/5 (6, 0); Grimsby Town on loan 95/6 (5, 0).

1992/93 – 1996/97

1992/93 – 1994/95

DAVID SEAMAN

'I paid top money and I got a top goalkeeper.' So spoke George Graham after one of David Seaman's many faultless displays during his first season between the Arsenal posts, the manager's matter-of-fact manner tacitly questioning why anyone should be remotely surprised at the vindication of his judgement. Yet in the spring of 1990, when George had announced his intention of replacing the popular and extremely able John Lukic, there *had* been a groundswell of doubt among large numbers of Highbury loyalists. Why, went the argument, get rid of a player who has proved himself in the most testing of battles - for the League Championship - and replace him with a man who would offer, at the most, only slightly higher quality? The answer, of course, is self evident. If there was an improvement to be had, then the ambitious Scot wanted it for Arsenal, and with all due respect to the admirable Lukic, he got it the day he signed David Seaman.

In terms of financial outlay, the Gunners were getting a bargain. Although David's transfer from Queen's Park Rangers cost £1.3 million, all but £300,000 was offset by the sale of his predecessor to Leeds, so an England international was acquired for the sort of price that might be paid cheerfully for a promising graduate from the lower divisions. The newcomer, however, was very much the finished article, his immense natural gifts honed by experience with four other clubs. Although his first employers, Leeds, had been so satisfied with the progress of another youthful custodian - a certain John Lukic - that they gave David a free transfer, the phlegmatic Yorkshireman had since established an impressive reputation with Peterborough, Birmingham and QPR.

Any doubts about David's ability to supplant a terrace favourite at Highbury were dispelled at the outset of 1990/91. Exuding a genial confidence rarely apparent in the high-pressure world of the First Division, he left supporters in little doubt that if it was humanly possible for a shot to be saved, then he would save it with the minimum of fuss. Likewise, crosses were claimed with calm dexterity, balls were plucked fearlessly from among flailing feet, and attacks were started with instant, incisive distribution. Importantly, too, if he did make a mistake, he remained unruffled, not allowing it to affect his game.

In early 1991, a succession of performances that were sensational even by David's standards did much to keep his side in the hunt for honours. In January at White Hart Lane, a series of reflex stops won a point against Spurs and left Gary Lineker marvelling at a world-class show; in February, four stupendous interventions at Elland Road preserved the North Londoners' interest in the FA Cup and, best of all, an omnipotent display at Anfield frustrated John Barnes and company in full cry, paving the way for a priceless 1-0 League victory. In each of those encounters, the full Seaman repertoire was in frequent demand, but he was equally effective in the closing stages of games in which he had scarcely touched the ball. Time and again he retained concentration to make crucial late contributions, and the error that allowed Lineker to clinch the FA Cup semi-final for Tottenham was wholly untypical.

Rather surprisingly, David appeared fallible at times in 1991/92, but that proved no more than a blip in a subsequent half-decade of sustained excellence. Blunders have been exceedingly rare, even if few will forget his mortifying misjudgement of Nayim's astonishing 50-yard lob which settled the 1995 Cup Winners' Cup Final. However, as loyal team-mates stressed on the night, without David the Gunners would never have survived to face Real Zaragoza in the first place. After all, he had shrugged off the pain of broken ribs to perform heroically in the quarter-final victory over Auxerre, then stopped three penalties in the semi-final shoot-out against Parma.

The occasional critic has muttered that the affable six-footer - who became something of a national institution through his heroics for England during Euro '96 - is too laid-back, that he needs a threat to his position, but his record and his reputation scream otherwise. It would take an awesomely exacting taskmaster to be dissatisfied with David Seaman.

BORN: Rotherham, Yorkshire, 19.9.63. GAMES: 337. GOALS: 0.
HONOURS: European Cup Winners' Cup 93/4; League Championship 90/1; FA Cup 92/3; League Cup 92/3. 33 England caps (88-).
OTHER CLUBS: Peterborough United 82/3-84/5 (91, 0); Birmingham City 84/5-85/6 (75, 0); Queen's Park Rangers 86/7-89/80 (141, 0).

1990/91 –

IAN WRIGHT

Ian Wright is a star. The word is chronically overused, and therefore devalued, but it fits this effervescent executioner to perfection. Unashamedly theatrical and with an ego as wide as his smile, he is a swaggering, volatile entertainer touched by a streak of rebelliousness which, like him or not, adds to his allure. Most of all, though, he is a goal-scorer made in heaven, among the finest the English game has seen.

Yet, ironically, when Ian moved from Crystal Palace to Arsenal in September 1991, there were critics who wondered whether the £2.5 million fee might be excessive for a 28-year-old. To be fair, it was a question worth the asking, but George Graham - not a man known for frittering away large sums of money - had no doubts, and his judgement was vindicated to the tune of some 173 goals in 252 starts

That ratio is staggering, yet it tells only half the story of Ian's contribution. What will linger in the memory when mere statistics have faded is the sensational manner of so many Wright strikes. Favourites differ from fan to fan, but this writer would select a sequence of almost balletic action which left onlookers slack-jawed at Highbury in August '93. Ian ran on to a Seaman clearance, juggling the ball from foot to foot before flipping it over the head of Everton's Matt Jackson; then the impudent predator snaked past his mesmerised marker before dispatching an audacious first-time lob beyond Neville Southall. The artistry was exquisite, the effect was deadly - pure Ian Wright.

The man is inspirational, then, and not only on the pitch. As though plugged into some magical independent life-force, he lights up the club when he arrives for work each day, bubbling irrepressibly no matter what the mood of mere mortals around him. The most public manifestations of this natural glee are the extravagant goal celebrations which have become the Wright trademark. The strutting bravado with which he salutes his own success has been denigrated by some but, surely, they are killjoys. His routines are harmless and bring much-needed colour to a modern soccer scene which, so we are told, lacks 'characters'.

It would be idle to deny, though, that there *is* a down-side to Ian's highly-strung nature. No less than ten times in six seasons he has suffered suspensions following petulant eruptions, both physical and verbal, his way of retaliating to wrongs real or imagined. However, having reached his thirties he is not going to change and his employers can do little else but accept that the occasional explosion - and any associated punishment - is all part of the unpredictable but hugely rewarding Wright cocktail.

Perhaps part, at least, of the fire that burns within Ian can be ascribed to his late start as a professional. Having worked as a brickie until he was 20, playing his football at non-League level, he has needed prodigious drive and aggression to reach the top and it is hardly surprising that those qualities have remained prominent in his game. Of course, he would not have travelled far on raw desire alone and his other assets read like a blueprint for the perfect striker. He boasts destructive pace and the deftness to gull defenders at speed; subtlety of touch and sublime finishing ability; and a capacity for invention that has produced some of the most spectacular goals of our time.

Disappointingly, Ian has not excelled in the international arena; also by way of criticism, it's been said that Arsenal have been too reliant on him, that there has been no spread of goals as in the title-winning years, that his presence has transformed the Gunners from League side to cup side. That's a matter for conjecture, but even those who advance the theory cannot blame the player. He has performed the only way he knows how and, on a personal level, could hardly have done better.

Despite establishing a promising rapport with Dennis Bergkamp in 1995/96, it seemed likely that the ebullient Londoner would leave Highbury, following a rumoured rift with Bruce Rioch. In the end it was the manager who departed and Ian enjoyed yet another memorable campaign, blemished only by a poisonous feud with Manchester United goalkeeper Peter Schmeichel. As 1997/98 began he was on the point of eclipsing Cliff Bastin's club scoring record; the Premiership's most tempestuous thirtysomething was showing no signs of slowing down.

BORN: Woolwich, London, 3.11.63. GAMES: 252 (7). GOALS: 173.
HONOURS: FA Cup 92/3; League Cup 92/3. 23 England caps (91-).
OTHER CLUBS: Crystal Palace 85/6-91/2 (225, 89).

1991/92 –

DAVID HILLIER

The Highbury career of David Hillier was a perplexing affair. Arsenal boasted few more accomplished passers during the half-decade following his arrival on the senior scene in time to make a sparky contribution to their 1990/91 title victory. Yet, come 1996, the unobtrusive but subtly effective midfielder found himself transfer-listed, his place in the side apparently dependent on the fitness of others, and it was no surprise when he sought a fresh start with Portsmouth.

True, David's progress had been hindered by injuries and there had been off-the-field problems which can have done little for his peace of mind. It is conceivable that such distractions resulted in a loss of direction and security, causing the accurate and enterprising distribution of earlier years to be replaced by a predictable, safety-first approach which few fans found to their liking. The workaday image was heightened still further by increased attention to ball-winning, an activity for which the waspish Hillier tackle equipped him admirably, and a comparative lack of pace which precluded attacking forays.

To be fair, as Arsenal became increasingly stereotyped in the twilight of George Graham's reign, it's reasonable to presume that David was subjugating his flair on the manager's orders. Indeed, that theory gained some credence in February 1996 with several displays that combined exquisite passing with ceaseless physical effort.

At that time he announced his intention of fighting for his Highbury future, which was encouraging but hardly a situation which might have been envisaged a few years earlier. After skippering the Gunners' 1988 Youth Cup-winning side, he developed rapidly, his composure and two-footed control, allied tellingly with strength and stamina, earned him senior outings in midfield and as an emergency sweeper in 1990/91.

The former proved to be David's forte and he was outstanding in Arsenal's splendid late surge in 1991/92 and during much of the following campaign. His troubles began with ruptured knee ligaments in April 1993, which cost him two Wembley outings, and over the next three years his star never quite regained its ascendancy. In November 1996 his £250,000 move offered new hope, but David Hillier could not afford to fail at Fratton Park.

BORN: Blackheath, Essex, 9.12.69.
GAMES: 108 (26). GOALS: 2.
HONOURS: League Championship 90/1.

OTHER CLUBS: Portsmouth 96/7- (21, 2).

1990/91 – 1996/97

RAY PARLOUR

1991/92 –

Ray Parlour represents the raw material – frantically raw at times – from which close observers of the Highbury scene expect a top midfielder to develop. With that straggly mop of blond curls flapping freely and limbs flailing wildly in every direction, Ray shifts mountains of work, he can tackle like a runaway scythe and his jaggedly menacing thrusts, usually down the right flank, can unsettle the most serene of defences.

There is so much about the Parlour game that is admirable – ceaseless commitment, an all-consuming will to win, ever-improving ball technique, aerial power, prodigious stamina – but still he has plenty to learn. Indeed, if the quantity of his effort has never been in question, it must be admitted that the quality has remained variable. Though Ray's all-round distribution was becoming more reliable by mid decade, his 'final ball' remained a lottery. At best, he could supply the most tantalising of whipped crosses, but too often he was imprecise, causing dire frustration at the end of many a sweet move.

His finishing, too, left plenty to be desired, as proved by his failure to score between a goal at Ipswich in March 1994 and another at home to Sunderland no less than two and a half years later. For an attacking midfielder, that was an abysmal record, especially as Ray's surging runs took him repeatedly into striking range.

Nevertheless, the Parlour potential was enormous, as travelling Gooners realised after watching his towering performance against Liverpool at Anfield in August 1992. In only his third League start, 19-year-old Ray commanded attention, laying on both goals – with a cross for Anders Limpar and a through-ball to Ian Wright – in an uplifting 2-0 victory.

Over subsequent terms he has been in the side more often than not, usually on the right but also performing capably in centre-field, notably during a spell in autumn '95 that was halted only by injury.

Under Arsene Wenger, the stringily resilient forager has pushed forward more than ever before, even doubling his goal tally for the season with an uncharacteristically accurate finish at West Ham in January. If experience brings more thought and composure to his game, and if he can avoid the type of off-duty scrapes which have produced unwelcome headlines in the past, then Ray Parlour should be a considerable Arsenal asset for the foreseeable future.

BORN: Romford, Essex, 7.3.73.
GAMES: 134 (41). GOALS: 7. HONOURS:
FA Cup 92/3; League Cup 92/3.

STEVE MORROW

It's monstrously unfair, of course, but it seems inevitable that Steve Morrow will be remembered better as the victim of a freak Wembley mishap than for his endlessly diligent efforts as an Arsenal utility man during the early and middle nineties.

The bizarre incident transformed what should have been the happiest day of the young Ulsterman's career to that point into a frightening, almost surreal interlude. The Gunners had just beaten Sheffield Wednesday in the 1993 League Cup Final and as the players cavorted joyously around the pitch, no doubt Steve was reflecting on his close-range strike which had won the match. It had been his first goal for Arsenal and had capped a fine midfield display in which he had neutralised the creative John Sheridan.

Then came the accident that halted the celebrations and ended Steve's season. The hero of the hour slipped from his skipper's grasp, broke his arm in the fall and then needed oxygen as his senses swam. He went on to make a full recovery but his most productive spell in the side to date had been interrupted traumatically.

That was a shame because Steve's progress had not been rapid since he had arrived in North London as a schoolboy in 1984. Indeed, so difficult did he find it to break into George Graham's successful squad that the quietly-spoken six-footer had already won full caps for Northern Ireland and been loaned to Reading before he made his senior Gunners debut as a substitute at Norwich in April 1992.

The following winter, Steve enjoyed a seven-match stint deputising for Nigel Winterburn at left-back, impressing with his tackling, aerial ability and sensible left-footed distribution. Thereafter most of his opportunities came in midfield, notably as a stand-in for John Jensen against Parma in the 1994 Cup Winners' Cup Final, when he excelled in a disciplined holding role in front of the back four.

Steve, who was also competent in central defence, was not the type to light up a game with a flash of magic, but he was reliability personified and many fans were sorry when Stewart Houston took him to Queen's Park Rangers for £500,000 in March 1997.

BORN: Belfast, 2.7.70. GAMES: 52 (33). GOALS: 6. HONOURS: European Cup Winners' Cup 93/4; League Cup 92/3. 27 Northern Ireland caps (90-).

OTHER CLUBS: Reading on loan 90/1 (10, 0); Watford on loan 91/2 (8, 0); Reading on loan 91/2 (3, 0); Barnet on loan 91/2 (1, 0); Queen's Park Rangers 96/7- (5, 1).

1991/92 – 1996/97

IAN SELLEY

1992/93 —

Ian Selley was emerging as one of the brighter sparks in Arsenal's crowded stable of thrusting young midfielders – a group renowned more for energy than enterprise, it must be said – when his light was dimmed, cruelly and suddenly, one dank and joyless Highbury afternoon in February 1995.

The wiry, agile 20-year-old, who had earned lavish praise for his spirit, mobility and skill in the latter stages of the Gunners' triumphant European Cup Winners' Cup campaign of 1993/94, suffered a shattered leg in a crunching accidental collision with Leicester City's Iwan Roberts and was consigned to the sidelines for more than a year.

It was a chronic setback for the England under-21 international, whose neat control, biting tackles and ceaseless industry offered a solid foundation for the perceptive, still-improving distribution which looked like giving him a distinct edge over many of his Highbury contemporaries.

A splendid, versatile all-round athlete who had deputised ably as a goalkeeper at youth and reserve-team level, Ian made his senior entrance as an 18-year-old at home to Blackburn Rovers in September 1992, going on to finish that term as a non-playing substitute in both League and FA Cup Finals.

Opportunities proved more plentiful in 1993/94, with Continental competition bringing the best out of him, notably at Highbury in the second leg of the semi-final against Paris St Germain.

Though the summer signing of Stefan Schwarz had restricted his progress towards a regular place, Ian made a further telling European contribution – the meaty volley that proved to be the winner against Brondby in the Cup Winners' Cup in November '94 – before that fateful clash with Leicester's Welshman laid him low.

The only consolation was that Ian Selley had youth on his side and could be expected to come again. Sure enough, after a stint on loan with Southend United midway through 1996/97, he returned to Highbury and earned a place on the substitutes' bench in the spring. But whether he figures in Arsene Wenger's long-term calaculations, time alone will tell.

BORN: Chertsey, Surrey, 14.6.74.
GAMES: 51 (9). GOALS: 2. HONOURS: European Cup Winners Cup 93/4.

OTHER CLUBS: Southend United on loan 96/7 (4, 0).

JOHN JENSEN

1992/93 – 1995/96

John Jensen excited – if that's not an inappropriate word – conflicting emotions in close observers of the Highbury scene.

There were those who lauded the much-capped Dane's consummate professionalism, who revelled in his ferocity as a midfield ball-winner and who offered unreserved admiration for his selflessness, stamina and ability to lift dressing-room morale. There were others who winced at John's party-spoiling presence, who were upset by tackles they saw as brutal, who cringed at the lack of ambition in his passing; indeed, they quoted him as the very embodiment of soccer negativity.

Still more saw John as a cult figure, thanks to the 98-game scoring drought which followed his £1.57 million signing from Brondby in August 1992, ironically a deal welcomed by Gunners fans not least because of his wonderful goal in the final of that summer's European Championships.

Finally, there was George Graham, who once referred to John as 'the new Peter Reid', an utterance which took on a distinctly surreal ring to those who recalled Reid's inspirational creative endeavours for Everton during the mid-eighties. Of course, the former manager's words have to be examined in the light of the infamous 'bung' allegations, to which the Jensen purchase was centrally relevant.

What, then, is the verdict on John's worth? First, it must be accepted that he was a footballer of considerable technique. Despite the cynical jibes of detractors, he *could* pass precisely and, as proved by his sole goal for the Gunners – a sweetly curled 20-yarder at home to QPR on New Year's Eve 1994/95 – he could strike the ball exquisitely. His challenges were invariably brusque, occasionally crude, but undeniably effective. He wasn't quick but he read the game well, and he never stopped trying.

At best, and wholly from a Highbury viewpoint, he exuded quiet authority and redoubtable strength in front of the back four. At his worst, from a neutral aspect, he was ineffably dull. In general, it was frustrating that he was not asked to play a more positive role, for which he was almost certainly equipped. In March 1996 John returned to Brondby, making the move permanent after an initial loan period.

BORN: Copenhagen, Denmark, 3.5.65.
GAMES: 129 (8). GOALS: 1.
HONOURS: European Cup Winners' Cup 93/4 (medal granted though he missed final); FA Cup 92/3. Denmark caps.

OTHER CLUBS: Brondby, Denmark (two spells); Hamburg, Germany.

STEFAN SCHWARZ

1994/95

'Stefan Schwarz . . . ah, now he was a tiger!' Those few words, redolent with respect and admiration, meant a lot, coming as they did from that monument to professionalism George Armstrong, the 1971 double-winning hero who is now an Arsenal coach. They summed up, with wistful simplicity, the regret among fans at the departure of the Swedish midfield star after just a single season at Highbury, an ill-affordable loss which capped the Gunners' *annus horribilis*.

For several years, since the pomp of Davis, Thomas and Rocastle, George Graham's side had been in urgent need of centre-field class and the £2 million signing of Stefan from Benfica in June 1994 went a long way towards providing it.

Fresh from helping his country claim third place in the World Cup, the baby-faced blond made a bright early impression. A beautifully balanced athlete, Stefan boasted reassuringly sound technique. He was quick both physically and mentally, his work-rate was enormous and he was unfailingly courageous, a fierce tackler and an uncomplaining taker of punishment.

The Schwarz left foot could be devastating, particularly at dead-ball situations and, crucially, he had plenty of experience of top-level competition. Here, it seemed, was a man who could take a pivotal role in realising Graham's ambition of regaining the League title, then making a real impact in the European Cup.

Admittedly, Stefan did not display the breadth of vision to become the play-maker for whom so many supporters longed, his passing being more precise than penetrative. Also, it could be argued that his four goals in 49 starts was not enough for one of Europe's leading midfielders, though it should be stressed that much of his work was done 'sitting' in front of his own back four or running selflessly to create space.

However, his overall quality was undeniable and his £2.5 million sale to Fiorentina in summer 1995 saddened all who wished Arsenal well. No doubt Stefan felt let down, too; he must have expected more of Arsenal than the distasteful distraction of the 'bung' scandal and membership of a side which, all too frequently, failed to rise above the mediocre.

BORN: Malmo, Sweden, 18.4.69.
GAMES: 49. GOALS: 4.
HONOURS: Sweden caps.

OTHER CLUBS: Malmo, Sweden, 88/9-89/90; Bayer Leverkusen, Germany, 89/90-90/1; Benfica, Portugal, 90/1-93/4; Fiorentina, Italy, 95/6-.

EDDIE McGOLDRICK

The summer of 1993 was redolent with promise for Arsenal fans. Two cups had just been won, the club had banked a lot of money, and the manager had not disguised his interest in acquiring a certain Irish international midfielder. But there was a problem. The man George Graham wanted was Roy Keane; the man he got was Eddie McGoldrick.

That's not to denigrate Eddie, an industrious and impeccably professional individual who was versatile enough to step in at full-back or sweeper in addition to his more familiar role shuttling up and down the right flank. But with Manchester United and Blackburn battling to shatter the British transfer record for the awesome potential of Keane, and with other clubs shelling out merrily for a variety of star names, Highbury regulars could be pardoned if they were a tad underwhelmed by the Gunners' sole gesture towards a renewed title challenge.

Eddie arrived at a cost of £1 million from newly-relegated Crystal Palace, for whom he had performed with consistent competence in the midst of their travails, and surprised many pundits by claiming a first-team place during the early months of the new term.

Quick, eager and a crisp striker of the ball who could float a tantalising cross, he made few mistakes but showed precious little guile in his touchline sorties. With Eddie wearing the shirt which might otherwise have been adorning the back of Anders Limpar, his perceived ordinariness as the season progressed made him a target for barrackers who saw him as a symbol of the Gunners' lack of adventure.

To be fair, before he receded to the fringe of the squad there were some exciting McGoldrick moments, several of them cropping up in the away annihilation of Standard Liege in November 1993. After laying on goals for Paul Merson and Kevin Campbell, Eddie ran half the length of the pitch before scoring Arsenal's seventh with a sharp 15-yard drive off the underside of the crossbar.

However, that was the exception rather than the rule and, having failed to secure a place in the plans of either Bruce Rioch or Arsene Wenger, he was sold to Manchester City for £300,000 in the autumn of 1996.

BORN: Islington, London, 30.4.65. GAMES: 44 (12). GOALS: 1. HONOURS: European Cup Winners' Cup 93/4. 15 Republic of Ireland caps (92-94). OTHER CLUBS: Northampton Town 86/7-88/9 (107, 9); Crystal Palace 88/9-92/3 (147, 11); Manchester City 96/7 (33, 0).

1993/94 – 1995/96

GLENN HELDER

Glenn Helder was the most frustrating player on Arsenal's books during most of his Highbury sojourn - and presumably the most frustrated, too.

The high-stepping Dutch international flankman endured a largely dismal stay, his form dipping so low that disillusioned fans dubbed him 'Graham's Revenge', a cynical reference to the fact that he was the disgraced former manager's final signing.

Yet there was no doubt about Glenn's ability. Though it was incongruous to recall in the midst of his subsequent travail, he had made a sparkling first impression following his £2.3 million purchase from Vitesse Arnhem in February 1995. On his home debut against Nottingham Forest, Glenn had illuminated Highbury with his daring runs, bewildering stepovers and penetrating crosses - yes, it was the same Glenn Helder - and followed up with several more enthralling displays.

The prospects of what he might achieve alongside his countryman Dennis Bergkamp - with whom he had risen through the Ajax youth system - seemed limitless, but dire anti-climax was in store. Shorn of the dreadlocks he had worn on arrival, Glenn was infuriatingly fitful throughout 1995/96. Even on those rare days when his left-wing speed and trickery threatened to open defences, he let himself down with poor distribution or finishing so woeful that he did not score until January. Come the spring, with no perceptible improvement, he was dropped.

Why did so much talent, albeit of the mercurial variety, go to waste? What transformed the once vigorously confident winger to distressingly peripheral, almost pathetic figure who was dispatched to Benfica on extended loan at the outset of Arsene Wenger's reign? Maybe Glenn could not come to terms with the work-rate required in the Premiership; perhaps he needed the freedom to rove, like Steve McManaman at Liverpool; certainly a goal or two would have helped.

Whatever, it was ironic to reflect that George Graham had frequently omitted Anders Limpar for his inconsistency, and then replaced him with Glenn Helder . . .

BORN: Leiden, Holland, 28.10.68. GAMES: 33 (16). GOALS: 1. HONOURS: Holland caps. OTHER CLUBS: Sparta Rotterdam, Holland; Vitesse Arnhem, Holland; Benfica, Portugal, on loan.

1994/95 –

JOHN HARTSON

1994/95 — 1996/97

When John Hartson joined West Ham for a fee which could tot up eventually to £5 million, there was no shortage of knowing smirks, even raucous laughter, among disbelieving Gooners. They should beware: the young Welshman has it within him to become a very fine centre-forward.

Admittedly, when the deal was announced in February 1997, the price *did* seem exorbitant, though Hammers boss Harry Redknapp was at pains to point out that the initial instalment was comparatively modest and that John would have to achieve near-miracles for the balance to be paid.

His chances? Pretty fair, given that nature has endowed the coltish redhead so admirably for his work. Tall and resilient, brave and spikily spirited, he positively oozes self-belief and, most important of all, he is laden with footballing talent. John is powerful in the air, but it is on the ground that he has the greatest capacity to excite. Belying a slightly clumsy gait, he boasts a deceptively slick turn, neat close control and can dispense lay-offs with delightful subtlety.

He can finish with an almighty thump, too, but rivets the attention most compellingly when he opts for finesse, never more notably than for Arsenal at home to Manchester City in March 1996. John was 30 yards from goal and marked tightly when Lee Dixon launched a long, curving pass in his direction; with his first touch, the young marksman stunned the ball immobile at his feet; with his second he floated it exquisitely over the City 'keeper for a goal that was deeply satisfying in every respect.

However, life was rarely tranquil for John after George Graham paid Luton £2.5 million in January 1995 to make him the most expensive British teenager. Soon he found himself in the exposed position of front-man in a struggling side, acquitting himself as well as could be expected of one so green. He notched a few goals as Arsenal inched their way to Premiership safety, then contributed the equaliser that inspired brief hope in the Cup Winners' Cup Final against Real Zaragoza.

Yet John could not command a regular place during 1995/96 and berated Bruce Rioch publicly, though spring found him in the side and scoring goals. Under Arsene Wenger the following term, he appeared happier and more committed, but then came the offer the Gunners seemingly couldn't refuse and a 21-year-old with vast potential had gone.

BORN: Swansea, Glamorgan, 5.4.75.
GAMES: 55 (16). GOALS: 17.
HONOURS: 9 Wales caps (95-).

OTHER CLUBS: Luton Town 93/4-94/5 (54, 11); West Ham United 96/7- (11, 5).

ALAN MILLER

Alan Miller was a sprightly young goal-keeper who had little option but to leave Highbury in an attempt to realise his undoubted potential.

The first graduate from the FA School of Excellence to win England under-21 caps - an honour which came his way before he had completed a full senior game for the Gunners - Alan tasted Premiership action for the first time when rising from the bench to replace the injured David Seaman at Leeds in November 1992.

Thereafter, George Graham had no qualms about promoting the capable rookie whenever the England custodian was indisposed. Agile and a brilliant shot-stopper, Alan had something to learn about claiming crosses and perhaps needed more aggression to dominate his penalty box, but the makings of a top-class 'keeper appeared to be in place.

The Miller talents were showcased spec-tacularly at home to Sheffield Wednesday in December 1993, when not only did he pull off a series of wonderful saves, but also originated the only goal of the game with a mammoth throw to Steve Morrow, who set up Ian Wright.

Inevitably, though, opportunities were sparse and long-term prospects severely limited, so it was no surprise when the tall 24-year-old accepted a £500,000 move to Middlesbrough in July 1994. He picked up a First Division title medal in his opening season on Teesside, then spoiled the Arsenal debuts of Dennis Bergkamp and David Platt with some blinding stops at Highbury on the first day of 1995/96. However, Alan's horizon was clouded by the arrival at the Riverside of Gary Walsh, and he was forced to move again in his quest for first-team football.

BORN: Epping, Essex, 29.3.70. GAMES: 6 (2). GOALS: 0. OTHER CLUBS: Plymouth Argyle on loan 88/9 (13, 0); West Bromwich Albion on loan 91/2 (3, 0); Birmingham City on loan 91/2 (15, 0); Middlesbrough 94/5-96/7 (57, 0); Grimsby Town on loan 96/7 (1, 0); West Bromwich Albion 96/7- (12, 0).

1992/93 – 1993/94

CHRIS KIWOMYA

It's difficult not to feel sorry for striker Chris Kiwomya, who joined Arsenal from Ipswich during the murky twilight of George Graham's managerial reign. Prior to the £1.2 million deal, the pacy Yorkshireman had been struggling to retain his place in a side waging a losing battle against relegation and it seemed that the Gunners' intervention might revitalise a once-promising career.

Presumably the beleaguered Graham thought that the 25-year-old, who could make markers look like statues as he raced on to long balls played into space, could lift an Arsenal side who were themselves disturbingly adjacent to the demotion dogfight.

Chris responded with spirit, looking lively if a little disorientated in a handful of substitute outings, before his deft chip secured three sorely-needed points at home to Nottingham Forest in February. However, the marksman's joy must have been marred slightly by the knowledge that, earlier in the day, the man who had just employed him had been sacked. Nothing daunted, Chris netted twice in a win over Crystal Palace four days later, only to lose his place because Ian Wright had returned from suspension. For the rest of the campaign the newcomer struggled for full fitness and found him-self on the fringe of the side. However, even that was preferable to his position in 1995/96, when Bruce Rioch failed to pick him at all, then transfer-listed him in January. Meanwhile, more injuries brought further woe.

A year earlier, Kiwomya goals had won two games for the Gunners, who had finished only six points clear of the drop. Demonstrably then, despite restricted opportunity, Chris had made a mark at Highbury. He deserved better luck elsewhere.

BORN: Huddersfield, Yorkshire, 2.12.69. GAMES: 6 (11). GOALS: 3. OTHER CLUBS: Ipswich Town 88/9-94/5 (225, 51); Le Havre, France, on loan 96/7.

1994/95 –

VINCE BARTRAM

Vince Bartram faces the same frustration as Alan Miller did before him: how to further his goalkeeping ambitions in the giant shadow cast by David Seaman.

The Brummie six-footer was signed from Bournemouth in August 1994 for £400,000 - the fee decided by a transfer tribunal - to replace the departing Miller as Arsenal's number-two custodian, and soon he was called on to show his mettle. That November the England 'keeper was injured in a League Cup encounter with Sheffield Wednesday at Highbury and Vince had to make the transition from the lower reaches of Division Two to the top level.

During a spell of six League games in December, and in another five the fol-lowing spring, he proved generally com-petent, an athletic performer on his line and sound enough at gathering crosses, though he did betray positional uncer-tainty at times.

Probably Vince's most convincing per-formance came at Newcastle in March, when he kept the Gunners in the game until the dying minutes, when he was finally beaten by an unstoppable 25-yarder from Peter Beardsley.

However, when Seaman was fit again, it was back to the bench for Bartram, who found himself facing a career crossroads. Having tasted the big time, was the man who once understudied Tim Flowers at Wolverhampton Wanderers content to remain a deputy? When the 1996 return of John Lukic and the emergence of Lee Harper pushed him further down the pecking order, it seemed that the answer was likely to be 'no'.

BORN: Birmingham, 7.8.68. GAMES: 11 (1). GOALS: 0. OTHER CLUBS: Wolverhampton Wanderers 86/7-90/1 (5, 0); Blackpool on loan 89/90 (9, 0); Bournemouth 91/2-93/4 (132, 0).

1994/95 –

STEVE HUGHES

1994/95 –

Steve Hughes is Arsenal's most exciting home-grown player of the nineties, a tall, left-sided midfielder who, well in advance of his 21st birthday, had done much to lay the foundations for an illustrious Highbury career.

An England youth and under-21 international who helped the Gunners to win the FA Youth Cup in 1994, he has the capacity to light up a hitherto-gloomy game, to shake it from a state of lethargy with a vivaciously confident run or a shot of explosive savagery.

In such a manner Steve lifted proceedings on several occasions in the spring of 1997, doing well enough as a substitute to secure a sequence of starts and put long-term pressure on more established performers such as David Platt.

Bright-eyed and sparky – now there's a quality for a lad named Hughes – he draws the eye and provokes expectation, especially when roaming in forward positions. Steve can control a pass neatly in his stride, then lacerate a defence with pace and skill. Also, when the occasion demands, he will hunt for the ball and either tackle waspishly or harrass opponents into making errors.

He's courageous, too, as he proved by diving to head a goal despite the close proximity of a flailing Sunderland boot during an FA Cup replay at Roker Park in January 1997.

Though Arsene Wenger is likely to introduce expensive new stars – almost certainly players with wide experience on the world stage – as he marshals his resources for 1997/98, it would be unthinkable for such a precocious talent as Steve Hughes to be excluded from the frame. Of course, he must learn to thrive on fierce competition and, at this early stage of his development, he shows every sign of doing so.

Steve still has plenty to learn about his trade and will have to attain the highest standards of industry and dedication if he is to reap the full harvest of his bountiful natural gifts.
Over to you, young man.

BORN: Wokingham, Berkshire, 18.9.76.
GAMES: 12 (7). GOALS: 2.

ADRIAN CLARKE

Adrian Clarke hasn't had the time or the opportunity to make a major impact in his short career to date, but already he has achieved something which has eluded better-known Arsenal midfielders of recent years - he has excited the Highbury crowd.

An old-fashioned winger at heart, the England schoolboy and youth international is adept at nipping past defenders and cutting inside, a guaranteed method of bringing fans to their feet. He did so, intermittently but thrillingly, during a brief senior stint in mid-1995/96, and many supporters were disappointed when he returned to the reserves.

Adrian's control is sure, he can cross with either foot, he uses the ball intelligently and he is not cowed by stern challenges, though like the majority of rookies, his off-the-ball work needs some attention. There is goal-scoring potential, too, as he showed with a crucial strike which helped the Gunners beat Millwall to lift the 1994 FA Youth Cup.

Such a skilful operator might have been expected to take the eye of Arsene Wenger, who values technique so highly, yet the only senior opportunities which fell to Adrian during 1996/97 came on loan at Rotherham and Southend.

It is notoriously difficult for home-grown youngsters, especially attackers, to make the grade at big clubs where costly imports are the norm. But Adrian, who made his first-team debut as a substitute at home to Queen's Park Rangers on New Year's Eve 1994/95, has both enormous natural talent and a calm temperament. He must have a chance.

BORN: Haverhill, Suffolk, 28.9.74. GAMES: 5 (4). GOALS: 0.
OTHER CLUBS: Rotherham United on loan 96/7 (2, 0);
Southend United on loan 96/7 (7, 0).

1994/95 −

PAUL SHAW

The situation of Paul Shaw embodies the problems facing so ma[ny] young footballers striving to break through at top clubs. Though obviously star material, he has bags of ability and soccer intellige[nce] and he's willing to work.

What he needs to further his development is top-level experien[ce] and lots of it. But with all the selection pressures that go with Arsenal's regular involvement in the quest for honours, such a pla[yer] is likely to hover on the fringe of the squad, filling in at times [of] injury and suspension but being denied the settled first-team sequence he craves.

Paul, an England youth international who scored heavily for th[e] Gunners' junior sides, is a clever forward endowed with enormo[us] amounts of skill and stamina who is perhaps most effectively employed in the space behind the front-runners.

After making his senior debut as a substitute at Nottingham For[est] in December 1994, he returned to the Highbury periphery befo[re] excelling on loan stints in the lower divisions, notably at Burnle[y] and Peterborough.

Having benefited from his travels, Paul was called from the ben[ch] intermittently by Arsene Wenger during 1996/97, finally starting [a] League game at Southampton in March. He responded to the opportunity with a competent all-round performance, which h[e] capped with a match-clinching goal, dispatched unfussily from [a] narrow angle.

Despite the prematurely receding Shaw hairline, Paul is still in h[is] early twenties and is good enough to earn a living in the Premiership. Whether that will be at Highbury or elsewhere rema[ins] to be seen.

BORN: Burnham, Berkshire, 4.9.73. GAMES: 1 (12). GOALS: [2]
OTHER CLUBS: Burnley on loan 94/5 (9, 4); Cardiff City 95/[6]
on loan (6, 0); Peterborough United on loan 95/6 (12, 5).

1994/95 −

SCOTT MARSHALL

REMI GARDE

Two successive springtimes have seen Scott Marshall continue to blossom as a sound, composed and admirably skilful young central defender. In 1995/96, some two months after being transfer-listed by Bruce Rioch, he won acclaim from the Highbury crowd for a series of enterprising displays when called in during an injury epidemic. Winning the ball cleanly and using it both sensibly and perceptively, he excelled alongside Keown and Linighan in the middle of a back-five formation.

In that same stint, already enjoying the fans' confidence through earlier efforts, he heightened his profile nationally by heading the Gunners into an early lead against League leaders Newcastle at Highbury. Thundering unstoppably into the six-yard box, he met a near-post nod-on from Linighan with power and precision, the execution of a favourite Arsenal ploy so perfect that Messrs Bould and Adams would have been proud to claim it for their own. For the rest of a pulsating match, the 22-year-old belied his comparative inexperience with a splendidly assured all-round performance, refusing to be fazed by the contrasting threats posed by Asprilla and Ferdinand. One year on, after a lengthy sojourn in the reserves, Scott rose to the occasion again when Arsene Wenger's resources were depleted, cutting an even more impressive figure, especially with his distribution. It seemed likely that Scott, whose progress since his senior debut in May 1993 had been blocked hitherto by the excellence of his elders, had done enough to earn a long-term future at the club. The son of former Newcastle 'keeper Gordon and the brother of Celtic custodian Gordon junior, Scott has a passion for soccer in his blood – and it shows.

BORN: Edinburgh, 1.5.73. GAMES: 18 (3). GOALS: 1.
OTHER CLUBS: Rotherham United on loan 93/4 (10, 1);
Sheffield United on loan 94/5 (17, 0).

1992/93 –

But for a recurrence of injury problems which have dogged him throughout his career, it is reasonable to suppose that Remi Garde would have exerted a major influence on Arsenal's 1996/97 campaign.

The versatile Frenchman's technical excellence is not in question. He controls the ball immaculately, uses it imaginatively and brings a decade's worth of experience in his homeland's top division to his reading of the game.

Best known as a central midfielder, the position in which he won his six international caps, Remi is unobtrusively impressive in a linking role alongside his young countryman, Patrick Vieira, helping to achieve a flowing movement for which the Gunners have hardly been renowned in recent years.

Equally, he is comfortable in the middle of defence, a calm gendarme martialling his forces, his anticipation and positional sense compensating for the fact that he stands three inches short of 6ft. Already 30 by the time of his summer '96 free transfer to North London from Strasbourg, nevertheless Remi has much to offer as the reign of Arsene Wenger moves into its second season. Whether bringing class and intelligence to the Premiership side or setting an impeccably professional example to the eager rookies rising through George Armstrong's reserve team, his input is likely to prove invaluable.

BORN: L'Arbrestle, France, 3.4.66. GAMES: 7 (4). GOALS: 0.
HONOURS: 6 France caps (90-).
OTHER CLUBS: Lyon, Strasbourg, both France.

1996/97 –

DAVID PLATT

He has cost five clubs a total of £22 million in transfer fees, he can point to a phenomenal scoring rate for England, and he captained his country; yet after two disappointing, injury-disrupted seasons at Highbury, David Platt remains something of an enigma.

For lengthy periods in a game, sometimes for the whole 90 minutes, he can look ordinary, even anonymous, patrolling back and forth in midfield, fetching and carrying fastidiously but contributing little that catches either the eye or the imagination. People wonder: what does he do?

Then, suddenly, the ball is played into the opponents' box, David has slipped away from his marker and he pops up, as if from nowhere, to plunder a crucial goal. It has happened too frequently to be dismissed as coincidence. In fact, the Platt knack of arriving 'late' on the scene of the action - actually, *he* is on cue, it's the rest of them who are early! - is a lethal mixture of rare instinct and cunning calculation.

Of course, intuitive timing alone would not have been enough to make David one of the most sought-after players in the world, which undeniably he was during the early nineties. He happens to be a top-quality finisher, too. Name a method of execution and he can apply it: the scorching drive, the subtle chip, the precise side-foot, the courageous header, they are all part of his repertoire, but it is the spectacular volley for which he will be remembered most vividly.

More specifically, the sensationally adroit last-gasp effort for England against Belgium in the 1990 World Cup Finals, the strike which underscored his already burgeoning international reputation; equally spectacularly, a stunning, hooked 16-yarder on the swivel for the Gunners against Nottingham Forest in August 1995.

That point-saving intervention, David's first Highbury goal following his £4.5 million arrival from Sampdoria in the summer, marked his final appearance before a two-month absence for a cartilage operation. Even on his return he was not fully fit and a series of lacklustre displays, understandable in the circumstances, gave rise to initially faint but unmistakable disenchantment among growing numbers of supporters.

They saw passing, control and tackling which were adequate but unremarkable; they perceived his much-vaunted goal threat as moderate; and, not fully aware of his physical strictures, they felt his customary athleticism was less apparent than expected. The fact that fellow newcomer Dennis Bergkamp was blossoming so brilliantly reduced general unease, perhaps, but nevertheless it offered a marked contrast to the midfielder's less rarified progress.

However, more surgery to David's knee was followed by a certain improvement in form which was rewarded by an England recall in the spring. The 1996/97 campaign brought further ins and outs, frustrating absences and brief upturns, and while the feeling persisted among most observers that he had ground to make up, there were even those who whispered that his time might be running out.

Yet a glance at the Platt record shows that unstinting determination has lifted David out of at least one far more unpromising situation, when he was rejected as a teenager by Manchester United. His reaction? To rebuild his career with Crewe, enhance it hugely with Aston Villa, then head for the stratosphere with Bari, Juventus and Sampdoria.

Somehow, though, despite his 27 goals in 62 games for England, David has never quite acquired the stature such statistics might suggest. Bruce Rioch bought him to give Arsenal the regular midfield goal-power they had lacked for years, Arsene Wenger has shown willingness to use him when he is fit; now, with two largely unsatisfying terms as a Gunner behind him, it is time for David Platt to deliver.

BORN: Chadderton, Lancashire, 10.6.66. GAMES: 63 (4). GOALS: 11.
HONOURS: 62 England caps (89-).
OTHER CLUBS: Crewe Alexandra 84/5-87/8 (134, 55); Aston Villa 87/8-90/1 (121, 50); Bari, Italy, 91/2 (29, 11); Juventus, Italy, 92/3 (16, 3); Sampdoria, Italy, 93/4-94/5 (55, 17).

1995/96 –

DENNIS BERGKAMP

Dennis Bergkamp of Arsenal: those very words carry a frisson of excitement, the like of which Highbury regulars have not experienced in modern times. The £7.5 million purchase of the multi-talented Dutchman from Inter Milan in the summer of 1995 was the most ambitious acquisition in the club's history, the deal's significance extending way beyond the enormity of the fee. Despite two unexpectedly arid years in Italy, Dennis was recognised as one of the world's finest footballers and his arrival signalled a deliciously daring change of outlook from the men who held the Gunners' purse-strings.

There was not even the faintest whiff of parsimony in the air, no curmudgeonly mutterings about shattered wage structures. What the Bergkamp transfer screamed to the world was that Arsenal wanted flair, the very best available, and that they were prepared to pay for it. Admirable sentiments, greeted rapturously by fans increasingly embittered by mediocrity, but would it prove practical? On the evidence of two seasons, the answer is a joyous, unequivocal 'yes'.

True, he got off to a fitful beginning as he came to terms with the frenetic demands of the English game. Even though manager Bruce Rioch maintained that his record buy was a major contributor from the off, crediting him with 'assists' towards 75 per-cent of the team's goals up to late September, the vultures gathered in force when the much-trumpeted newcomer failed to score in his first seven senior outings. Indeed, in denouncing Dennis the tabloid press reached shameful heights of hysteria - until the stirring events of one sunlit autumn afternoon at Highbury began force-feeding them a diet of their own asinine words.

Southampton were the visitors as the real Dennis Bergkamp stood up. He opened his account after nearly 11 hours of football with an emphatic 12-yard volley, then heaped ridicule on his doubters with a beautifully poised, swerving sprint past several defenders before netting with a fulminating 25-yard drive. Thunderous approval, tinged with a soupcon of relief, announced the symbolic baptimism of a new Highbury hero.

Thereafter, Dennis began to turn in the kind of thoroughbred displays that had won him world renown before his misadventure in Milan. At his most effective in the so-called 'Dalglish zone', tucked in between front-runners and midfielders, he revealed a technique that is as close to perfection as can be imagined, his control and distribution impeccable with either foot, his finish deft or explosive at will.

There was much more, too, over which to drool: the quickness of thought, the fluidity of movement, the intelligent creation and ruthless exploitation of space, the apparently unshakeable composure which some mistake, at their peril, for lack of commitment. But it is his sheer range which intimidates opponents the most. Dennis can strike like a thief in the night, all subtle incision, or batter a defence by brutally spectacular frontal assault, offering a variety which did much to reduce the Gunners' erstwhile predictability (Ian Wright honourably excepted).

Yet for all that, the Dutchman remains essentially a team player rather than an individualist, ever mindful of colleagues' needs, though clearly there were occasions during his first two North London campaigns when he was thinking too quickly for those around him. Happily, the imaginative Arsene Wenger can be relied upon to create an enlightened climate in which thoroughbreds will thrive. By January 1997 Dennis was doing just that, seeming more relaxed and therefore more expressive, witness his delectably chipped FA Cup goal at Roker Park, fashioned out of nothing by bewildering manoeuvres with the sole of either boot.

In his career to date, Dennis Bergkamp has been at his most devastating in smooth, flowing sides that made passing a priority, the likes of Ajax and Holland, rather than when shackled in a more rigid system as he was in Serie A. Now, on the threshold of his prime at 28 and with Wenger to guide him, Highbury awaits . . .

BORN: Amsterdam, Holland, 10.5.69. GAMES: 74 (1). GOALS: 30.
HONOURS: Holland caps (90-).

OTHER CLUBS: Ajax, Amsterdam, 86/7-92/3 (185,103);
Inter Milan 93/4-94/5 (52,11).

1995/96 −

PATRICK VIEIRA

If Arsene Wenger is going to make Arsenal great again, it's a fair bet that his fellow Frenchman, Patrick Vieira, will be the centrepiece of the Gunners' brave new order.

By the end of his first season in North London, the rangy, stringily lean midfielder was emerging as one of the most complete all-round performers in the Premiership. Mixing iron with invention, authority with sophistication, he was being tipped freely as a future captain of both club and country – and he was only just 21 when the 1997/98 campaign got under way.

Patrick was recruited for £3.5 million from AC Milan in August 1996 in what was clearly a Wenger-inspired transaction, though Arsene had not yet been officially installed at Highbury. The Senegal-born six-footer made an immediate impact on his new team-mates, even those seasoned professionals who had seen it all. To a man they were impressed by Patrick's easy command of a football, the range and accuracy of his distribution and the vision with which he deployed these stylish qualities. There was admiration, too, for his lithe athleticism and strength, tellingly underpinned by a ruthless streak which proclaimed 'winner', as surely as if the word were emblazoned across his forehead.

After a brief acclimatisation to English football among George Armstrong's reserves, Patrick became a fixture in the senior side, his classy presence auguring well for the new manager's intentions.

Until he turned down Ajax for Arsenal, few Gooners knew the name of Vieira. After all, he had not been long at Cannes before being whisked away to the San Siro, where he was granted a mere half-dozen outings for AC Milan before becoming a Gunner. Now, quickly, he became a favourite, his craft allowing Dennis Bergkamp more freedom to go forward and his understanding with Ian Wright showing devastating potential.

Patrick's contribution was summed up by one sequence of action against Wimbledon at Selhurst Park in November, when he won a tackle on the edge of his own box, brushed off another challenge during a long-striding 60-yard run, then delivered a perfect pass for Wright to score.

He needs to net more himself – two goals were inadequate return for a fellow who hits the ball so crisply with either foot – but surely that will come. For now it's enough to reflect that Patrick Vieira has become a pivotal Arsenal figure in just one term, and that his potential knows no bounds.

BORN: Dakar, Senegal, 23.6.76.
GAMES: 37 (1). GOALS: 2.
HONOURS: 1 France cap (97-).

OTHER CLUBS: Cannes, France;
AC Milan, Italy, 95/6.

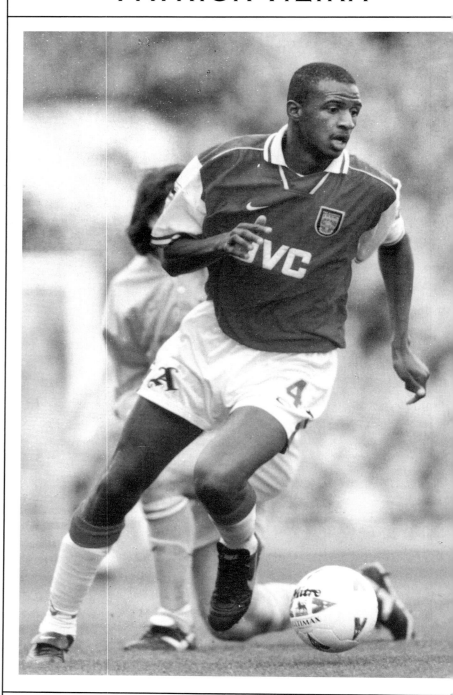

1996/97 –

JACK CRAYSTON

Lancastrian Jack Crayston was a popular choice to fill the void left by Tom Whittaker's death in October 1956. As an elegant wing-half, he had helped the Gunners attain glory in the thirties, and had been Tom's assistant since 1947; clearly, no one was more steeped in the Highbury tradition.

After taking over in mid-season with Arsenal 12th in the First Division, Jack completed a creditable initial term, lifting them to fifth place and leading them to the FA Cup quarter-finals. But during the next campaign, the team slumped to mid-table and nose-dived out of the Cup at Northampton. Jack wanted to buy new players, but when he asked the board for cash, it was not forthcoming, and he resigned in frustration.

Perhaps a clue to his problems in the seat of power lies in his nick-name, 'Gentleman Jack'. He was immensely courteous and well-liked, but never showed the ruthlessness needed by all successful managers. His appointment proved that the obvious choice is not always the best.

Later he managed Doncaster Rovers before running a shop in the Midlands until his retirement in 1972. Jack died on Boxing Day 1992.

MANAGER 1956 –1958

GEORGE SWINDIN

In February 1959, with Arsenal topping the First Division table, it seemed that George Swindin had worked a soccer miracle. At the start of the season he had taken over a distinctly average side for which the road to resurrection looked long and hard.

But after wreaking wholesale changes, he was apparently on the verge of leading the Gunners out of the mire. Even when they slipped to third place by season's end, the forecasts were of honours merely postponed.

Cue anti-climax, and three years of mediocrity which were to bring George the sack from the club he had served so well as a goalkeeper on either side of the war.

What went wrong? A savage spate of injuries to key players at vital times hampered his quest for a winning blend, and the all-conquering achievements of neighbouring Spurs did not help. There were also mistakes, such as the sale of David Herd, and it is a fact that George, a dry Yorkshireman, upset some people by a lack of tact.

But he was honest, dedicated and positive, and his sorrow on the day he left Highbury was genuinely moving. After going on to manage Norwich and Cardiff, he ran a garage business before moving to Spain.

MANAGER 1958 –1962

BILLY WRIGHT

Billy Wright's appointment in the summer of 1962 was greeted with wild enthusiasm by the fans; after all, an illustrious playing career with Wolves, a record 105 England caps, a spotless reputation for fair play and clean living, and a marriage to a glamorous pop star – Joy Beverley – all combined to create an image of golden perfection entirely in accord with their aspirations for the Gunners. But Billy had no management experience – and it showed.

A genial and thoroughly decent fellow, he was in his element with youngsters, and it is to his eternal credit that so many of his protégés subsequently became stars of Arsenal's League and FA Cup double triumph.

But he was less adept at dealing with senior players, being regarded in some quarters as 'too nice' and badly equipped to take difficult decisions. Cliques developed, ill-feeling crept in and team spirit was not enhanced as a consequence.

In fact, Billy got off to an encouraging start in management with the club he had favoured as a boy. He bought a brilliant centre-forward, Joe Baker, and presided over an attractive side, which ended the 1962/63 season occupying a respectable seventh place in the First Division.

His second campaign brought a comparable return, with the Gunners scoring freely though afflicted by a sieve-like defence, but then two finishes in the bottom half of the table sealed his fate. The one-time hero of all England was sacked in July 1966, after which he was so disillusioned that he left the professional game.

Thereafter Billy Wright forged a career as a top TV administrator, retiring in 1989. He died in 1994.

MANAGER 1962 – 1966

BERTIE MEE

Bertie Mee was Arsenal's physiotherapist and little known outside Highbury when he took on the job of rescuing the club from the doldrums. That he did so to such dramatic effect - with the 1970/71 League and FA Cup double representing the pinnacle of his success - is a tribute to his talents as organiser, motivator, psychologist, disciplinarian and, not least, delegator.

He was honest enough not to claim vast technical knowledge of soccer, his playing experience, as a winger with Derby County and Mansfield Town, having been distinctly modest. But Bertie had been around the game for many years, the last six of them spent mostly in the Highbury dressing-room, and he had divined plenty.

In particular, he had no doubt about who could do the parts of the job that he couldn't. Accordingly, he enlisted the help of top-class coaches, first Dave Sexton and then Don Howe, both inspired choices which did much to enhance outsiders' perceptions of the Mee acumen.

What Bertie excelled at was man management and, though polite and ostensibly shy, he left no one in any doubt about what was required of them. After accepting the job - at first with the option of reverting to his previous post after a year - he lost no time in laying down stringent ground rules. He knew Arsenal had plenty of talented footballers, but also he knew that in certain cases there was a pronounced lack of the dedication and pride that was indispensable in prospective big-time winners. Thus prima donnas were out, workaholics were in and, slowly at first, the ambience of Arsenal began to change.

Veins of steel and determination began to run through all levels of the club, standards were set and maintained, and the Gunners inched, with sometimes agonising tread, towards better days.

The traumas of League Cup Final defeats in 1968 (to Leeds) and 1969 (even worse, to Swindon Town) were survived and, Bertie ensured, learned from. The result was a hard-earned return to glory via European Fairs Cup triumph over Anderlecht in 1970.

The manager had laid formidable foundations and on them, a season later, was constructed the double, an astonishing achievement which would have been deemed unthinkable only a short time earlier.

Harrowingly, though, anti-climax was to follow: an FA Cup Final reverse against Leeds in 1972 and a title runners-up spot in 1973 did little to deflect widespread accusations that the team was dull. The wave of criticism hurt Bertie far more than his brave public face revealed and, by mid-decade, he was no longer enjoying his work.

The situation deteriorated so far that the Gunners flirted with relegation in two successive campaigns and, even before they had secured their safety in 1976, an emotional Bertie, clearly over-stretched by the constant pressure, announced that he would resign at season's end.

It was a bitterly poignant sign-off to an epoch-making era, and though he was panned in some quarters for breaking up his fine team too soon, none could question his prime achievement - Bertie Mee was the man who had made Arsenal great again.

After a short, but much-needed sabbatical from soccer, he became general manager of Watford, continuing to serve the Hornets as a director until 1991.

MANAGER 1966 – 1976

TERRY NEILL

Under Terry Neill, the Gunners were rarely out of the hunt for honours. They reached three consecutive FA Cup Finals, lifting the trophy once; lost a European final in the cruellest fashion, by dint of a penalty shoot-out; and were permanently ensconced in the upper half of the First Division, usually in the top six.
Many clubs would have viewed such a record as eminently acceptable but for Arsenal, with their vast resources and demanding support, it was simply not good enough.

In some respects, the Ulsterman was unlucky. Soon after arriving at Highbury, fresh from the White Hart Lane hot seat, he signed Malcolm Macdonald, only to see the free-scoring centre-forward's career wrecked by injury; and through no fault of his own, he lost the outstanding services of Liam Brady and Frank Stapleton.
Against that, his subsequent bold excursions into the transfer market were not consistently successful, and he failed to achieve rapport with a number of key players, notably the far-from-finished Alan Ball.

Terry was more adept at administration than motivation - most on-the-field matters were handled by coach Don Howe - and it was no surprise that after the Gunners sacked him, he bowed out of football management.

MANAGER 1976 –1983

DON HOWE

Don Howe was a players' manager, first and last. When he took over from Terry Neill - initially on a caretaker basis, but confirmed in the job after four months - every footballer at Highbury knew that if they were honest with their new boss, he would give them the fairest of deals.
Don had impeccable coaching credentials: he had been the tactician behind Arsenal's double of 1970/71, and as chief coach had played a mammoth part in the club's cup exploits during his predecessor's reign. In between the two North London spells he had managed West Bromwich Albion, coached in Turkey and at Leeds, and assisted Ron Greenwood with the England team.
Somehow, though, his undeniable expertise and burning enthusiasm failed to translate themselves into renewed success for the Gunners. Keeping a lower profile than Terry in the transfer market, Don brought through numerous promising youngsters and constructed a formidable squad, without attaining the desired blend.
Even so, when widespread reports of Arsenal's interest in Terry Venables as his replacement prompted Don's resignation in the spring of 1986, his side were not far adrift of the First Division pacesetters.
Later he coached Wimbledon to FA Cup glory, before returning to management with Queen's Park Rangers and Coventry City, then going on to wield further huge influence in the England set-up.

MANAGER 1983 – 1986

STEVE BURTENSHAW

Steve Burtenshaw was an experienced coach who served as Arsenal's caretaker manager from late March, 1986, until George Graham's appointment that May. Steve, who had a lengthy playing career with Brighton followed by spells as boss of Sheffield Wednesday and Queen's Park Rangers in the seventies, went on to become the Gunners' chief scout. He left Highbury in August 1996, during the turbulent period which saw the dismissal of Bruce Rioch.

ACTING MANAGER 1986

GEORGE GRAHAM

What, exactly, are we considering here? The football manager who led Arsenal to one European triumph, two League titles, one FA Cup and two League Cups, all in the space of eight and a half seasons? Or the fellow who - it is alleged, but still strenuously denied - pocketed large amounts of cash which should have gone to his club? Sadly, in moral terms, the two are indivisible and it must be accepted that if George Graham did defraud the Gunners then he was taking the fans' money, too. If he didn't, if the sum he banked was the 'unsolicited gift' he maintains it was, then his sacking for financial irregularities over the incoming transfers of John Jensen and Pal Lydersen is a monstrous injustice. Either way, both aspects of his tenure are relevant to those who pay to pass their leisure hours at Highbury.

Arguments about ethics and greed seem a world away from the healthy optimism in the air on that spring day in 1986 when George took charge of Arsenal. Even at that point, his managerial achievements had surprised many of his team-mates in the Gunners' 1970/71 double-winning side. As a player, he had been firmly in the easy-going category, exhibiting few leadership tendencies, but what a change was wrought in his football persona after he took over as boss of Millwall in 1982. At The Den, where he rescued the Lions from the brink of the Fourth Division and prepared them to take their place in the First, the Scot studied hard and learnt quickly, becoming known as a single-minded, resourceful young boss with a high regard for discipline.

On his return to Highbury, George lost little time in enhancing that reputation, winning the Littlewoods Cup in his first season without significant recourse to the transfer market. Too realistic to become complacent, he proclaimed that it was only the beginning, and set about assembling a squad of formidable power and depth. Eschewing megastars, he bought brilliantly - Marwood, Dixon, Bould and Winterburn were all outstanding bargains, while Smith, Seaman and Limpar were more expensive, but devastatingly effective - as well as developing the young talent already at his disposal.

George's grasp of tactics and readiness to adapt to changing circumstances offered further evidence of his burgeoning expertise, which Championships in '89 and '91 underlined with a flourish. Indeed, though it has been fashionable to denigrate the Gunners as negative, the title-winning teams most emphatically were not, and their manager has received insufficient credit for that.

However, with the priceless benefit of hindsight, it is possible to trace a downhill trend since '91, the North Londoners' magnificent cup record notwithstanding. Most damningly, George Graham never led another meaningful title challenge, and while no one can *expect* to lift that most coveted of domestic prizes on a frequent basis, a club the size of Arsenal must be in the running for it, at least.

His transfer record fell away badly, too, there being precious little to excite the fans after the purchase of Ian Wright. While Manchester United, Liverpool and Blackburn built splendid squads through heavy but wise spending, Graham's Arsenal merely built a reputation for blind parsimony. He was content with his defence and that was fair enough; but the midfield (particularly) and attacking areas screamed out for quality reinforcements which never arrived. George paid lip service to flair but never paid cash to secure it. The cup successes, admirable though they were, spoke more eloquently of industry and commitment than beauty and entertainment; in reality, they papered over the cracks while the situation deteriorated.

Throughout the reign of the man once known as 'Stroller' - later, less kindly but tellingly, to be dubbed 'Gaddafi' - he was adept at using adversity to the club's benefit. Though some of his players have had little reason to hold such a stern martinet in affection, they all respected him and invariably pulled together when the going got tough. However, such an ethos must be wearing to maintain and, perhaps, can only cover other deficiencies for a limited period. Thus when events closed in during 1994/95, Arsenal were a colourless side, struggling in the League, difficult to like. There was an inescapable feeling that, never mind the 'bung' issue, it was time for a change.

That it should come in the way it did - dismissal and a subsequent 12-month ban from all football activities - was overwhelmingly sad for this proud, independent, immensely talented fellow, and for everyone associated with the club for whom he had procured such spectacular success. Years before he had spoken of founding a footballing dynasty in the manner of Bill Shankly's at Liverpool, but it was not to be. Perhaps he may yet do so elsewhere; he is not an old man and, certainly, he has the ambition.

Unavoidably, at Highbury he will be remembered with ambivalence. No manager, not even Herbert Chapman, led the Gunners to more trophies. But where honour is concerned, the name of George Graham is tarnished, probably forever. Whether that is just, only he can know.

MANAGER 1986 – 1995

BRUCE RIOCH

STEWART HOUSTON

Bruce Rioch took over a club in turmoil. He imported one of the world's top players and the England captain; he made the Gunners infinitely easier on the eye than they had been for several years; he led them to a top-five Premiership finish, qualifying for Europe in the process, and a League Cup semi-final. Then he was sacked.

The foregoing is a bald summation but one which addresses the salient issues as identified by Arsenal's mystified fans. It would seem that Rioch's inability to cope with club politics, particularly the board's handling of transfer policy, cost him his job. It could hardly have been failure on the field.

Bruce had a harder act to follow, in terms of tangible success, than any Arsenal manager since George Allison took over from Herbert Chapman in 1934. But there were certain consolations for the briskly ambitious new incumbent when he arrived at Highbury in the summer of 1995.

Firstly, it was evident to all who cared about the Gunners that the club's image needed radical restoration. George Graham's sad exit, the Merson situation, other unhappy off-the-field incidents, and the team's widely perceived dullness had conspired to create a climate for change. Clearly, such a wide-ranging remit could not be discharged overnight; accordingly, by any reasonable reckoning, the boss who had just led Bolton into the Premiership had a certain amount of time on his side.

Secondly, he was allowed to shatter the hitherto sacrosanct wage structure which Graham had protected so remorselessly, leaving the fans agog with excitement over possibilities for the future. Of course, such comparative financial freedom carried with it an awesomely onerous responsibility, one which could be vested only in a leader who combined strength, judgement and integrity with a beautiful vision of how the game should be played. At first, the board seemed confident that they had found such a man in Bruce Rioch. The son of a regimental sergeant major, he had a

reputation as a tough taskmaster with a ruthless streak, a moralist who exuded sobriety and who would not shrink from difficult decisions. Those who clamoured for some sort of clean-up crusade could rest easy.

Football-wise, too, his pedigree offered realistic, if cautious, grounds for hope. After an accomplished playing career as a polished midfielder - highlights included winning a title medal with Derby County and skippering Scotland in the 1978 World Cup Finals - he made a promising start in management with Torquay. There followed stints with Middlesbrough, whom he guided from near-bankruptcy in the Third Division to the top flight before subsequent relegation resulted in his sacking; Millwall, where early optimism tailed away; and Bolton, where he ran an excitingly creative team which he must have been loath to leave behind.

Bruce's soccer creed was to entertain. He demanded an attractive passing game and to that end he invested heavily in Bergkamp and Platt; both renowned, significantly, as squeaky-clean characters.

Naturally, the reshaped Gunners needed time to settle, but by late autumn there was clear evidence of progress, style having been injected without the sacrifice of competitiveness or discipline. For protracted passages in a succession of matches, their football flowed enthrallingly and the fans adored it. There were even whispers of a possible Championship challenge but, with consistency yet to be attained and other purchases patently necessary, these were rash in the extreme.

Rioch himself never indulged in such flights of fancy, maintaining throughout that his team had considerable development to make up on such benchmark rivals as Manchester United and Liverpool. The wisdom of this caution became apparent as the season progressed in up-and-down manner, though his achievements offered proof of invigorating consolidation.

However, before long there were ominous rumblings of a rift between Rioch and various players, particularly Ian Wright, who had a transfer request turned down. More worryingly still, there was speculation that the manager was disillusioned by the board's reported unwillingness to back his New Year quest for further playing reinforcements, that there were damaging personality clashes, and that Bruce was reluctant to tie himself to the club. However, he signed a contract after more than a year's delay, only to be dismissed two weeks later on the very threshold of the 1996/97 campaign. Following a season which had produced green shoots of undeniable if tantalising promise, the board's decision was viewed widely as both harsh and bizarre. To what heights might Bruce Rioch's Arsenal have risen? Frustratingly, that must remain a matter for puzzled speculation.

Stewart Houston was given first chance at leading the Gunners towards the light after the George Graham affair had cast a pall of gloom over Highbury - and he made a fair fist of it. Appointed caretaker manager in the wake of his boss's traumatic departure in February 1995, the personable Scot presided over gradual if unspectacular progress towards Premiership safety and guided the side to the European Cup Winners' Cup Final.

Having declared his interest in taking the post full-time, Stewart went about his work with cool dignity as his long-term employment prospects were discussed in the glare of unremitting publicity.

Industrious, determined and an extremely able coach, he impressed many observers during his taxing three-and-a-half-month stint until season's end, yet there was always the feeling that he would make way in the summer.

Though not implicated in any way in the 'bung' scandal, the former number-two was indelibly associated with Graham's teams and his footballing methods, which had been perceived increasingly as less-than-lovely. What the club needed, the thinking went, was a fresh start.

Therefore it was no surprise when Stewart - who had arrived at Highbury to coach the reserves in 1987, becoming assistant manager three years later - missed out on the top job.

Predictably in the circumstances, the ex-Manchester United and Scotland full-back was passed over again following Rioch's exit in August 1996. For an uneasy month, during which he spoke of his confusion and bitterness over the way Graham and Rioch had been treated, he served a second stint as Arsenal's caretaker before leaving to take over at Queen's Park Rangers.

MANAGER JULY 1995 – AUGUST 1996

ACTING MANAGER 1995 & 1996

ARSENE WENGER

Though Bruce Rioch can be quietly satisfied with his achievements as manager of Arsenal, a straw poll at Highbury some eight months after his controversial exit would have revealed that few fans were mourning his departure. Such apparent callousness reflected no criticism of the unfortunate Anglo-Scot, merely utter delight with his successor.

It would be fair to say that when Arsene Wenger was first mooted seriously as the next boss of the Gunners in the summer of 1996, he was unfamiliar to most English football supporters. True, he had known considerable success with Monaco and the Japanese club Nagoya Grampus Eight, and he had turned down the job of technical director to the English FA because he wanted the involvement that only club football can bring, but few could have fitted a face to the name.

Of course, the introduction process was hardly helped by the farcical situation which the board had allowed to develop, whereby everyone knew the identity of the new manager but Arsenal refused to announce it. This was resolved in late September when Arsene Wenger became the first Frenchman to take charge of an English club.

In many ways he cut a deliciously improbable figure. An economics graduate who was fluent in at least half-a-dozen languages, the tall, slim, bespectacled Wenger seemed a world away from the popular conception of a soccer boss. Intellectual, professorial, scholarly . . . the adjectives poured forth from pressmen eager to find a convenient pigeonhole for this fascinating newcomer and, in fairness, they all fitted.

However, none of that mattered because, quite simply, he knew his business. Without making unnecessary waves - while he is a strong man, that is not his way - Arsene subtly overhauled the Highbury approach to football. Training became more ball-orientated than ever before - even running was done with a ball at the players' feet - and everyone was encouraged to be more positive, less hidebound by fear. Thus, pretty soon, such defensive bulwarks as Tony Adams and Martin Keown were to be found *overlapping*, if not with carefree abandon then certainly with fewer inhibitions than ever before.

Remarkably this change in emphasis was achieved without sacrificing too much of the Gunners' renowned solidity at the back. Wenger had merely looked at what he had inherited, been pleasantly surprised at the ability at his disposal and re-created the old unit in a slightly different form. Meanwhile his introduction of the vastly promising Patrick Vieira, his deployment of flair-merchants Wright, Bergkamp and Merson and his encouragement of talented youngsters, especially the lively Steve Hughes, offered an attacking feast more readily associated with Manchester United and Liverpool than the traditionally more cautious North Londoners.

Thus, against the odds for a fresh incumbent, Arsene led a genuine challenge for the Championship which began to peter out only in March. No doubt boosted by top-class incomers - George Weah and Paul Ince were two of his most persistently rumoured transfer targets - the Gunners can expect to be even more competitive in 1997/98, though the manager will be seeking to attain a better disciplinary record. After all, in a tight finish suspensions could be the difference between winning and losing the title.

In general, though, Arsene Wenger's first end-of-term report is highly encouraging. The team is playing attractively, the players appear to enjoy life under the Frenchman's regime and clearly they respect their charming and innovative new leader. For his part, for all his apparent enlightenment, when they transgress he will defend them publicly with George Graham-type fervour while, reportedly, being unremittingly firm in private.

As for the supporters, they can rejoice in the knowledge that the footballing future of their beloved Arsenal is in the hands of a perfectionist, a soccer fanatic who will fly halfway round the world just to get a glimpse of a new tactic - and that's on his day off! An intriguing future awaits.

MANAGER 1996 –

PAT RICE

For a little more than two weeks in September 1996, arch Highbury loyalist Pat Rice took charge of his beloved Arsenal. Serving in the interregnum between fellow caretaker Stewart Houston and manager-in-waiting Arsene Wenger, Pat presided over three League victories and the second leg of the UEFA Cup elimination by Borussia Moenchengladbach.

With engaging candour, the Gunners' former skipper, who had returned to the club as a coach after a spell at Watford, admitted that he wasn't ready for the number-one job. However, he applied himself wholeheartedly to his stand-in duties and was rewarded by his appointment as assistant to the incoming Frenchman.

ACTING MANAGER 1996

PLAYERS' STATISTICS

Player	Seas	LEAGUE			FA CUP			L CUP			EUROPE			TOTAL		
		Ap	Sb	Gl	Ap	Sb	Gl	Ap	Sb	Gl	Ap	Sb	Gl	Ap	Sb	Gl
Adams T	83-	391	(4)	27	34	(1)	5	56	(1)	5	23	(0)	2	504	(6)	39
Addison C	66-67	27	(1)	9	2	(0)	0	2	(0)	1	0	(0)	0	31	(1)	10
Allinson I	83-86	60	(23)	16	7	(2)	4	8	(5)	3	0	(0)	0	75	(30)	23
Ampadu K	1989	0	(2)	0	0	(0)	0	0	(0)	0	0	(0)	0	0	(2)	0
Anderson T	62-64	25	(0)	6	0	(0)	0	0	(0)	0	1	(0)	1	26	(0)	7
Anderson V	84-86	120	(0)	9	12	(0)	3	18	(0)	3	0	(0)	0	150	(0)	15
Anelka N	96-	0	(4)	0	0	(0)	0	0	(0)	0	0	(0)	0	0	(4)	0
Armstrong G	61-77	490	(10)	53	58	(2)	10	35	(0)	3	24	(2)	2	607	(14)	68
Bacuzzi D	60-63	46	(0)	0	2	(0)	0	0	(0)	0	0	(0)	0	48	(0)	0
Baker J	62-65	144	(0)	93	10	(0)	4	0	(0)	0	2	(0)	3	156	(0)	100
Baldwin T	64-66	17	(0)	7	0	(0)	0	3	(0)	4	0	(0)	0	20	(0)	11
Ball A	71-76	177	(0)	45	28	(0)	7	12	(0)	0	0	(0)	0	217	(0)	52
Barnett G	69-75	39	(0)	0	3	(0)	0	5	(0)	0	2	(0)	0	49	(0)	0
Barnwell J	56-63	138	(0)	23	10	(0)	0	0	(0)	0	3	(0)	1	151	(0)	24
Barron P	78-79	8	(0)	0	0	(0)	0	0	(0)	0	0	(0)	0	8	(0)	0
Bartram V	94-	11	(0)	0	0	(0)	0	0	(1)	0	0	(0)	0	11	(1)	0
Batson B	71-73	6	(4)	0	0	(0)	0	0	(0)	0	0	(0)	0	6	(4)	0
Bergkamp D	95-	61	(1)	23	3	(0)	1	9	(0)	6	1	(0)	0	74	(1)	30
Biggs T	57-58	4	(0)	1	0	(0)	0	0	(0)	0	0	(0)	0	4	(0)	1
Blockley J	72-74	52	(0)	1	7	(0)	0	3	(0)	0	0	(0)	0	62	(0)	1
Bloomfield J	54-60	210	(0)	54	17	(0)	2	0	(0)	0	0	(0)	0	227	(0)	56
Boot M	1966	3	(1)	2	0	(0)	0	1	(0)	0	0	(0)	0	4	(1)	2
Bould S	88-	236	(8)	5	20	(0)	0	30	(0)	1	13	(4)	2	299	(12)	8
Bowen D	50-58	146	(0)	2	16	(0)	0	0	(0)	0	0	(0)	0	162	(0)	2
Brady L	73-79	227	(8)	43	31	(4)	2	23	(0)	10	13	(0)	4	294	(12)	59
Brignall S	1978	0	(1)	0	0	(0)	0	0	(0)	0	0	(0)	0	0	(1)	0
Brown L	61-63	101	(0)	2	5	(0)	0	0	(0)	0	3	(0)	0	109	(0)	2
Burns T	64-65	31	(0)	0	2	(0)	0	0	(0)	0	0	(0)	0	33	(0)	0
Caesar G	85-90	27	(17)	0	0	(1)	0	3	(2)	0	0	(0)	0	30	(20)	0
Campbell K	87-94	124	(42)	46	13	(6)	2	14	(10)	6	13	(4)	5	164	(62)	59
Carter J	91-94	18	(7)	2	2	(1)	0	1	(0)	0	0	(0)	0	21	(8)	2
Caton T	83-85	81	(0)	2	4	(0)	0	10	(0)	1	0	(0)	0	95	(0)	3
Chambers B	72-73	1	(0)	0	0	(0)	0	0	(1)	0	0	(0)	0	1	(1)	0
Chapman L	82-83	15	(8)	4	0	(1)	0	0	(2)	0	2	(0)	2	17	(11)	6
Charles M	59-61	60	(0)	26	4	(0)	2	0	(0)	0	0	(0)	0	64	(0)	28
Charlton S	55-58	99	(0)	0	11	(0)	3	0	(0)	0	0	(0)	0	110	(0)	3
Clamp E	61-62	22	(0)	1	2	(0)	0	0	(0)	0	0	(0)	0	24	(0)	1
Clapton Danny	54-61	207	(0)	25	18	(0)	2	0	(0)	0	0	(0)	0	225	(0)	27
Clapton Dennis	59-60	4	(0)	0	0	(0)	0	0	(0)	0	0	(0)	0	4	(0)	0
Clarke A	94-	4	(3)	0	1	(1)	0	0	(0)	0	0	(0)	0	5	(4)	0
Clarke F	61-64	26	(0)	0	2	(0)	0	0	(0)	0	0	(0)	0	28	(0)	0
Coakley T	1966	9	(0)	1	0	(0)	0	4	(0)	1	0	(0)	0	13	(0)	2
Cole A	1990	0	(1)	0	0	(0)	0	0	(0)	0	0	(0)	0	0	(1)	0
Cork D	1983	5	(2)	1	1	(0)	0	0	(0)	0	0	(0)	0	6	(2)	1
Court D	62-69	168	(7)	17	9	(1)	0	9	(2)	1	8	(0)	0	194	(10)	18
Cropley A	74-76	29	(1)	5	2	(0)	0	2	(0)	1	0	(0)	0	33	(1)	6
Davidson R	1967	0	(1)	0	0	(0)	0	0	(0)	0	0	(0)	0	0	(1)	0
Davies P	1971	0	(1)	0	0	(0)	0	0	(0)	0	0	(1)	0	0	(2)	0
Davis P	79-94	331	(20)	30	22	(5)	3	46	(5)	4	15	(1)	0	414	(31)	37
Devine J	77-82	86	(3)	0	6	(0)	0	8	(0)	0	8	(0)	0	108	(3)	0
Dickov P	92-96	6	(15)	3	0	(0)	0	2	(2)	3	0	(0)	0	8	(17)	6
Dixon L	87-	320	(4)	20	29	(0)	1	42	(0)	0	24	(0)	0	415	(4)	21
Docherty T	58-60	83	(0)	1	7	(0)	0	0	(0)	0	0	(0)	0	90	(0)	1
Dodgin W	52-59	191	(0)	0	16	(0)	1	0	(0)	0	0	(0)	0	207	(0)	1
Eastham G	60-65	207	(0)	41	13	(0)	0	0	(0)	0	3	(0)	0	223	(0)	41
Evans D	53-59	189	(0)	10	18	(0)	2	0	(0)	0	0	(0)	0	207	(0)	12
Everitt M	59-60	9	(0)	1	0	(0)	0	0	(0)	0	0	(0)	0	9	(0)	1
Ferry G	1964	11	(0)	0	0	(0)	0	0	(0)	0	0	(0)	0	11	(0)	0
Flatts M	92-94	9	(7)	0	0	(1)	0	1	(0)	0	0	(0)	0	10	(8)	0
Fotheringham J	54-58	72	(0)	0	4	(0)	0	0	(0)	0	0	(0)	0	76	(0)	0
Furnell J	63-67	141	(0)	0	13	(0)	0	12	(0)	0	1	(0)	0	167	(0)	0
Garde R	96-	7	(4)	0	0	(0)	0	0	(0)	0	0	(0)	0	7	(4)	0
Gatting S	78-80	50	(8)	5	9	(1)	1	3	(1)	0	3	(1)	0	65	(11)	6
George C	69-74	113	(20)	31	21	(1)	11	8	(0)	2	15	(1)	5	157	(22)	49
Goring P	49-58	220	(0)	51	20	(0)	2	0	(0)	0	0	(0)	0	240	(0)	53
Gorman P	81-83	5	(1)	0	0	(0)	0	0	(0)	0	0	(0)	0	5	(1)	0
Gould R	67-69	57	(8)	16	7	(0)	3	6	(3)	3	2	(0)	1	72	(11)	23
Goulden R	1958	1	(0)	0	0	(0)	0	0	(0)	0	0	(0)	0	1	(0)	0
Goy P	1958	2	(0)	0	0	(0)	0	0	(0)	0	0	(0)	0	2	(0)	0
Graham G	66-72	219	(8)	59	27	(0)	2	27	(2)	9	23	(2)	7	296	(12)	77
Griffiths A	60-61	15	(0)	2	0	(0)	0	0	(0)	0	0	(0)	0	15	(0)	2
Groves P	86-92	91	(65)	21	11	(6)	1	18	(8)	6	0	(4)	0	120	(83)	28
Groves V	55-63	185	(0)	31	16	(0)	6	0	(0)	0	2	(0)	0	203	(0)	37

PLAYERS' STATISTICS

Player	Seas	LEAGUE Ap	Sb	Gl	FA CUP Ap	Sb	Gl	L CUP Ap	Sb	Gl	EUROPE Ap	Sb	Gl	TOTAL Ap	Sb	Gl
Hankin R	1981	0	(0)	0	0	(0)	0	0	(2)	0	0	(0)	0	0	(2)	0
Harper L	96-	1	(0)	0	0	(0)	0	0	(0)	0	0	(0)	0	1	(0)	0
Hartson J	94-96	43	(10)	14	2	(1)	1	2	(4)	1	8	(1)	1	55	(16)	17
Harvey J	77-78	2	(1)	0	0	(0)	0	0	(0)	0	1	(0)	0	3	(1)	0
Haverty J	54-60	114	(0)	25	8	(0)	1	0	(0)	0	0	(0)	0	122	(0)	26
Hawley J	81-82	14	(6)	3	0	(0)	0	1	(0)	0	0	(0)	0	15	(6)	3
Hayes M	85-89	70	(32)	26	8	(1)	3	14	(7)	5	0	(0)	0	92	(40)	34
Heaney N	91-93	4	(3)	0	0	(0)	0	0	(1)	0	0	(0)	0	4	(4)	0
Heeley M	77-78	9	(6)	1	0	(0)	0	0	(0)	0	4	(1)	0	13	(7)	1
Helder G	94-96	27	(12)	1	2	(0)	0	4	(2)	0	0	(2)	0	33	(16)	1
Henderson J	58-61	103	(0)	29	8	(0)	0	0	(0)	0	0	(0)	0	111	(0)	29
Herd D	54-60	166	(0)	97	14	(0)	10	0	(0)	0	0	(0)	0	180	(0)	107
Hill C	82-84	46	(0)	1	1	(0)	0	4	(0)	0	0	(0)	0	51	(0)	1
Hillier D	90-96	82	(22)	2	13	(2)	0	13	(2)	0	0	(0)	0	108	(26)	2
Hollins J	79-82	123	(4)	9	12	(0)	0	19	(1)	3	10	(3)	1	164	(8)	13
Holton C	50-58	198	(0)	83	18	(0)	5	0	(0)	0	0	(0)	0	216	(0)	88
Hornsby B	72-75	23	(3)	6	0	(0)	0	0	(0)	0	0	(0)	0	23	(3)	6
Howard P	1976	15	(1)	0	0	(0)	0	4	(0)	0	0	(0)	0	19	(1)	0
Howe D	64-66	70	(0)	1	3	(0)	0	1	(0)	0	0	(0)	0	74	(0)	1
Hudson A	76-77	36	(0)	0	7	(0)	0	3	(1)	0	0	(0)	0	46	(1)	0
Hughes S	94-	10	(6)	1	2	(0)	1	0	(1)	0	0	(0)	0	12	(7)	2
Jenkins D	66-68	16	(1)	3	2	(0)	1	6	(0)	5	0	(0)	0	24	(1)	9
Jennings P	77-84	237	(0)	0	38	(0)	0	32	(0)	0	19	(0)	0	326	(0)	0
Jensen J	92-95	93	(5)	1	8	(1)	0	14	(2)	0	14	(0)	0	129	(8)	1
Johnston G	67-68	17	(4)	3	0	(0)	0	3	(1)	0	0	(0)	0	20	(5)	3
Jonsson S	89-90	2	(6)	1	0	(1)	0	1	(0)	0	0	(0)	0	3	(7)	1
Julians L	58-59	18	(0)	7	6	(0)	3	0	(0)	0	0	(0)	0	24	(0)	10
Kane P	1960	4	(0)	1	0	(0)	0	0	(0)	0	0	(0)	0	4	(0)	1
Kay J	82-83	13	(1)	0	0	(0)	0	0	(0)	0	0	(0)	0	13	(1)	0
Kelly E	69-75	168	(7)	13	15	(2)	4	15	(0)	0	13	(2)	2	211	(11)	19
Kelsey J	50-61	327	(0)	0	24	(0)	0	0	(0)	0	0	(0)	0	351	(0)	0
Kennedy R	69-73	156	(2)	53	25	(2)	6	11	(0)	4	14	(2)	8	206	(6)	71
Keown M	1985 and 92-	151	(18)	2	13	(2)	0	14	(2)	1	11	(4)	0	189	(26)	3
Kidd B	74-75	77	(0)	30	9	(0)	3	4	(0)	1	0	(0)	0	90	(0)	34
Kiwomya C	1994	5	(9)	3	0	(0)	0	0	(0)	0	1	(2)	0	6	(11)	3
Kosmina J	1978	0	(1)	0	0	(0)	0	0	(0)	0	1	(2)	0	1	(3)	0
Le Roux D	1957	5	(0)	0	0	(0)	0	0	(0)	0	0	(0)	0	5	(0)	0
Limpar A	90-93	76	(20)	17	7	(0)	2	9	(0)	0	3	(0)	1	95	(20)	20
Linighan A	90-96	101	(17)	5	12	(2)	1	13	(1)	1	8	(1)	1	134	(21)	8
Lukic J	83-89 and 96-	238	(0)	0	22	(0)	0	33	(0)	0	0	(0)	0	293	(0)	0
Lydersen P	91-92	12	(3)	0	0	(0)	0	1	(0)	0	0	(0)	0	13	(3)	0
McClelland J	60-63	46	(0)	0	3	(0)	0	0	(0)	0	0	(0)	0	49	(0)	0
McCullough W	58-65	253	(0)	4	11	(0)	0	0	(0)	0	4	(0)	1	268	(0)	5
McDermott B	78-83	38	(23)	12	0	(1)	0	3	(1)	0	3	(3)	1	44	(28)	13
Macdonald M	76-78	84	(0)	42	9	(0)	10	14	(0)	5	0	(1)	0	107	(1)	57
McGill J	65-66	6	(4)	0	0	(0)	0	2	(0)	0	0	(0)	0	8	(4)	0
McGoldrick E	93-95	32	(6)	0	1	(1)	0	7	(2)	0	4	(3)	1	44	(12)	1
McGowan G	92-	3	(2)	0	1	(0)	0	0	(0)	0	0	(0)	0	4	(2)	0
McKechnie I	61-63	23	(0)	0	0	(0)	0	0	(0)	0	2	(0)	0	25	(0)	0
MacLeod J	61-64	101	(0)	23	8	(0)	4	0	(0)	0	3	(0)	1	112	(0)	28
McLintock F	64-72	312	(2)	26	36	(0)	1	34	(0)	4	19	(0)	1	401	(2)	32
McNab R	66-74	277	(1)	4	39	(0)	0	26	(1)	2	20	(1)	0	362	(3)	6
Madden D	1983	2	(0)	0	0	(0)	0	0	(0)	0	0	(0)	0	2	(0)	0
Magill J	59-64	116	(0)	0	11	(0)	0	0	(0)	0	4	(0)	0	131	(0)	0
Mancini T	74-75	52	(0)	1	8	(0)	0	2	(0)	0	0	(0)	0	62	(0)	1
Marinello P	69-72	32	(6)	3	0	(1)	0	5	(0)	1	6	(1)	1	43	(8)	5
Mariner P	83-85	52	(8)	14	5	(1)	2	3	(1)	1	0	(0)	0	60	(10)	17
Marshall S	92-	18	(3)	1	0	(0)	0	0	(0)	0	0	(0)	0	18	(3)	1
Marwood B	87-89	52	(0)	16	2	(0)	0	6	(0)	1	0	(0)	0	60	(0)	17
Matthews J	74-77	38	(7)	2	4	(2)	1	6	(0)	2	0	(0)	0	48	(9)	5
Meade R	81-84	25	(16)	14	2	(1)	0	3	(1)	1	2	(1)	1	32	(19)	16
Merson P	86-	289	(38)	78	28	(3)	4	38	(2)	10	23	(1)	7	378	(44)	99
Miller A	92-93	6	(2)	0	0	(0)	0	0	(0)	0	0	(0)	0	6	(2)	0
Morrow S	91-96	39	(23)	4	5	(2)	0	7	(4)	2	1	(4)	0	52	(33)	6
Neill T	60-69	240	(1)	8	12	(1)	0	15	(1)	2	5	(0)	0	272	(3)	10
Neilson G	65-66	14	(0)	2	3	(0)	1	0	(0)	0	0	(0)	0	17	(0)	3
Nelson S	69-80	245	(10)	10	33	(2)	1	27	(0)	1	19	(2)	0	324	(14)	12
Nicholas C	83-87	145	(6)	34	11	(2)	10	20	(0)	10	0	(0)	0	176	(8)	54
Nicholas P	80-82	57	(3)	1	8	(0)	0	8	(0)	2	4	(0)	0	77	(3)	3
Nutt G	55-59	49	(0)	10	2	(0)	0	0	(0)	0	0	(0)	0	51	(0)	10
O'Leary D	75-92	523	(35)	11	66	(4)	1	68	(2)	2	21	(0)	0	678	(41)	14
O'Neill F	1960	2	(0)	0	0	(0)	0	0	(0)	0	0	(0)	0	2	(0)	0
O'Shea D	1982	6	(0)	0	0	(0)	0	3	(0)	0	0	(0)	0	9	(0)	0

PLAYERS' STATISTICS

Player	Seas	LEAGUE			FA CUP			L CUP			EUROPE			TOTAL		
		Ap	Sb	Gl	Ap	Sb	Gl	Ap	Sb	Gl	Ap	Sb	Gl	Ap	Sb	Gl
Pack R	1965	1	(0)	0	0	(0)	0	0	(0)	0	0	(0)	0	1	(0)	0
Parlour R	91-	101	(35)	6	12	(0)	1	13	(3)	0	8	(3)	0	134	(41)	7
Pates C	89-92	12	(9)	0	0	(0)	0	2	(0)	0	2	(0)	1	16	(9)	1
Petrovic V	1982	10	(3)	2	6	(0)	1	3	(0)	0	0	(0)	0	19	(3)	3
Petts J	57-61	32	(0)	0	0	(0)	0	0	(0)	0	0	(0)	0	32	(0)	0
Platt D	95-	54	(3)	10	2	(0)	0	5	(1)	1	2	(0)	0	63	(4)	11
Powling R	73-77	50	(5)	3	2	(0)	0	2	(0)	0	0	(0)	0	54	(5)	3
Price D	72-80	116	(10)	16	26	(0)	1	11	(0)	0	11	(1)	2	164	(11)	19
Quinn N	85-89	59	(8)	14	8	(2)	2	14	(2)	4	0	(0)	0	81	(12)	20
Radford J	63-76	375	(4)	111	42	(2)	15	34	(0)	12	24	(0)	11	475	(6)	149
Rice P	67-80	391	(6)	12	67	(0)	1	36	(0)	0	26	(1)	0	520	(7)	13
Richardson K	87-89	88	(8)	5	9	(0)	1	13	(3)	2	0	(0)	0	110	(11)	8
Rimmer J	73-76	124	(0)	0	12	(0)	0	10	(0)	0	0	(0)	0	146	(0)	0
Rix G	76-87	338	(13)	41	42	(2)	7	45	(2)	2	21	(0)	1	446	(17)	51
Roberts J	69-72	56	(3)	4	0	(0)	0	12	(0)	1	9	(1)	0	77	(4)	5
Robertson J	68-69	45	(1)	7	4	(0)	1	4	(0)	0	5	(0)	0	58	(1)	8
Robson S	81-86	150	(1)	16	13	(0)	1	20	(0)	3	2	(0)	1	185	(1)	21
Rocastle D	85-91	204	(14)	24	18	(2)	4	32	(1)	6	4	(0)	0	258	(17)	34
Rose M	95-96	2	(3)	0	0	(0)	0	0	(0)	0	0	(0)	0	2	(3)	0
Ross T	74-77	57	(1)	5	3	(0)	1	6	(0)	3	0	(0)	0	66	(1)	9
Rostron W	74-76	12	(5)	2	1	(0)	0	1	(0)	0	0	(0)	0	14	(5)	2
Sammels J	62-70	212	(3)	39	20	(1)	3	19	(0)	3	15	(0)	7	266	(4)	52
Sansom K	80-87	314	(0)	6	26	(0)	0	48	(0)	0	6	(0)	0	394	(0)	6
Schwarz S	1994	34	(0)	2	1	(0)	0	4	(0)	0	10	(0)	2	49	(0)	4
Seaman D	.90-	249	(0)	0	26	(0)	0	36	(0)	0	26	(0)	0	337	(0)	0
Selley I	92-	35	(6)	0	3	(0)	0	5	(1)	0	8	(2)	2	51	(9)	2
Shaw P	94-	1	(11)	2	0	(1)	0	0	(0)	0	0	(0)	0	1	(12)	2
Simpson P	63-77	353	(17)	10	53	(0)	1	32	(1)	3	20	(1)	1	458	(19)	15
Skirton A	60-66	144	(1)	53	8	(0)	0	0	(0)	0	1	(0)	1	153	(1)	54
Smith A	87-94	242	(22)	86	23	(3)	6	36	(2)	16	15	(2)	7	316	(29)	115
Smithson R	1962	2	(0)	0	0	(0)	0	0	(0)	0	0	(0)	0	2	(0)	0
Snedden J	59-64	83	(0)	0	10	(0)	0	0	(0)	0	1	(0)	0	94	(0)	0
Sparrow B	1983	2	(0)	0	0	(0)	0	0	(0)	0	0	(0)	0	2	(0)	0
Standen J	57-60	35	(0)	0	3	(0)	0	0	(0)	0	0	(0)	0	38	(0)	0
Stapleton F	74-80	223	(2)	75	32	(0)	15	26	(1)	14	15	(0)	4	296	(3)	108
Stead K	1978	1	(1)	0	0	(0)	0	0	(0)	0	0	(0)	0	1	(1)	0
Storey P	65-76	387	(4)	9	49	(2)	4	36	(1)	2	22	(0)	2	494	(7)	17
Strong G	60-64	125	(0)	69	8	(0)	5	0	(0)	0	4	(0)	3	137	(0)	77
Sullivan C	53-57	28	(0)	0	4	(0)	0	0	(0)	0	0	(0)	0	32	(0)	0
Sunderland A	77-83	204	(2)	55	34	(0)	16	26	(0)	13	13	(1)	7	277	(3)	91
Swallow R	54-57	13	(0)	4	0	(0)	0	0	(0)	0	0	(0)	0	13	(0)	4
Talbot B	78-84	245	(9)	40	29	(1)	7	26	(1)	1	15	(0)	1	315	(11)	49
Tapscott D	53-57	119	(0)	62	13	(0)	6	0	(0)	0	0	(0)	0	132	(0)	68
Tawse B	1964	5	(0)	0	0	(0)	0	0	(0)	0	0	(0)	0	5	(0)	0
Thomas M	86-91	149	(14)	24	14	(3)	1	22	(2)	5	1	(1)	0	186	(20)	30
Tiddy M	55-57	48	(0)	8	4	(0)	0	0	(0)	0	0	(0)	0	52	(0)	8
Tyrer A	1966	0	(0)	0	0	(0)	0	1	(1)	0	0	(0)	0	1	(1)	0
Ure I	63-69	168	(0)	2	16	(0)	0	14	(0)	0	4	(0)	0	202	(0)	2
Vaessen P	78-81	23	(9)	6	0	(0)	0	1	(1)	2	3	(4)	1	27	(14)	9
Vieira P	96-	30	(1)	2	3	(0)	0	3	(0)	0	1	(0)	0	37	(1)	2
Walford S	77-80	64	(13)	3	5	(5)	0	5	(0)	1	3	(2)	0	77	(20)	4
Walley T	65-66	10	(4)	1	1	(0)	0	3	(0)	0	0	(0)	0	14	(4)	1
Ward G	53-62	81	(0)	10	3	(0)	0	0	(0)	0	0	(0)	0	84	(0)	10
Webster M	1969	3	(0)	0	0	(0)	0	2	(0)	0	1	(0)	0	6	(0)	0
Whyte C	81-85	86	(4)	8	5	(0)	0	14	(0)	0	3	(1)	0	108	(5)	8
Williams S	84-87	93	(2)	4	11	(0)	0	15	(0)	1	0	(0)	0	119	(2)	5
Wills L	53-60	195	(0)	4	13	(0)	0	0	(0)	0	0	(0)	0	208	(0)	4
Wilmot R	85-86	8	(0)	0	0	(0)	0	1	(0)	0	0	(0)	0	9	(0)	0
Wilson R	63-73	234	(0)	0	32	(0)	0	18	(0)	0	24	(0)	0	308	(0)	0
Winterburn N	87-	345	(1)	7	32	(0)	0	45	(0)	3	26	(0)	0	449	(1)	10
Wood G	80-82	60	(0)	0	1	(0)	0	7	(0)	0	2	(0)	0	70	(0)	0
Woodcock T	82-85	129	(2)	56	13	(1)	7	20	(2)	5	2	(0)	0	164	(5)	68
Woodward J	1966	2	(1)	0	0	(0)	0	1	(0)	0	0	(0)	0	3	(1)	0
Wright I	91-	190	(7)	118	15	(0)	12	28	(0)	28	19	(0)	15	252	(7)	173
Young A	1960	4	(0)	0	0	(0)	0	0	(0)	0	0	(0)	0	4	(0)	0
Young W	76-81	170	(0)	11	28	(0)	3	20	(0)	1	18	(0)	4	236	(0)	19

Dates shown indicate first year of each season. Thus 70-77 means 1970/71 to 1977/78. A single entry indicates one season only, eg 1964 refers to 1964/65.